D0890483

A
Z
A

Volume
Two

L

E

A

Journal of Korean Literature
& Culture

Korea Institute Harvard University

2008

AZALEA

Journal of Korean Literature & Culture

Volume Two ∼ 2008

Publisher: Korea Institute, Harvard University

Editor: David R. McCann

Editor-in-Chief: Young-Jun Lee

Editorial Board: Bruce Fulton, Brother Anthony, Hwang Jong-yŏn,
Kwon Youngmin, Heinz Insu Fenkl

Copy Editor: K.E. Duffin

Design: Wayne de Fremery

Proofreader: Phyllis Coyne et al.

AZALEA is published yearly by the Korea Institute, Harvard University,
with generous funding by the International Communication Foundation,
Seoul, Korea.

Subscriptions: $30 (one year); $55 (two years); $80 (three years).
Overseas subscriptions: $45 (one year, air mail only).

Inquiries to: *AZALEA*, Korea Institute, Harvard University, Center for
Government and International Studies, South Building Room S228,
1730 Cambridge Street, Cambridge, MA 02138
Phone: (617) 496-2141 Fax: (617) 496-1144 Email: korea@fas.harvard.edu

Submissions are welcome. Submitted manuscripts and books sent for
review become the property of *AZALEA*.

Printed on acid-free paper, in Seoul, Korea by Haingraph Co., Ltd.

ISSN 1939-6120
ISBN-13: 978-0-9795800-1-7
ISBN-10: 0-9795800-1-3

CONTENTS

KOREA FROM THE OUTSIDE

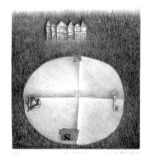

Editor's Note

This second issue of *AZALEA* continues our efforts to present exemplary works of current literature and literary art from Korea. We have altered the frame of the term "exemplary," however. For a start, the reader will find illustrated work, *manhwa*, from the DPRK, or North Korea, in the selection of materials gathered, translated, and introduced by Heinz Insu Fenkl. This may remind us that the illustrated page, the cartoon, is a major feature in the current publishing world, while also helping us to remember the other Korea from which the materials came.

A selection of illustrated work, from North or South, brings its own challenges as expressive form. The cartoon simplifies: black and white; sometimes line figures; clear, perhaps obvious, point; power and resonance accumulated through that simplification. The inclusion of the current selection may bring to mind the cartoonish quality of American notions of North Korea, its government and people, and vice versa.

I recall a weeklong journey to North Korea some ten years or so ago. I was traveling in a group accompanied by government guides and drivers. One evening I watched a TV program, an hour or more of army chorus songs interspersed with elderly individuals heatedly denouncing the United States for its actions during the Korean War and since. The presentation resembled a cartoon.

The next day at lunch as I was sitting across the table from one of the drivers, I plucked up my courage, told him about the show, and asked if he saw me as his enemy. He did not hesitate in his reply. He pointed up and then back and forth, saying, "No, no. The problem is between our governments. Between you and me as human beings, there is not a problem." Seeing the TV show, having an opportunity to bring it up in a conversation—the exchange was important.

A rather different sort of exchange informs the section in the current issue on the sijo poetic form and practice. As the introductory essay notes, the sijo has a long history in Korea and continues to find avid, inventive practitioners. I have selected three writers for this issue. Cho Ohyǒn and Hong Sǒng-ran are both esteemed as sijo poets, widely recognized and honored in today's literary circles. Kim Dae Jung, former President of South Korea, turned to the sijo form during his political imprisonment in the 1980s. Hong Sǒng-ran offers a most poignant comment on the political and literary resonances of that act.

We plan to offer sijo work by other Korean writers in future issues, but we have also presented several sijo poems written in English. This past spring, the Sejong Cultural Society in Chicago sponsored a sijo writing contest for middle and high school students. As a contest judge, I read all the entries and felt delighted that such a number of students had found the form interesting, workable, and expressive in English. Our congratulations go out to all the participants, and our thanks also to the Sejong Cultural Society.

The contest might be viewed as a stage on which the sijo form presented itself to a young, contemporary audience, in a language entirely different from Korean. I would judge the performance a success, and hope that we may be able to find others who are using the sijo form in English, or yet more languages, to bring into the pages of future issues of *Azalea*. Such realms of practice and performance are further dimensions of the literary universe the editors and translators of *Azalea* wish to explore. We shall welcome our readers' comments, suggestions, and submissions for future issues.

David R. McCann
September 2008

AZALEA

Volume

Two

Writer in
Focus

Shin Kyung Sook

The Strawberry Field

by Shin Kyung Sook
Translated by Gabriel Sylvian

I'm forgetting everything about my life. The amnesia is progressing now inside me. I went to give my lecture today, and sweated bullets for more than half an hour in class. Some dead poet. I wrote a dissertation on his literary world, yet I spent the whole day trying to remember his name, and with it, endless writings and episodes stored in my brain—all lost. Suddenly my once formidable associative functions and imaginative powers were unavailable to my memory—all gone, together with the name. That name—I must have seen it a thousand, ten thousand times.

What was the title of the book of poems you dropped under the desk, Yu, the day I discovered you?

Even that memory's gone. My students were looking at me. Their stares cut right through to the hollow of my being. I think my amnesia was worsening even at that moment. My forehead oozing sweat. *You seem unwell. How about just stopping the class now.* Startled, amnesic eye. . . . My eyes.

I got a surprise telephone call from a man yesterday afternoon. I was pouring some Yaksan germanium spring water into a kettle for tea. A silence welled up inside me when I heard his voice. It

AZALEA

*The
Strawberry
Field:
Shin Kyung
Sook*

was a silence I've experienced at other times, when watching a sudden flurry of snow in April, or when examining old knife marks I once carved into an old table. Had twelve years really gone by? He said he'd seen me two days before at the Hoam Art Hall, at a concert called "Thirty Years of the Folk Song." I'd been sitting in the audience, he said, holding hands with a little girl. A little girl? No, but I'd been at the concert that day. The man was connecting with me again after twelve years. I never imagined he would phone me again. Still holding the water bottle in midair, I just listened to the sound of the man's voice. Then the silence gave way to a feeling of emptiness. Although we hadn't spoken in twelve years, I didn't feel estranged from him at all. He said that after I stood him up at the Open Space in the Forest, he'd donned work gloves, learned auto mechanics, and was now operating a car repair shop, selling gas and washing cars. His life was nothing to brag about, he said, but he never missed a Pak Ŭn-ok or Chŏng T'ae-ch'un concert. Whom had he seen? He asked me if the girl by my side was my daughter. "No, I was alone." The man fell silent for a while at my answer. After a few moments, he told me four years had passed before he'd stopped wondering about that unkept appointment twelve years ago, about why he'd never received a call or a word of explanation. The reason he'd taken the trouble to find my phone number and call me, he said, was because I'd seemed so peaceful at the concert. He wanted to tell me he'd be able to forget me now. He told me that when he'd seen my face, fair with no makeup, and wrinkles beginning to set in the corners of my eyes, my eyes were even more beautiful than they'd been when I was twenty-three. He paused again, then continued. Someday if you see me alone in some subway station or at a tourist attraction, or maybe at a hospital or gas station, I hope your eyes still look as beautiful. That's my hope. Although I'm no longer a part of your life, my heart hasn't changed. Now I'll forget about you.

That day, the singer said, "Some people say a song is just a song; don't preach to your listeners. Other people think songs should say something about society. Which is right? I still can't decide."

Now, a day after the phone call, I want to tell the man's story. Actually, I've wanted to tell his story for a long time, the story that began to well up inside me after we lost contact. The story of his life and of my desire when I was twenty-three. I think I've always been looking for somebody to listen to my story about him—someone who would listen and then immediately forget. But my steadily progressing condition will soon devour the man's story. If I wait much longer, the memory living in the corners of my mind will start to decay. The amnesia, advancing at this very moment, will scatter the images of him that I have in my heart, just as it has already begun to faintly take its toll on the contours of my face.

The singer sang.

Why plant red flowers by the road, mountain, or gate, when flowers redder than any canna lily or balsam flower still grow in the hearts of those left behind? Why plant red flowers anywhere? On the day those flowers were cut, ah! The stars vanished! At the army base at Songjŏngni, helicopter blades soared upward into the faded sunlight, ripping open the crimson sky, blood-red . . . What did you see, my son? I saw flagless anti-rebel armies. What did you hear, my daughters? The roaring advance of army tanks. Ah, it was still the month of May. Not a single general was decorated with a gold medal that day. Don't plant red flowers anywhere, not till we've buried the young men's medals at their graves. Oh . . . what did you . . . see?

No matter what the man said, I am witness to the slow advance of time in the mirror. How my outward features—eyes, nose, and mouth—have already begun to lose their definition, and how this will not change. I understand the fragility of it all. One day when I was twenty-three, I looked into the mirror and an

AZALEA

*The
Strawberry
Field:
Shin Kyung
Sook*

alarm sounded within me. Something flared up in my mind like a fiery orange sunset over a dusky plain. My eyes couldn't believe what they were seeing. Through the glare, there behind the western mountains in the background, lurked the menace of my extinction. Death was at my door, or so I thought. I didn't realize it was my face losing its youthfulness. The lackluster pupils, the high-bridged nose by them, seemed to be crying out for help. The contours of my face were gradually beginning to sag and wrinkle, and the process has been continuing ever since. Now past their prime, my outer contours will soon waste away for good. But my inner contours have already come this far from when I was twenty-three, from the warehouse on the hill, from the strawberry field. From that time on, I was no longer the same woman.

In my memory Father is wearing white rubber shoes. That's what he always wore, even on those winter days when he'd return after a long absence. Whenever he came back, Mother would shine them up to a bright white. Two white rubber shoes placed on the dirt floor was a sign that he was home again. Years later, I remembered his shoes but I couldn't remember his face. I was still very young when he left us for the final time. First I forgot his face; then I forgot his shoes. Because I had no real memories of Father to speak of, forgetting him wasn't painful. I thought I'd forgotten all about him until I met the man.

Mother sometimes used to blame Father's absences on the war, rather than on character flaws or personal shortcomings. Shirking military duty, she said, forced him to spend life on the lam. Even when sleeping, he would awaken if he heard footsteps and announce he had to leave again. In the process of repeatedly adjusting to new environments and adverse situations, he became a man for whom the security of a home meant nothing, a man unable to settle down in one place.

Even before taking leave of us forever, Father sometimes would go missing for strange reasons. Mother never had a chance to ask him where he was going. As though it were business as usual, he would stroll to the end of the street looking for a sawmill where he could purchase some lumber. Finding no sawmill there, he'd decide to search for one across the street, and cross the road at the traffic light. Then he'd cross at another light, and slip away, just like that. Or, after getting up from the dinner table, he would put on his slippers as if going out to buy cigarettes, and then not come back for a month or two. Because Mother acted as though nothing was the matter, Father's abrupt disappearances gained an air of naturalness. Then there was his final absence. After disappearing for six or seven months, Father returned one day looking more dead than alive. He opened the door of the room nearest the entrance, went inside, passed out, and stayed that way for two or three days. I sat by his pillow while he slept. I was still a small girl. The room had a deathlike stillness. I remember the wooden pillow and its finger marks, and the wardrobe closet door left halfway open. A gob of gum was stuck to the wall where he'd hung up his baggy pants. After waking up, Father put his belongings into the biggest suitcase in the house: the pants he always hung on the wall, the pillow—all his personal things. A lot of room remained in the suitcase even with all his things inside it. Worn-out objects you'd wonder why anyone would want to keep. That was the first time I saw Mother cry. Years later I realized why. It wasn't a trip to the cigarette store this time, but Father's final goodbye. He was leaving us forever. Mother knew it then.

Father's absence from my life gives me the suggestion of a horizon. A horizon of endless want. Something must lie beyond it, you'd think; but nothing was ever there. Nothing new, no different boundary line, no milepost pointing out a path. Like an empty cave bathed in sunlight. It seems to mean something, yet defies analysis. "Fading hope suffused with absence" are the only words that come close to describing it.

Azalea

The
Strawberry
Field:
Shin Kyung
Sook

Sometimes money orders would arrive in the mail, but even they stopped coming, and so I was aware of Father's presence only rarely. Gradually, the man called "Father" was erased from my consciousness. That is, until the year I turned twenty-three, during my first year of college, when I saw the man on the school campus, a traveling salesman hawking reprinted editions of old literary magazines.

March had turned to April. The man was standing at one end of the campus by a paperboard sign announcing a welcome party for new students. He'd found a shady spot and set up a table on which he spread out informative brochures. A few students were searching through the sample volumes he'd also set out. Why couldn't I have just passed him by? Was I charmed by the black covers of the bulky reprinted editions? Was it sheer chance that I noticed him? Only much later did I realize that as I was walking with my head lowered, it was the rubber shoes on his feet that had caught my attention. Noticing his shoes, my gaze then slowly traveled up his body. And there was the man's face. Frizzled hair, bloodshot eyes gazing slightly upward, skin that invited repugnance. A reddish-tipped nose, uncommonly tough, lumpy cheeks, a black turtleneck shirt showing beneath a grayish safari-style jacket, a worn-out belt, faded blue jeans—and those white rubber shoes that threw off any balance to his outfit.

I'd thought that forgetting about something was like hurling it into a chasm and shutting the door after it. My father's existence had vanished from my memory, cut off at some point like his money orders. But the door was opened again by the white shoes the man was wearing on the school grounds that April. I felt as though my heart were being rent as my father's existence—the man who carved the image of his absence onto the entryway of my life and then never returned—was led back out through the door I thought I'd closed up and sealed shut.

16

My life is devoid of desire now. Sometimes I think about what it means to be human; what life means to us, or rather, to me. But my focus now is different from before. It's no longer about expanding my field of experience, nor is it directed at universal love, sacrifice, intellectual curiosity, or at cultivating an aesthetic. Only the dreary thought that, while knowing change is impossible, an unambitious pocket of craving still exists within me that yearns to transcend the humdrum reality cast as my lot.

But in those days I had desire—like the desire I had when I took the order form the man gave me and aggressively penciled in my address, phone number, and preferred date for monthly payment, my face set with a small measure of determination.

Several images come to my mind when I think of him.

A Chong'am district alley at sundown. Stacks of wooden boxes, a scattering of flowerpots with annuals growing in them, dark, porchless houses visible from the open front gate. A water spigot wrapped with garden hose, standing in the middle of the house's narrow open courtyard. There I was, at twenty-three, following the smell of the waste-fouled river, snooping around to catch a glimpse of where the man lived. He does not know this. He does not know that just as he secretly watched me two days ago while I listened to songs at the Hoam Art Hall, as a twenty-three-year-old—that young woman who has long since vanished in the mists of time—I once went looking for his home in the Chong'am district, an abode, as I remember, that was hideously dark. Looking in through the front gate, its door just slightly ajar, I watched the man emerge through a narrow kitchen door in knee-length trousers, carrying a dinner tray. Dark house, tiny courtyard, outdoor toilets with signs reading "Gents," "Ladies," a few rabbits in a hutch, a half-opened door, the man's mother, or possibly his grandmother, sitting at the doorsill with ashy white complexion, hands reaching out to take hold of the dinner tray he'd fixed for her. He stood there, the young man, holding that tray against a background of squalor and loneliness. That was the way he lived.

AZALEA

The
Strawberry
Field:
Shin Kyung
Sook

Every time the man and I walked around together, he never once failed to attract the attention of the street inspectors. In those days inspections were a common enough nuisance; all young people had to put up with them. But inspections were never just a routine matter for him. His outer appearance seemed to set off warning bells in people's minds. It was as if he were carrying a sign reading "Stay away!" and no person, much less a community, could pass by him without taking notice. There was a strange misshapenness about him that discouraged others' approach, something people intuited long before they got any sense of his personality. There was an inexplicable weirdness about him that even impinged on the heartfelt moments when I felt love for him. His despair and frustration were of an entirely different order from the despair and frustration of other young people. While searching through the man's bag or his pockets, the street inspectors would glance at me, and there were always questions in their glances. Some inspectors even felt it necessary to ask me, "Are you OK?" The man understood those people. In a friendly voice he would say, "I look like a criminal, right?"

I believe it was last year, during a trip alone to Cheju Island. I rented a car at the airport and while driving to my lodgings I tuned into a radio station. A program was on the air introducing men and women callers to each other like a dating game. The radio host told the male caller to introduce himself. "I'm thirty-nine, I own a cake and pastry shop." The man's voice sounded like any other. But when the host asked the man to describe his appearance, the man answered, "Frankly, I'd describe myself as looking like a criminal." Taking the comment as a joke, the host laughed. "You must have gotten stopped by the street inspectors a lot!," to which the man casually answered yes. "Yes, my ID card has to be ready at all times when I go out. Everybody says I look like a criminal." The woman on the program did not opt to date the man. The man told the truth like it was. The cake shop owner with the countenance of a lawbreaker told the host, "My cakes are out of this world. I'd sure like to send one to your station. How would I deliver that?"

The man with the sign on his face reading "Keep away from me!" or "Steer clear of this man!" shot a curt glance at the young girl tagging along behind him. What do you want? He didn't look directly at her. He'd recognized her instantly because she'd been his only customer that day. They came to the front of a small snack restaurant where a small throng of students just out of school were holding signboards with anti-government slogans. The man lost his patience. He turned around to the girl bumping against his heels as she trailed behind him and asked her, "Did you make an error on your form?" "No." "Then why are you following me around?" "I have a question for you." "What?" "Why do you wear white rubber shoes?" The man's threatening appearance registered most intensely in his eyes. When they looked at you they seemed to cut right through you. When they turned away they seemed to mock you. When they stared at you they seemed the height of cruelty. The man's gaze rested on me briefly, then quickly he looked away. He couldn't look at anybody for very long. I cast him a fierce look, staring him right in the eyes. He couldn't focus on one spot for very long, so his gaze floated from my eyes to my nose to my neck. Later he told me. The first reason he wore the shoes was that he had to walk great distances. The second reason was that white rubber shoes were out of style. This man, whose very appearance seemed to scream "forbidden territory," wore white shoes hoping they would distract people's attention from his face. Because half the success of a salesman depends on his face, the white shoes figured as part of his sales strategy.

Azalea

The
Strawberry
Field:
Shin Kyung
Sook

Still, as I think about it now, I can't get over the idea that the warning sign in his appearance was the same one present in Yu's beauty, which, when I think back on her, could only be described as "artistic." I am drawn to the thought that the forbidden territory of their two utterly different appearances had a singular meaning.

What does memory loss mean to a person's existence? Now, as my stockpile of memories is vanishing, what critical point have I come to in my life? I initially thought my amnesic symptoms were the result of a traffic accident. One day after the Christmas holidays two years ago, I was sitting talking with my friend in the back seat of her car. Her husband was driving. I forget where we were heading. I only recall that we were leaving the city. We'd already passed Kup'abal, I think, so it was probably Illyŏng or Changhŭng. We'd planned the outing, but not so much as an end-of-the-year party as one of the casual get-togethers people usually have before the New Year. Outside it was dark as far as the eye could see, but we were in good spirits. Beautiful lights flickered from the banks of the rice fields spread out on either side of the highway. My attention was drawn momentarily to the dark space between the distant lights and the road, when suddenly a barrage of neon lights swept into my field of vision: flashing lights from restaurants, pizzerias, and motels, and lights decorating trees and shrubs between local eateries and barbecue houses. It happened at one moment during the repeated sequences of stillness and light. The car suddenly took a sharp turn and screeched to a halt. At the same time, a white Sonata that had been trailing our black Sonata crashed into us. At the jolting impact from the rear collision, and just as my friend was calling out my name, I lost consciousness. I'm told I passed out for only three or four minutes. A construction site sign reading "Turn Around" had suddenly sprung into view, causing my friend's husband to slam on the brakes. That's when the car directly behind us smashed into our rear bumper. Before I was loaded into the ambulance and taken to the nearest hospital, I saw that the front of the white car and the trunk of my friend's car had been totaled. I was mortified by the sight of my friend's automobile with its trunk popped open and a huge gash in its rear. I was probably in a complete daze. Although I'd blacked out on impact, I wasn't the one who required hospitalization. It was my friend, who had called out my name fearing for my safety. My friend's husband was also unhurt. For a few days afterwards, the ear-splitting sound of the car crash remained as a ringing in my ears. When I tried to fall asleep, I would experience a startled or fearful feeling; but I thought that would be the end of the accident for me. Some two months later I began to notice some symptoms of memory loss. How can I describe it? It was as if everything was being pushed to the back of my brain, or like a curtain falling over what once had been crystal-clear images. Everything seemed very distant and faint. In the morning I would open the refrigerator door to take out some milk and suddenly forget what I'd wanted, and just stand there in a daze. Or I would go to the bookshelf for a book of poems, only to forget the title I was looking for. I would just linger there, my mind blank.

The symptoms gradually became more severe. Once I got into a taxi to go to the department store before realizing I'd left my purse at home. So I had the taxi turn around and take me back. *Just a moment, sir.* I had the taxi stop on the street in front of my house. I folded up the thin cardigan sweater that had been hanging on my arm and there, beneath the cardigan, was my purse. I'd put the straps over my arm and then forgotten about it. Or once, I took my car out for a drive and parked it in the basement parking lot of the Kyobo Bookstore. Then, after meeting someone at the business hall tearoom with the large ceiling on Kyobo Building's first floor, I caught a taxi to go home. Only after I arrived at the parking area in front of my house did it hit me: "Where's my car?" The distress I experienced after that. I felt like I was spinning out of control.

Yu. Will you also disappear from my memory? Your laugh, your pale arms, the delicate nape of your neck. . . . The picnic that day, the mystery of you.

AZALEA

The
Strawberry
Field:
Shin Kyung
Sook

Yu. I don't remember the first time we met. Maybe it was on a bus, or maybe at the marketplace. At the beginning I didn't really notice you. I'd sense a kind of brightness flashing nearby, but then it disappeared. Or at times, on my way home from school, I would catch the scent of perfume, or while at the market on an errand for Mother, I would see someone with a dazzling white neck but she would quickly disappear into an alleyway. Could that have been you? It was over a month after the new semester began that I first came to know who you were. I was twenty-three, and had arrived at the classroom early. I took a seat near a window and was resting my head on the desk, listening to a boom of voices coming from the student hall. Behind me, I heard the sound of a chair being moved. And then silence. As I slowly opened my eyes, your legs came into view as you stretched them out while seating yourself. Your calves were delicately shaped, with smooth, downy hairs on them. I looked at your bright, white outstretched legs as I leaned over the desk. I also saw the small floral print designs on the hem of your low-slung skirt. I wondered who you were. I decided to resist the impulse to turn around and look, when suddenly a book of poems by a dead poet fell onto the floor. You leaned forward to pick it up, but you couldn't reach it without bending your knees. Your slender white hand fumbled frantically for the book. I, twenty-three, raised my head from my desk, picked up the book, then turned to look behind me. There were your eyes. Your eyes that seemed to encompass everything. Only you could go around wearing such a bright skirt without caring what anybody thought. Nobody wore skirts and things like that back then. Nobody curled their hair with rollers. Oppression seeped into even the smallest day-to-day affairs: When someone laughed, they knew they had to be careful about laughing. When a good thing happened to someone, they knew they didn't deserve it. The impossibility of complete happiness was deep-dyed into the emotions of young people then. We didn't laugh, we felt uncomfortable when something good happened, or when feeling happy about it. Yu. How different you were! The clarity suffusing the images I still have of you remains an unsolved riddle. How could you be so free, how could you avoid the oppression looming everywhere then, even in the air we breathed? How could your laughter sparkle? How could you show off your smooth calves in the midst of all that tear gas? How could you?

After coming back from the strawberry field, I never saw you again. Some time later, I received a letter in the mail from your mother.

. . . she called me Dear Miss.

Dear Miss

I am the mother of the deceased Yu. I got your name and address from the address page of her diary. The page contained information about her friends. Judging from your prominent place on my daughter's address list, I imagine you two were very close. Perhaps you have already heard. Although it is now long after the fact, I just wanted to let you know of Yu's sudden passing.

One day and part of a morning after Yu's disappearance, her body was discovered in a small, secluded stream in Minnesota. It was covered with light abrasions. She had been staying with friends there over the summer vacation. Yu had taken their dog for a walk that day and never returned. According to the investigation conducted by the local authorities and the direct confirmations of our family and friends at the scene, Yu lost her footing on a stony hill leading down to the stream from the road, and sustained a brain injury. She probably lost consciousness when she fell into the water. The stream was only

*knee deep, but she was unable to pull herself out or call for help. It
was this way, at the age of twenty-seven, that Yu reached the end of
her life. Her remains were transported back home and buried at the
family burial ground at Ch'ŏngna in Ch'ungnam Province.*

I was a young woman of twenty-three.

The moment the young woman realized Yu was the owner
of the brightness she'd sensed brushing past her, she'd felt an
immediate attraction to her. It's difficult to say exactly why. Looking
back on what the young woman discovered in her, it now seems
such a common thing; but at the time, what was so special were
those characteristics that the young woman had never felt in
herself. Freedom of movement, subdued tranquility, an attitude of
acceptance that seemed to embrace everything, even death.

Yu. Sunlight was shining down on us. We were both about to
cross the road at the traffic light. The sky was a mix of white and
blue. Across the road, leaves. Light green leaves of a gingko tree.
I was never to see you again after that day, but even now with my
amnesia progressing, your face as it was at that time appears so
vividly to my eyes. Had we once been in love? Can it be expressed
in that way? The abundance of your hair. Your laughter. Your
soft hands. Can I speak about you? After we returned from the
strawberry field, you did not appear in my life again. You vanished
just like my father. You never came back. Yu. Even if we had met
again, it would have already been too late for us to recognize each
other. We were about to cross at the traffic light. Were we bored? As
we waited for the light to change, you snuck a kick at my leg with
your foot. I kicked back. You poked at my hips with your hand. I
poked at your hips with my hand. You turned your body all the
way around and clobbered me in the back and waist with your two
fists. I beat at your back and waist. We simultaneously set down the
bags we were carrying at the foot of the traffic light and beat each
other's backs, stepped on each other's feet, and kicked each other's

backsides with our feet. Playfulness without oppression. Meanwhile, the light changed. We both quickly picked up our bags and crossed the street. I can still hear our peals of laughter.

Yu. I grew up an only child. Did you know that? Did you know of my longing as you passed through my heart?

I had always wished for a sister ever since I was a little girl. Sisters standing with their backs against the wall blowing soap bubbles into the air, big sisters carrying little sisters on their backs, rosy-complexioned cheeks of the little sisters riding piggyback, little sisters bawling and pulling at the hair of whomever their older sisters were fighting. Those sorts of sisters. Which role did the young woman want? Big sister? Little sister? Her cousins used to pick pointless fights with each other in front of her. When they were lying on the floor doing homework, the older sister would kick her little sister's backside with her toes, and then the little sister would kick the older sister's back with her tiny feet. Hey, you! The big sister would get up. Then the little sister would get up. Later, it would be forgotten who started the fight, and then, teary-eyed, "I hit you once, why did you kick me twice?" "I hit you soft, why did you hit me hard?" Yu. Your pointless kicks at the traffic light kindled my desire. The color of light green above us. The light, so bright, shining down on us from between the leaves. Yu, the woman.

Mother used to glance at the two-story house with its nice yard a block down from ours whenever she passed by it. Sometimes, the sound of a piano came from the house, and mother would listen intently. "I should have given you piano lessons." Mother seemed to enjoy piano music. How amazed I was to learn that it was your house. Yu. That was also the moment the sisterly love I'd felt for you died. Violence sprouted up at the site of its disappearance, and emptiness coiled in the space beneath.

AZALEA

The
Strawberry
Field:
Shin Kyung
Sook

Dear Miss

I thought for quite some time that I would have to forget about Yu as quickly as possible in order to overcome the grief of losing her. Because of that, I never told anyone about Yu's death and turned away from everything connected with her. But I knew in some way the sadness of losing Yu would never heal. And so for a long time I have been trying as often as possible to reconstruct Yu in my mind. I try to ease the remaining sadness by retracing Yu's steps. The fact that I must work through the grief by collecting and recording Yu's steps no doubt says a good deal about my circumstances.

When everything seemed at an end, when it all seemed to have come to a dead stop, Mother would make an astounding new start. That was the way she lived. She was a woman who, when the money orders stopped coming, sat in her hole-filled socks peeling garlic cloves until her fingers gave out. A woman who, when she saw that peeling garlic would not give us the basic necessities for living, wandered around Namsan carrying a sack on her shoulders. A woman who went around all day long picking up acorns. Squirrel food. My mother. A woman who made acorn jelly, who complained about my studies eating into her finances, but who always sent me to school. A woman who set up a cooking stove at the marketplace and started frying griddle cakes with green onions, who boasted of her ability to finance her own midsized shop, and who brewed her own moonshine. By the time I was twenty-three, Mother had three employees working for her. She bought a home: two rooms on the first floor and one room on the second. She rented out the second floor, but having a house with a proper kitchen changed Mother's life. Stacks of extra soap dishes and tubes of toothpaste piled up in the bathroom. She planted her favorite flowers in pots and set them out on the windowsills. As the house changed, Mother also tried to change herself. She stopped using bar soap to wash her hair and began using the shampoo she'd previously reserved for me. And then one day, Mother, who would fall into bed exhausted in just her everyday clothes, brought home some sleepwear and a nightgown she'd just purchased. Sometimes she complained, "I can't sleep comfortably in these," and changed back into her day clothes and tried getting back to sleep that way. On the whole, she began to change her lifestyle to conform to that of other women her age. Mom brought home cartons of milk, hundred-gram boxes of butter, and croissants and other breads, and tried having them instead of our usual breakfast. I didn't dislike bread and adjusted well, but mother didn't last three days. She said it all looked delicious on TV, so refined!—but afterwards she went back to rice and soup.

This was the woman who brought me into this world. There was always a certain indescribable gap between us. I spent my childhood years afraid of letting her out of my sight, afraid of being abandoned and becoming an orphan. While Mother spent her days in street stalls selling acorn jelly, I sometimes truly wished she'd never have the opportunity to see what life was like elsewhere, that she would stay trapped in the house. That way she would never abandon me. It was only in her early twilight years, after we got the new kitchen and the new house that her gestures, her actions, began to arouse any compassion in me. She'd never once thought to betray me. I saw then that she wasn't the tough, strong woman I'd made her out to be, but a weak and insecure woman, a typical single mother. A woman to be pitied. But I saw this all too late. In the meantime, I was watching her trying to form new habits and failing.

. . . Recalling him now, the appearance of the man no one seemed to look at, or rather, whom they avoided altogether, gave the twenty-three-year-old woman a strange feeling of relief. Perhaps it was precisely that sense of relief she loved, not the man.

AZALEA

The
Strawberry
Field:
Shin Kyung
Sook

I want to know about the personal and spiritual connections Yu formed during her short lifetime. If you can help me, Miss, to complete Yu's existence, she will not be forgotten. She will remain in her mother's mind. Through conversations with Yu, I was able to know that Yu loved people and nature, was concerned about problems like hunger, the fair distribution of wealth, and environmental protection. But what I have learned through retracing her steps is that she did not just talk about these things, but took initiatives to do something about them.

Before she was found in the stream, she had been interested in the way of life described in the book Walden. *Yu was in the process of narrowing her life down to very simple basics. Since I have turned from trying to forget about Yu to reconstructing her, I have derived satisfaction from what I have learned from Yu's friends and from her writings. Yu's sincerity and thoroughness far exceeded what I had known only vaguely. Now that I have set many of her writings in order, I have discovered something else. Her writings were diverse, ranging from a literary thesis, to poems, novels, essays, and diaries.*

The Yu described in the letter her mother sent was unfamiliar to me. Twenty-three years old. A completely different Yu from the Yu of that time. She was beautiful. It seems that after Yu slipped from my life she lived another sort of existence. Yes, everyone's life has two layers. Opposing natures dwell simultaneously in us, natures as different as plants are from animals.

I opened the window that had been shut all winter long. The sound as I pushed it from the thick window frame dug into my ears like a cry of pain. A disagreeable sensation came over me. Frowning, I rested my weight against the frame and looked out at the grapevines by the front gate. The new, light-green leaves were quivering at intervals in the morning breeze like so many tiny, flapping bird tongues. Each time I'd passed by the front gate during the winter, I'd glanced up at those dried-up things all twisted and tangled, and wondered what they were. Thin and leafless, those wire-like things, so stiff, so neglected, looked like nothing living. One day I became so annoyed with them that I was on the verge of tearing them down once and for all. Several times I actually reached out, intending to rip them down, but when I saw the vine prop standing below them, I remembered they were grapevines and let them alone. Now those vines, revived in the springtime breeze, had cast off their barren nakedness and were putting forth soft, light-colored leaves.

Maybe that color will carry over into my next life despite my forgetting. That earnest, light-green color!

An Open Space in the Forest.

The restaurant is gone now. Even with my amnesia worsening, I still sometimes pass by the spot. I wait for the bus at the bus stop there. I often follow the route the man followed the day Yu and I went on our strawberry field picnic. But I do not associate those things with him. Still, there are times when I unwittingly find myself staring at the Wedding Plaza where An Open Space in the Forest used to be. One day I even crossed to the other side of the street and went inside the wedding hall. I'd thought they held only marriage ceremonies there, but found that the Wedding Plaza also doubles as a buffet restaurant for traditional 1st and 61st birthday celebrations. As though I were a party guest, I watched a family crowd around a one-year-old baby to take its photograph. The hall was lined with displays of Chinese food: pretty arrangements of fresh vegetables, abalone and pumpkin soups, breads and rice, meatballs and sliced sausages, slices of raw fish, sweet and sour pork, an assortment of vegetable salads. Spreads of covered and open dishes filled with warm food. Foods laid out in abundance to celebrate the ongoing life of the one-year-old birthday baby. After the commemorative photos were taken, there was the pencil, the money, the bunch of thread . . .which one did the baby grab?

AZALEA

The
Strawberry
Field:
Shin Kyung
Sook

An Open Space in the Forest.

The place is gone now. The man and the young woman usually met there. They discovered An Open Space in the Forest late one night when the man was seeing the young woman home. Like all new couples, they wanted to spend a little more time together. When they came to her house, she'd see him as far as the bus stop. They'd pass the intersection, and after arriving at the bus stop, he would again see her to her front gate, and then walk back to the bus stop alone. Having done that several times, the two of them looked across the road from the bus stop where they were standing. An Open Space in the Forest. Hoping it was a place where they could be alone together, they walked a few paces from the bus stop towards the traffic light. An Open Space in the Forest was tucked away in a four-story building, in the basement with signs advertising a billiard hall, a Chinese herbal medicine shop, and a veterinarian's clinic. A small sign reading "Tea and Light Western Fare" seemed to be dancing in the hazy neon light. Once they descended the stairs and pushed open the wooden door, they felt safe.

A central seating area, a deejay booth opposite the counter, partitions facing the wall obscured by curtains. "Good evening everyone. Welcome once again to An Open Space in the Forest. We appreciate your patronage! If there is a song you would like to hear during your visit, please make a request. We'll do our best to play your requested number promptly." Listening to the voice of the deejay, they were directed to a narrow space behind a partition where they took a seat at a table, facing each other. The partition and the curtain made the two feel awkward. They both coughed in embarrassment. Coffee was served and then the waiter, with a courteous greeting, gently closed the curtain. The space was so narrow their knees touched and they could hear each other breathe. Under the café lights, his appearance seemed to gradually become more misshapen. He did not raise his face to look at her. He was not confident enough to look at her from such a close distance. She got up and crossed over to sit beside him. She took a memo pad from her purse and wrote out the question, "Do you want to request a song?" and pushed it toward him. Then, raising his head, he took the ballpoint pen from her and wrote, At the Pukhan River.

The singer said,

"This next song goes way back. I wrote it during an intense period in my life, at a time when I was closest to being 'me,' and really happy to be 'lost' in myself. I hope you like it."

Morning. The whole night through, dark clouds hidden by the night sky weighed heavily on your mind. I've come alone, here to the river at daybreak, to soak my legs in its cold water. I think about Seoul, that stranger city; and of your name, and of the empty streets, as the fog, the fog, rolls, rolls, along the beach.

That day, "At the Pukhan River" rang out across the concert grounds from the stage. It mingled with the other sounds. As the song was being played, the man and I thought of one another, there, in the same space. Perhaps the song was playing the moment he spotted me.

An Open Space in the Forest.

It was late at night, and there was no other place the man and young woman could go. The awkwardness they experienced when they first sat down behind the partition disappeared with time. They

AZALEA

The
Strawberry
Field:
Shin Kyung
Sook

did not sit facing one another any more. She sat next to him. She tried to keep him from bowing his head. While they were singing "At the Pukhan River" together, the man and young woman touched cheeks, touched shoulders. The man's complex about his appearance incited her to boldness. One day after listening to the song, the young woman took the man's face reverently into her two hands. He tried to turn away, but she looked deeply into his eyes, then kissed the corner of one of them. "Look at me. You have to look someone straight in the eye once in your life. Think of me as the person you have to look at."

As the man shifted his gaze to look at her directly, she started to be reconstructed by him. Her eyelids of unequal size were like a doll's. When he looked at her, the black birthmark near the right corner of her mouth, which had always given her an indolent and lazy air, suddenly became sensual. Her girlish body, stunted from malnutrition, stirred up an incestuous love within him. The man always carried her on his back and never wanted to put her down. He had a strong back. It suddenly occurred to the young woman: Do other girls grow up being carried on their father's back like this? Do other girls grow up feeling protected from this sense of existential insecurity? They were passing by the Myŏngdong district. Finding themselves in the path of a group of political demonstrators coming down from Myŏngdong Cathedral, she asked him if he would carry her on his back. She was testing him. If he did not agree to carry her, she would tell herself that the satisfaction she'd felt during their piggyback rides had meant nothing. It was something she could do without. Without any hesitation, the man hoisted the young woman onto his back, and steering clear of the demonstrators, he quickly moved toward the Exchange Bank. While he did so, she clung to his neck and tried swinging her feet. A feeling of satisfaction spread through her body, filling her heart. As long as his face was turned away from her, the man showed no sign of having a complex. When she rode on his back, he acted like any other person. But when his face was turned toward her, he always seemed to be feeling guilty about something. If the young woman looked away from him for any reason, he at once bowed his head and lost all heart. He said that the young woman was the only person in the world who looked at him without prejudice. Sometimes, he said, he felt that even his own mother, the woman who bore him, looked at him as though to say, "You're my kid, but ugh! What a mug!"

When he left home every morning, the man's mother gave him a homemade boxed lunch and two small bills. No matter where he happened to be, at noon he would come with his lunch to the front gate of the young woman's school. They met each other there, and making their way through the crowds of demonstrators, went to a small restaurant where they ordered a bowl of *ramyŏn* noodles between them and shared the lunch he brought along. His mother seemed to know everything about cooking with various grains like corn, millet, black beans, and barley. She always mixed them into the rice she cooked, so her rice always left a sweet taste in their mouths as they chewed. They ate their lunch as slowly as possible because he had to go back to work the minute they finished. The young woman's attempts to prolong their lunchtime meetings by five or ten minutes with her chatter disrupted his schedule, interfering with his job-related appointments, deliveries, and visits. But he accepted these consequences because his restless gaze, unable to settle for long on anyone or anything, could at last rest upon her.

Mother had awoken and gotten up from bed. Because I had grown up, she was now old. I watched her from the second floor as she descended the stairs leading to the front door carrying her plastic basket containing bath items—shampoo, rinse, toothpaste, toothbrush, and soap. The only thing Mother had left, this woman who always made a fresh start when everything seemed hopeless, was her two-story home with its grapevines. It had taken her

33

Azalea

The
Strawberry
Field:
Shin Kyung
Sook

fourteen years to get that house after the money orders stopped coming. Mother's wrinkly nape showed beneath her hair, which was combed back and knotted into a tight bun. She walked by the grapevines I'd just been staring at, and suddenly, as though remembering something, stooped down to peer inside the doghouse not far from her feet. As she crouched on her knees to look inside it, the white sweater she knit for herself rode up, exposing her feeble back. What was she looking for? There was little chance our dog Happy had come home last night. Mother stood up again, wearily. She picked up her bath bucket and dragged herself along in her slippers to the front gate. She snapped off a grapevine branch looped tendril-like around the prop, and examined it closely. I felt afraid for her. Someday mother might not be able to remember anything. Someday she might go to the bathhouse just as she was doing now, and not be able to find her way back. My dread was accompanied by the sound of the gate crashing shut, which could be heard from the second story where I was standing. Mother would walk down the alley and gaze intently at the drops of melted snow on the grapevine. And she would think, Will I be able to see the water on the grapevines next year? How many springs are left for me? On my way out yesterday, I, too, cut off a piece of grapevine just like mother did that day, and just gazed at it, there in my hands, as I made my way down the same alley.

One day at An Open Space in the Forest, the man said, "I can't meet you at night anymore. I took a part-time job as a guard at a warehouse. Because my mother is sick." He had to earn money. Although he was just barely twenty-three, he had been working all sorts of jobs since he was seventeen. He had been a delivery boy for a supermarket, an assistant technician at a boiler repair shop, and an employee at a newspaper distribution office. From the year he turned seventeen, he was obliged to support his ailing mother and grandmother. He'd never dreamed of going to college. Never having had such a dream, he never felt inferior for not going. Such a place existed in the world, and I, his lover, went there. That was all. Having dropped out of high school his freshman year in order to earn money, the man did not speak of college as a place of any importance.

A public telephone booth at midnight. Every night after the man reported for his part-time job as warehouse guard, the young woman walked to the market to call him. Everything was all right as long as he was there on the other end of the line. People were lined up waiting for her to finish her call. "There are people waiting in line. I'll call back soon." She would then walk back to the end of the line. She repeated this several times. She wished she had a telephone booth for her own private use. She stood in the public telephone booth late at night. She clung to the public phone past midnight, going on endlessly about some story or other. The man was in the dark warehouse, the young woman in a public telephone booth. Yu. While on the phone with the man, the young woman gazed through the glass door of the booth and spotted Yu walking past the intersection. Yu slid a hand over her seemingly fragrant neck, then walked along swinging her arms freely. As she walked, she seemed to leisurely thrust aside the soft evening air as though she lacked nothing, as though nothing was impossible for her. The young woman finished her call to the man in the warehouse, and was on her way home. She looked at Yu's house a block ahead of her. She looked up at Yu's bedroom on the second floor. The lights were turned on in Yu's upper-story room. As the young woman stood facing the wall of Yu's house with its undulating vines of red roses, she stared at Yu's silhouette appearing and disappearing at the window. Yu, moving back and forth, was changing clothes. For a brief moment, she saw a silhouette of Yu with her clothes removed.

The young woman instinctively motioned with her hand to an empty taxi passing in front of the two-story house with its flowering

Azalea

The
Strawberry
Field:
Shin Kyung
Sook

vine roses. Her face was hot. Also her hands, her legs. "Take me to Ch'angdong!" The man, who had just fallen asleep in the dark warehouse, got a phone call from the young woman, whom he'd just hung up with, saying she was near the warehouse. He gasped and sprang to his feet. The dark warehouse stood halfway up a hill upon which an acacia tree stretched out its roots tenaciously. It was dark because there were no streetlamps around. Opening the creaking door and entering the warehouse, she found herself surrounded on all sides by stacks of white paper cut to various sizes. The young woman looked at the bundles of paper, boxed and stacked high. For the first time, she began to worry about the man. Does he really sleep here alone, with all this paper? Does this man, who has cared for his mother and grandmother since he was seventeen, really guard this cold and dreary warehouse? If someone came to steal paper, would he have to fight them? She sat down on his cot. A military blanket lay spread out in a jumble across a pillow. The scent of acacia blossoms wafted in through a window cracked open for ventilation. Something was about to take place between the man and the young woman in the warehouse. It had been decided the moment she saw the beautiful outline of Yu's nude body in the window. The young woman could no longer repress her desire for the man. The whole thing had been set in motion the minute she caught the empty taxi in front of Yu's house. She sat on the man's cot and looked down at the indoor slippers hanging from her toes. That was all. She said nothing, keeping her desire hidden. His hands were trembling. He asked her if she was afraid. She did not answer. The young woman waited. Her mother at that moment was at home awaiting her daughter's return. Perhaps her mother had already been everywhere she could think of, searching for her daughter. The playground in front of the house, the market, the telephone booth the young woman was standing inside a few hours ago. The man was trembling violently. Because he was shaking so hard, the young woman blurted out, "I'm not afraid." Birds were singing on the hill. His trembling. He held out his hand and touched her face. In that

36

cautious reaching of his hand was an earnestness possessed only by people who have never had an opportunity to refuse anything. "You love me just like you do others," he said. She had no choice but to say, "Only you." She looked up at him. She told him to hold her. The first kind words she spoke since entering the warehouse. The man was still shaking. The young woman took off her one-piece dress by herself. She tossed it onto the dark warehouse floor with its stacks of white paper. She led his shaking hand and placed it on the hem of her white cotton slip. The man's hand fell away. He was weeping. He could not raise his head. "I know you're going to leave me," he said sadly. The young woman said she was longing for him. She said this did not mean anything. This is just what people in love do. The man stopped crying. "I can't do it." He shook his head. The young woman knelt on the cot and started to take off the man's clothes, revealing soft, pale skin under his shirt. His bare skin was like a child's, so unlike his face with its "stay away" scowl. His thin body that had stopped maturing at seventeen had a softness like the instinct for life itself. The young woman started crying. The man was pitiful. It was as if the desire within her was trying to violate him. It was only then that he pulled her to him and embraced her. The man who out of shyness could not look her in the face now could not take his eyes off her. The warmer they became, the more they felt pain, as though thorns had sprung from their bodies. The pain made them clasp each other even more tightly. They felt pain but were drenched in pleasure. The thorns pressed in deeply, sticking into the body of the other. The young woman, not knowing herself to be bleeding, pressed the thorns on her body deep into the man's flesh. The man, bloodied, wiped off the blood and embraced her again. Their faces were puffy from weeping. Waves of intense passion brought emptiness and then were swept away. Having no words to say, they lay on the narrow cot, one on top of the other. The man spoke. The other day, he was passing by Chogye Temple. He was on his way to an Insa district tearoom to meet an office worker interested in purchasing his prints. Suddenly a wave of demonstrators swept

AZALEA

*The
Strawberry
Field:
Shin Kyung
Sook*

toward him from the Susong district. Soon after that, there had been an explosion of tear gas bombs. He was just about to take cover in a basement tearoom, when suddenly he saw a group of Buddhist monks walking his way. Some were the age of schoolboys. Their shaved heads glistened in the sun. How beautiful that shimmer was, he said. One of the little monks was grasping the robe of a big monk and playing pranks; another was licking a popsicle and tripping the boy monk walking ahead of him; another was lagging behind, trying to get a look at the oncoming demonstrators, while a big monk was urging him to "Hurry up!" "I found myself holding out my hand and patting the boys' heads." The man kept talking. He said he'd kept on rubbing the tops of the little monks' crowns. It was so cute the way they tried gently to avoid the tickling sensation when he touched them. Before the sensation of touching their heads had left his fingertips, "Another tear gas bomb exploded. I hid in an alleyway, and when I came out they were already gone." The man spoke shyly. "Seeing your body just now reminded me of those boy monks' shiny heads," he said. "What were you thinking about?" he asked. The young woman spoke only in her thoughts. It felt like flames shooting up from a desert, and sand catching fire. She did not speak aloud. She did not want to tell the man about the feeling of loneliness that came rushing in after the flames subsided. Nor did she want to say something she did not mean. But even more, she did not wish to hurt his feelings. For a moment, the expression on the face of the young woman who did not want to say something unintended went awry. Somewhere a night bird called. The sound of the evening wind seemed to be climbing up the walls outside and creeping in through the window. Acacia blossoms seemed to float in the night air. Instead of answering, she looked emptily at her dress fallen on the warehouse floor. She knew she would never forget this night. The pleasure welling up through the pain, the scent of the acacias and the paper, the cry of the night bird. The story about the boy monks, and this emptiness remaining after desire.

38

These images, which have nothing to do with his existence:

The riot police buses lined up on the streets of An'guk district. Flags fluttering stoically at the Plaza Hilton, and the sweltering sun. My friend Yu with her bright, glowing cheeks. Her long, moist eyelashes casting shadows on the corners of her eyes. And again, the blaring heat from the sun. Was it at the Kanghwa Gate? The young riot police with red, sunburned faces and their stinking feet stuffed into army boots had received their rations and were chomping their food. Why we were passing by then, I do not know. The moment Yu saw their beads of sweat dripping into their soup, soup which seemed to give off a sour odor, she couldn't keep from gagging, and had to stoop down at the base of a tree to collect herself. Although these images have no connection with him, whenever I think of him, they flash in and out of my mind like automatic associations, these images that have no relation to him.

From then on, the young woman went every night to the warehouse where the man worked. That is, until she went to the strawberry field. There was no longer any pain in the act. The man could now embrace her without crying. Without trembling. After they finished, he moistened a towel with water and wiped the young woman's breasts and forehead glistening with her perspiration, and entered her again. Even in the silence, the man and the young woman lost themselves in the desire of wanting each other. The man gradually lost more and more weight. The young woman's mother began beating her daughter when she came home after sunup, her face drained from exhaustion. But the pain left by her mother's blows could not stop the young woman's desire. With swollen cheeks, she went again the following night to the warehouse where the man waited. The man licked her swollen cheeks. She thought suddenly that she could die now with no regrets. She did not care if the world forgot about her. Everywhere her mind was filled with thoughts of

AZALEA

*The
Strawberry
Field:
Shin Kyung
Sook*

him, even when she was signing some petition or other to investigate instances of forced enlistment or in support of reforestation projects. Even at those moments when her hand was signing a petition, her desire for him never left her mind. Gradually he lost even more weight. He perspired when they shared his boxed lunch with the rice and mixed grains. She wiped away his sweat. When their skin brushed lightly, they both wished night would come quickly. They missed the warehouse on the hill. That dark warehouse on the hill, filled with stacks of paper to be delivered to stationery stores and printing shops, was the place that suited them best.

I cannot remember when something began to erode the young woman's pure desire. Maybe she was unable to notice this erosion, right up to the end. But this much is clear. She was finding it harder and harder to sleep. When she wasn't with the man, she couldn't concentrate on anything. It was hard to attend classes. She had violent mood swings. She would be in the highest of spirits, then before long, she would fall into a deathlike state. She would be combing her hair in front of the mirror, and without thinking would open a drawer, take out all of her panties and brassieres, and then put them right back where they'd been, for absolutely no reason.

It was as if her friends, other young people of that time, were being fed daily rations of cheerlessness and despair. There was the frustration born of demonstrations that lasted for days on end, and the transfusions—not of blood but of tear gas fumes—that followed. This frustration seeped into their posture, the way they walked, how they stared. The pursuit of truth has never been easy but their frustration was fed by shocks they had never experienced before. Along the campus roads, fledgling birds died and trees wilted helplessly. Wherever they were, whatever they did, despair would rear its head. Not a soul could escape its smell. No one except Yu. Frustration bred cynicism, ruined the complexions of schoolgirls, fueled hatred, and, sometimes, summoned death.

The man spoke.

He said he wondered for years why I didn't show up for our appointment twelve years ago, why I didn't even try to contact him. Do I know even now, all these years later, why I did those things? What caused me to do them?

It was a day in May, a Sunday.

A telephone call came from the man. He said he was at An Open Space in the Forest. She looked at her watch. It was eleven. He sat waiting for her behind the partition in the basement restaurant. She spoke evasively, saying she could not go to meet him. She had not been to school for several days. Nor had she gone to the warehouse on the hill where he now spent his nights alone. She had not phoned him. When the telephone rang, she had not answered it. If it kept ringing, her mother would answer. The young woman hoped he would just hang up. On Sundays, he went to the cathedral for eleven o'clock mass. She had picked up the phone, thinking he was at mass. But he was at An Open Space in the Forest. She had been staying at home all morning, washing her hair, changing her clothes, just loafing around. He called again. He said he would wait for her until she got there. She couldn't say, "I don't want to see you." She had never said such a thing to him before. Anything was possible when she was with him. Going, coming, waiting. It was never a problem for him if she showed up later than expected. "I'll wait. I'll wait here until you show up." He hung up. She didn't know why she felt the way she did. He had done nothing wrong to her. But she thought she could no longer see him. But she could not say those words to him. Those words did not exist in the language between them. She was tired of the whole situation. She took her bag and slipped through the long alley without looking up. Even then, she didn't know she would end up ringing the doorbell of

AZALEA

The
Strawberry
Field:
Shin Kyung
Sook

Yu's house. Not even when she was looking at the red vine roses embroidering the walls of Yu's gate. The moment the clusters of red roses caught her eye, she could no longer stand the fact that the man was waiting for her behind the partition at An Open Space in the Forest. Someone was playing a Chopin nocturne at Yu's house. Was it Yu? An accomplished technique. She stared at the red roses, kicked at the red wall and listened to the passionate rush of the music. The image of Yu's white fingers bouncing over the white and black keys danced before her eyes. The May sunshine poured down limpidly through the red roses. On impulse, she pressed long and hard on the doorbell next to a white mail basket. "Who is it?" Yu's voice came streaming out. Seeing the young woman at the gate, Yu buzzed her in. As soon as she stepped through the gate, flowers from the garden rushed into her field of vision. Crowds of marigolds, pansies, and pinks stirred gently in the breeze. As she stood there dazzled by the wave of color, the front door at the top of the steps opened and Yu appeared, wearing a white tee shirt and blue shorts, holding a dog with plush fur in her arms. Her long hair was pulled back into a bun and secured with a ribbon. Who was playing the piano? The nocturne continued even after Yu came outside. Yu did not ask the reason for the young woman's visit. She had never invited Yu inside her own house. Once when they were walking home together, Yu had asked, "Are you going to invite me in?" but she pretended not to hear. Nor did she ever go inside Yu's house. Yu pointed to her front door and asked, "Won't you come in?" The young woman shook her head. You are too bright. Too radiant. If she had felt even a little uncertainty or longing on Yu's part, she would have asked her in, or she would have gone inside Yu's house. A budding desire emerged from the empty space where sisterly love had once existed. Yu set down the dog she was holding. "What's its name?" "Happy." "Such a common name!" "Mom picked it out and you know what she said? She said nobody else would ever name their dog that. But if you let all the dogs in the city out and called out 'Happy!' about half of 'em would come running." The young woman laughed at Yu's words. "She's a Chinese shih tzu . . . she's clever and very jealous. That's why I love her." A Chinese shih tzu. The young woman tried pronouncing it, mumbling it to herself. Standing at the gate, Yu watched the Chinese shih tzu as it stepped onto the lawn. Unexpectedly, Yu asked, "Wanna go to a strawberry field?" She said she'd planned to go to one with her mother that day, but her mother had suddenly changed her mind and was playing the piano instead. "Your mom plays the piano?" She thought about her own mother, who went around Namsan picking up acorns. Her mother, standing in front of griddle cakes and moonshine. "How about coming along with me?" The young woman was suddenly carried away by Yu's charming invitation. "Do you know where it is?" "Sure, we go to the same one every year. I'm wild about strawberries!" Yu told her to wait a moment. The instant Yu jumped up and ran to her front door, the Chinese shih tzu that had been lying languidly on the grass bolted up and scampered after her.

The young woman left the man waiting behind the partition in the dark basement restaurant at the intersection in front of her house, to follow Yu. In order to get to the strawberry field near Suwŏn, they took Bus 153 to Seoul Station and from there changed to the subway. So many people were looking at Yu. Her brightness made one forget about everything, even the noise of the subway trains. At Seoul Station, demonstrators were setting up camp. The stinging odor of tear gas was dank inside the subway. Yu's eyes teared up. On the train, Yu's brightness was obvious to everyone. She was dressed in a translucent sky-blue jacket over the cotton tee shirt she'd been wearing at her house. Her short, A-line skirt was printed with sky-blue water drops on a white background. At home, when she'd taken out the ribbon pin she'd been wearing in her hair, her long brown braided tresses had cascaded below her shoulders. Yu, with her smooth calves, below which she wore white, ankle-high sneakers. Yu was so very clean and dazzling, no one could pass her by without looking.

Azalea

The
Strawberry
Field:
Shin Kyung
Sook

Yu was beautiful. That much was clear. She had the aura of a glamorous movie star—though in truth the young woman had never seen a movie. That was the charm Yu exuded. The sun was scorching hot. Getting off the subway train, Yu and the young woman both bought themselves straw hats from a street stall. Although the hats were exactly the same, the one Yu wore seemed of a much higher quality because she was so lovely. A woman standing in front of the stall glanced at the straw hat the young woman was wearing, and just lowered her eyes; but when she saw Yu, she was transfixed. The unique texture of the straw hat seemed to stand out just because Yu was wearing it. The woman asked for a straw hat like Yu's and bought it. People gazed at Yu with awe, as if compelled to admire her. And it was true—so many people looked at Yu that the young woman beside her felt a kind of pride. She was so caught up in wonder that she almost forgot the man waiting for her behind the partition in the basement restaurant.

The singer said,

I went to see Chŏng T'ae-ch'un once when he performed in Kangwŏn Province. The story goes that after the performance he went with some younger friends to Chŏngdongjin. Now T'ae-ch'un had never seen the drama *Hourglass* when it was on TV. People call our generation the "hourglass" generation, and always associate it with Chŏngdongjin, where the drama was set. Everyone says that if you go to Chŏngdongjin, you can recollect traces of your long-vanished hopes. Well, the story has it that T'ae-ch'un and his friends went there with that kind of expectation. Besides a beautiful beach, they saw the train station and the pine tree that the director Ko Hyŏn-jŏng used as the background for some of the scenes in the drama. Then a sudden rain shower hit. It came on so quickly that they all ran to the train station for cover. There wasn't a soul there. While they were sheltering from the rain, a beautiful rainbow appeared outside the station window. They said it was so beautiful they watched it for a long, long time. They arrived in downtown Sokch'o, keeping their eyes on the rainbow all the while. At Sokch'o there's a land bridge near the marketplace. T'ae-ch'un is a knife collector, so he was strolling around the land bridge thinking he should buy a traditional knife from the area if any were to be had. Just then, a double rainbow appeared with that land bridge in the background. Because he's a thoughtful man, when T'ae-ch'un saw that double rainbow—although nothing else changed in the least—when he saw that single rainbow become a double one, he interpreted the doubling as a message: "There's still hope here." That night, he came back to Seoul and wrote the song "Chŏngdongjin." I'd like to sing it for you now:

From the window of the empty station room, we watched the rainbow. Waves in endless billows rushed towards the shore. A passing shower over the water at Chŏngdongjin, and a passing freight car on the railroad tracks, seven colors in the azure sky. . . .

The strawberry field was on the outskirts of Suwŏn. The hills, where the mountain cherry blossoms had fallen, were covered in dense greenery. As we came off a long, narrow dirt path, a strawberry field spread out before our eyes. Red letters on a white wooden sign marking the entrance to the field caught my attention: *Please pick your fresh strawberries. 5000 wŏn a basket.* Amid the shadows of May, in the midst of the green leaves, red strawberries dangled close to the damp earth. Each time the wind blew, green leaves were swept aside, and red berries with parched dry fuzz shyly revealed themselves. A woman with a towel on her head was picking berries and filling up her basket. When she caught sight of Yu, she said, "Oh, it's the daughter!" and came up from the ridge marking the boundary of the field. The palms of her hands were covered with strawberry juice. "Your mother's not here?" "She said she couldn't come. She decided to play piano for my uncle's kids at lunchtime." "I'd have enjoyed seeing her." "She told me to say

AZALEA

The
Strawberry
Field:
Shin Kyung
Sook

'hello.'" The strawberry field belonged to Yu's family. So even at the strawberry field, Yu was a free spirit. In a shed there were large baskets of similar size, neatly stacked one on top of the other. Here and there, people who had come to eat strawberries were sitting on mats with baskets of fresh-picked, just-washed fruit set in front of them. "Let's go!" Yu pushed a big basket at the young woman. The woman who called Yu "the daughter" shouted out to Yu as we were about to enter the strawberry field, and offered her a pair of white cotton gloves. Yu accepted the gloves and then handed them to the young woman. The young woman at once took the gloves from Yu, then asked as though remembering, "What about you?" "I hate wearing gloves . . . it takes the fun out of it. I like the sensation in my fingers when I break the stems." The young woman placed the gloves in her own basket. A young man who had entered the field carrying his young daughter stole glances at Yu, who was bending over, opening up the spaces between the green leaves and picking the ripe fruit. He glanced at the strawberries touched by Yu's fingertips, and at Yu's white thighs revealed as her A-line skirt hitched up in the sunshine among the green leaves and red berries. The young woman understood the heaviness of desire in the man's furtive glances. She had seen those eyes before. They were hers just before she went to the warehouse on the hill. Even after splashing cold water on her face and neck, that look in the mirror was still there.

Her basket was brimful with berries she'd picked. When she pulled out the white cotton gloves lying at the bottom of the basket, she found them soaked with red juice. The young woman stared for a while at the juice from the strawberries saturating the cotton. She tried to focus on her own picking, avoiding raising her head as much as possible. If she raised her head or looked to the side a little, she glimpsed Yu's brown braided hair in the sunlight, her beautiful neck between the braids, her white thighs among the red strawberries and green leaves. Yu was absorbed in her own harvesting, entirely unaware of her own sensuality. Yu did not know that each time she knelt down, her small breasts, still virgin to another's touch, were clearly exposed. The sight pained the young woman, with her underdeveloped body. Because the cleft at the center of Yu's collarbone seemed to invite the touch of the young woman's pinky. Because of Yu's sensual movements. Because the bright light seemed to dye her fleshy earlobes.

Dear Miss

I would like to preserve the traces Yu left behind. But by that, I do not mean those traces she left in the form of a book or other kinds of writing. I want to create just one journal that will exist in the world in my own handwriting. I want to think of the journal as being Yu. Perhaps it is presumptuous of me, this decision of mine; but rather than memorialize her, I want to preserve her existence, as her mother. I want to give birth to her again. The biggest reason is because through the process, I can feel her friends, I can feel her breath.

They wandered too far from the shed, too far from the woman who gave Yu cotton gloves to protect her. Too far . . . following the sunlight, following the green, following the red berries.

Was the young woman unaware that no one was around, that the people sitting on the outstretched mats were now just a flicker in the distance? She was. What was keeping her from raising her head was not Yu's sensuality, but her desire to kill her. The young woman did not know of her deep murderous desire to damage and pollute what Yu had. That is, until she placed her hand on Yu's white neck while Yu was absorbed in berry-picking.

She put her hands around Yu's neck while Yu busily attended to what her own hands were doing. The nape of Yu's white neck was hot from the sun and soft like jelly. When she slowly began to

Azalea

*The
Strawberry
Field:
Shin Kyung
Sook*

tighten her grip, Yu looked into her eyes. Yu's eyes were beautiful, so cold they reflected the sky. "That hurts," she giggled, looking at the young woman. There was an earnestness in those beautiful, clear, pure eyes. That was all. There was no sadness in Yu. There was no pain. There was no want. There was no impossibility. "Does it hurt a lot?" "Hm." The young woman released her grip and pulled Yu towards her in an embrace. At that, the red strawberries heaped up in Yu's basket spilled onto the field and were flattened. Red juice from the strawberries dripped down Yu's A-line skirt. The young woman stealthily picked up a handful of strawberries from her own basket and mashed them onto Yu's clean skirt. Yu did not resist, and just stared blankly at the red juice spreading over her clothes. Yu's skin was translucent. Her entire development had been untroubled. Nothing in her life had ever gone wrong. She was not oppressed in any way. The young woman placed her tongue on Yu's red earlobe. Her reddish handprints were already on Yu's white neck, and she traced them, caressing them. Yu's innocence. Even when the young woman pushed her tongue into Yu's partially opened mouth, Yu did not resist. It was subtle. It was peaceful. There was no malice. But when the young woman put her tongue deep into Yu's mouth, Yu suddenly pushed her away. "Lie down!" Suddenly Yu gave the order. It was decisive. It was as though her non-resistance up to that point had all been for the purpose of executing this command to "lie down!" "You were trying to kill me!" Yu suddenly became rough. She pinned the young woman down, opened up her blouse, and poured strawberries onto her breasts. Yu's outstretched hand was soft and dexterous. Sweetness, completeness. The young woman closed her eyes. She could not resist. The feeling of strawberries squashed on her cheeks, on her stomach, on her thighs, keeping her from resisting Yu. Yu's sugar-sweet fingers, lips, there was nothing left. Not a speck of anything. Everything fell into the caprices of their desire: the faint scent of sweat and the smell of the earth that yielded the strawberries, and the loneliness remaining after the act with the man, gone.

Already, from the moment she was in the lecture room that first semester, listening to the shouts of the demonstrators while leaning over her desk, from the time she chanced to see Yu's white calves as Yu sat behind her, the desire to kill Yu that she felt at the strawberry field had been sprouting up in her heart. She realized that her image of Yu, which had begun as a strange fixation, and at times fell apart dizzyingly, had been fermenting into exactly this moment in the strawberry field. Yu's ambiguous image had now come sharply into focus.

When they left the strawberry field, the woman who handed them the cotton gloves clucked her tongue. "You two ladies are too big for mischief!" At the woman's house adjoining the field, the young woman and Yu washed each other's bodies. They scrubbed their elbows and knees stained with red juice. They dried each other off with towels and put on the clothes the woman had given them: a blouse with blue amoebas and skirt pantaloons for the young woman, and an old brown one-piece dress with a Chinese collar for Yu. Even the woman's baggy, countrified clothing couldn't detract from Yu's beauty. After the young woman and Yu slipped into these rustic, worn-out clothes, they embraced each other like sisters, then fell into a long sleep. When the young woman awoke, darkness had already fallen. Where was she? She'd been here once before. A silent room. A wooden pillow stained with fingerprints, a closet with its door halfway open, a wall stuck with chewing gum, a man's baggy pants hanging from a nail on the wall. The young woman's heart felt as though it were being rent as she looked around this room. Yu was still asleep next to her. She placed her hand on Yu's heart. The sound of her regular breathing. The young woman raised herself up halfway, then buried her face in the spot where Yu's heart was hidden, and wept. She now knew she could never go back to the man, that she had parted from him forever. The woman had washed both their outfits, but they were so heavily stained with red juice from the strawberries they could never be worn again. Still in their borrowed clothes, they took baskets of strawberries the woman had wrapped up for them, donned their straw hats and boarded the subway train again.

AZALEA

The
Strawberry
Field:
Shin Kyung
Sook

After the young woman got off the train and was exiting the station, she saw the man with his head hung low. Was her face different now? She was on her way up the steps and the man was on his way down. Had her face changed in the strawberry field? Though his gaze met hers, he did not recognize her. His expression betrayed a downhearted resignation. The "stay away" sign had reappeared. He descended the steps to catch the subway, his head cast downwards. Looking away from his retreating form, she glanced at her watch. 11:00 P.M. Had he waited for her the entire twelve hours behind the partition in that basement? Yu had been behind her as they were coming out of the station, but now she was gone too. The young woman wandered around confused, looking for Yu. Yu had vanished. She had left, without even a goodbye. Now in her place there were only noises coming from above ground, the sound of car horns, and the colors of the neon lights at night.

That was the last time I saw her. For some reason, we often lose someone close to us while passing through the tunnel leading to age thirty. They are too young to die; so when they disappear, their image is carved deeply in the hearts of those who knew them. I heard nothing about Yu after she came back from the strawberry field: how she spent her days, about her life at the time she was approaching her death, about the funeral. I just received the one letter from her mother.

Dear Miss

But please do not view remembering Yu as a chore. I would only wish for volunteer contributions. Not only would doing so give meaning to Yu's existence, but it will keep me from experiencing

50

misunderstandings as I preserve her; not just as my child, but as a human being. This is the reason I am asking you, miss, for your help, though I do so with trepidation. Might you feel inclined to help me retrace the footsteps Yu left behind? I do not know what your relationship to my daughter was, but if you, miss, feel that you want to help me, please let me know. Any kind of input is fine—Yu's humanity, thoughts you shared with her, something she said—if it helps one understand what kind of person Yu was. I promise that if you help me I will not reveal your identity for any reason.

After returning from the strawberry field, I no longer traveled to forbidden places. I now accept the impossibilities of life. I accept the fact that different worlds I cannot know are unfolding in other people's lives, and that such circumstances can change a person. In passing through the man and Yu, my desire reached its end. All that remains is forgetting. That I was once a young woman who raced toward the forbidden is now nothing more than a dim recollection.

To Yu's mother, who called me Dear Miss, I did not send anything.

*The letter from Yu's mother was adapted from the preface to the posthumous collected writings of An Sŭng-jun.

계룡정인 2님 2006 지수

Gabriel Sylvian

Gabriel Sylvian: After reading "The Strawberry Field" for the first time, I knew I wanted to translate it to let English-language readers get a sense of the intricacy and beauty of the original. What was the response of Korean readers to the work when it first came out in the year 2000?

Shin Kyung Sook: It was publicized as being quite a different work from the things I had previously written. My works until that time had been noted for their lack of sex scenes between lovers, but "The Strawberry Field" contains strong sexual images. One critic quoted a passage from one of the love scenes in "The Strawberry Field" and said it would be long remembered as one of the most beautifully written love scenes in Korean literature. That pleased me very much. Some people said they'd barely recognized the work as mine. "The Strawberry Field" is set in the context of 1980s Korea. The narrator is reflecting back on the period of military dictatorship when she grew up. The adolescent lives cast into the midst of oppression and violence during the 1980s, which is the environment that the "I" in the novel experienced, survived in odd ways. The characters appearing in the novel are not of the kind that gain easy acceptance, and they have not had a place in existing Korean novels dealing with the 1980s. They're not people participating on the social stage of history, but rather young people who experience loss and dejection, and who have neglected themselves. Some people couldn't believe that the author of *Where the Harmonium Used to Be* (P'ung'gǔm i ittǒn chari)[1] had written this story.

GS: SF seems to be one of those works that both attracts translators and yet discourages them from attempting to translate it. Discouraged, perhaps, by its intricate narrative design, such as its intertwining timelines and points of view, but drawn to it because of its "sense of melancholy" and also because it provides some of the most memorable seduction scenes in recent memory. You mentioned in 2000 that releasing SF gave you a feeling similar to one you experienced when you published your very first work back in the 1980s. That implies a deep personal investment in the story. Is this story at all about you?

SKS: You're asking me to answer about my own desire! (Laughs) The male character in the story with "the face like a criminal" and the luxurious character "Yu" both exist in me, to some extent. The "I" in the story experiences both people. I created the narrative "I" and then had her experience what I had inside me but could never realize. The word "seduction" is so interesting. I agree there are lots of seduction scenes. I totally censored myself in word choice, though. I wanted to make it a beautiful work yet with a sense of emptiness through the "I" who seems to embody both "the man" and Yu. Conditions in Korea in the 1980s had both of those qualities. The entirety of my adolescence is in there.

GS: You have stated before that you prefer the term "empathy" to "sadness" when describing the basis of your own work. "Empathy" foregrounds a deep emotional connection between a work and its reader. Could you talk about that?

1. A translation of the work was published in *Harvard Review*, No. 23, Fall 2002, with the title "The Blind Calf."

SKS: I was talking about the emotion of being well disposed toward people who suffer from lack or want. The people I find burdensome are those with strong beliefs. People who try to accomplish something with those beliefs. People with strong beliefs oppress others without knowing they are doing it. If the world were made up of people who see themselves as forever unshakable in their resolution, what space could ever exist for seeing eye to eye? My novelistic world is always a search for vulnerable and imperfect people.

GS: "Lack" and "want" are often rooted in childhood experience. Healing from childhood trauma is a large theme in your writing, and this has made for very affecting narratives like *The Outer Room* (Oettan pang) that reference the oppression and frustration of female subjects by their historical and socioeconomic conditions, as well as by gender-based double standards. Women's knowledge, as a zone separate from male knowledge, seems to be an important source of this healing in many of your novels. And as the critic Paik Nak-chung (Paek Nak-ch'ŏng) wrote of *The Outer Room* that the change (or healing) of the female protagonist in your novels perhaps might lead to change in society (he wasn't sure), have you ever hoped inwardly that your writings might contribute to concrete social change? Do you consider yourself a feminist?

SGS: My girlhood was not a typical one. I had an uncommon growing-up period. What was uncommon was not that I was a laborer by day and wearing a school uniform and attending classes at night but rather the things that I saw and felt—what I experienced. Of course Korean society from the 1970s to the early 1980s had a huge impact on that. The social reality was just too unbearable to be directly withstood by a sixteen-year-old girl. Even though I had colleagues who were fighting to improve human rights within the space for change that was possible, I could not join them in their activities because I had to attend school. This led to my harboring feelings of guilt and similar frustrations. I couldn't be a subject, after all. Because I experienced those feelings during my sensitive girlhood, there was a long period of time during which I could not love myself. Underlying that experience was the fact that I was a female, and that I was poor, but I don't think those weighed in as the biggest issue. It was suddenly moving to the city and suddenly being surrounded by all the poverty there. The home of my birth wasn't a poor one. I was the fourth child with three older brothers, so at such times as advancing to a school of a higher grade or some choice in my life, I was sometimes put behind my brothers. But I never experienced that as significant psychological suffering. And then there was the particular situation of my family. Our family members were always extremely protective of one another, to the point of being very conservative. We looked out for each other and worried about one another, and I grew up as a member of that family. It was after leaving home that I came to experience "want." If my novels are highly feminine in character, it's because I am a woman and know women better than I do men. I've never thought that my novels would ever lead Korean society to social change. I'd rather say, my novels seem to have no objective at all. But I think that through the individuals appearing in my novels one can get an idea of what Korean society was like at the time. Because it is the society I live in, and novels are always based in reality. And I would rather be a woman than a feminist. Now I want to express through my writing the things I have experienced and felt as a woman. Therefore, inevitably my understanding of the women in my novels is deeper. Therefore, I would like men to read my novels more than women. Men who want to understand women. But they are not "women's novels"; they are human stories told through the eyes of women. It's the same as saying that male writers who write using male narrators are not writing "men's novels."

Nowadays Korean society's view of women has become equal to that of men. We've matured to the point that we don't have to portray women as weak anymore. Contemporary women in contemporary Korea don't feel inferior because they are women. From the late 1980s through the 1990s, feminism swept over Korean society and that had an influence. Now as then, I feel that men and women have clear differences, and would like those differences to be accepted as ontological differences, not as "prejudices" marking a power relationship.

I think we've practically reached that point. Now, naturally, it's just a matter of how men and women can coexist. In that sense, I think women have gained more possibilities for action. I often have times when I discover myself being considerate of others, and at those times I have a strong sense that, "Yes, I am a woman!" It's the same when I'm writing. The language system existing in that world is closer to that of men than to that of women. Subtle and sensitive. Bringing language into cultivation, harvesting it, and then replanting it with new seeds—that's the feeling I get from being a writer. In that sense, I think the idea that "things feminine will save the world" has resonance and meaning. That feeling has grown deeper in me the older I've become.

GS: Certainly in your work until 2000, including SF, there seems to be no escape from the legacy of oppression of 1970s and 1980s Korea that haunts the past, present, and future of your recollecting narrators. I'd like to ask you about the role "amnesia" plays in the work. Is it a negative strategy to deal with an oppressive past, for example, of the kind we find in Eun Hee Kyung's *The Bird's Present* (Sae ŭi sŏnmul)?

SGS: In the first sentence of the story, the character states that she is forgetting about her life. So underlying the work is the ambition to write the story down before she forgets it to the amnesia. It's neither a refusal to grow up nor is it a form of resignation, but she wants to conjure up the story from her memory. To not forget it, but remember it. The singer in the story is an actual singer. At one point he says that some people think a song is just a song, and others think it should contain something about society, but that he doesn't know which one is right. If you just change the word "song" to "story" that's the way I felt when I wrote "The Strawberry Field." Although I debuted in the 1980s, I have always been concerned with the individual. Even when social problems have overshadowed the individual, I have always thought individuals have to be happy in society. But in one part of me, I had always been weighted down by the feeling that I had avoided dealing with that directly. I wrote works like *Where the Harmonium Used to Be* still feeling that weight. Ironically, people say that I am a 90s writer who negates the 1980s, but I grew up in the 1980s and debuted as an author in the 1980s. People who participated in society through the student movement or in other ways had already been excessively novelized. I thought it was proper to take another route, to rediscover the individuals of the 1980s who lived among that oppression and violence. A majority of my novels written in the early 1990s try to do that. The strongest works in that area are "The Strawberry Field" among my shorter works, and *The Train Leaves at 7* among my longer novels.

GS: In SF, the ghost of the absent father seems to haunt the mind of the narrator. Interestingly, the ghost is accessed through the incestuous relationship with the unnamed man, and then that access is lost through the encounter with Yu. Can you mention something about the meaning mechanism of the novel?

SGS: The narrator "I" in "The Strawberry Field" grew up without a father. The mother raises her by herself. The father in the novel leaves the house as though he's going for a stroll and never comes back. The basis for the narrator's desire is the suddenly disappearing "father." Well, things have changed now, but up until ten years ago in Korea, growing up without a father meant being ostracized from society. In order to give her a fundamentally unhealed longing, I brought in the "absent father." Her encounter with "the man" who comes to love her comes about because of the white rubber shoes he wears that remind her of the ones her dad wore. By unilaterally ending the relationship with "the man" she hurts him ("the man"). That was partially because of the emergence of "Yu," but "Yu" is a girl, like herself. The unconscious which was abruptly abandoned by the father in her youth is thus manifested. In fact, "the man" is in the same boat as "I." The bright, luxurious "Yu" captivates "I" from their first encounter. That's because she is so different from "I." She is also very different from "the man." Therefore, "the man" is the woman's reality, and "Yu" is her dream. . . . [As for incest] That's a tough question. I don't see the relationship between "the man" and "I" as an incestuous one, even if she does recollect the father when she sees his white shoes. The father's white shoes on the ground symbolize the vagabond father's return. When they first meet, "the man" is wearing white shoes. So she remembers her father, that's all.

GS: Well, since we're on the topic of desire, I'd like to ask you something. In an interview in 2000 shortly after SF was published, you were asked about what you intended by including a same-sex theme. You commented that in SF, the characters were more at a distance from yourself than previous novels, and suggested that, within the context of the story, readers might look at the same-sex theme as being "sisterly love" rather than homosexuality. Yet the latter half of the 1990s was the peak of the gay rights movement in Korea, and other mainstream authors like Yun Dae Nyung, Sŏ Yŏng-Ŭn, and Yi Nam-hŭi also began variously employing same-sex themes in their fiction for the first time, after 1995. Do you prefer to distance SF entirely from the sexual-political developments of that decade?

SGS: The characters "Yu" and "I" are entirely different people, in everything from their home lives to their clothing, even in appearance. "I," who grew up amidst a great sense of personal loss, sees "Yu," who is so very bright and splendid, and she almost wants to kill her. That's expressed in "The Strawberry Field" impulsively and sexually. The connection between the two women is not sexual-political. But I think there is a gist there that can be read that way. I don't pursue just one theme when I write. I choose to keep a door open so that the story will be variously interpreted. It's similar to my personality, which tends to just want to run and hide when someone tries to persuade me of something. I hope that everyone who reads it will come away with a different story. That's one of the reasons I choose ambiguity.

GS: In the 21st century, as Korea increasingly distances itself from the martial law period, how has your own aesthetic approach to the past, present, and future also changed?

SGS: I'm now almost entirely free of the burden placed on me by 70s and 80s Korea. That was possible because I could write novels. But one can't divide time into past, present, and future. Time is not a straight line, but a curve. They're mixed up and then they meet. So you never know what's going to come popping out, and in what form. Last year I wrote *Li Chin*, a novel set in the late 19th century. Since then I've become free in terms of narrativity/plot as well. A long time ago, I would have said "I can't do that [kind of writing]" but now it feels like I can write about anything. The novel I'm currently working on is a full-length novel called *Take Care of My Mom* (Ŏmma rŭl put' hae). It's a narrative I'm dedicating to the things that have restricted me until now. Recently I've been thinking each person is a book. And I'm spending more time on those who have lived their life beyond the realm of morality, as well as those who lived within morality and finished their lives beautifully. I may write a really extreme work based on this idea. It might be a work full of partiality.

GS: Who are the greatest influences in your writing? How did you come to write, especially female "coming-of-age" stories?

SKS: Rather than influence, I'll talk about the works I enjoyed reading. I was deeply impressed as a high school girl with Cho Se-hŭi's *Small Ball Thrown Upwards by a Dwarf* (Nanjang'i ka ssoaollin chagŭn kong).[2] In college, I was an avid reader of Korean novels by O Chŏng-hŭi, Choe In-hun, and Yi Ch'ŏng-jun. Until reading Milan Kundera in my late 20s, I'd thought, "I have to be a novelist like Oh Chŏng-hŭi." I was totally charmed by her deep insights and tragic worldview. When Kundera's *The Unbearable Lightness of Being* was first translated and released in Korea, it was so fresh and new. I enjoyed discovering its language, which contained not only tragic things, but also elegantly mixed in analytical aspects, and even jokes. In recent years, I've been reading Ismail Kadare's works. I like the feeling I get when I face his earnest, weighty writing style, like muscles popping out when running a marathon.

The reason I became a writer was because it was something I could do without any help from others. I guess I had thought I would always live alone. My dream as a writer was to have a feeling of existence that matched me like a piece of clothing that fit perfectly. I think that's what I have been pursuing all this time. As I was writing, I didn't think of my work as "female coming-of-age stories." I wrote about time periods. Time periods I couldn't just let go by, that I felt stuck in.

GS: How about your more recent reading interests?

SKS: I just returned from a month-long trip to Italy. The books I read in my baggage were Cormac McCarthy's *The Road*, Ian McEwan's *On Chesil Beach*, and the latest works by young Korean writers Jo Kyung Ran and Kim Yŏnsu, *I Bought a Balloon* (P'ungsŏn ŭl sassŏ) and *The Right to Travel* (Yŏhaeng hal kwŏlli). Also Orhan Pamuk's *Istanbul*. I left them at the hotels where I finished reading them. The novel I mentioned that I'm writing now called *Take Care*

2. Translated by Bruce and Ju-Chan Fulton and published as *The Dwarf* by University of Hawai'i Press, 2006.

of My Mom (Ŏmma rŭl put'akhae) is now being serialized in the journal *Creation and Criticism* (Ch'angjak kwa pip'yŏng). The first part that I've already written I made into a book for my own use. So that I don't forget the rhythm. I kept reading the first section during my trip.

GS: Best wishes for your upcoming novel. Thank you.

Five Poems by Yi Seong-Bok

Translated by Hye-Jin Juhn and George Sydney

ABOUT TIME

1

a mason's life is breaking stone, and a grocer's life is

standing all day   my friend who looked like Montgomery Clift
        used to

hang around a third-class double-feature movie house   I don't
        know what's become of him

time has passed and will continue to pass   on the morning of the
        first day

of the year two thousand I'll have a grandson   well, I've got to go

the cars to paradise flash past,

the roadside trees stand in straight rows   over there, a child grins,
        twirling

a mouse by its tail

time, frozen days

sisters who after working all night at the factory slept through sun-
        bright days

2

as I followed the river of weariness, from time to time on my
        forehead

a wild strawberry bloomed, most of that is

fantasy, in reality, from time to time my elder brother sired

a son   laughter burbled from my father   again some fruit fell

from a naked tree   from time to time

a red horse crossed the iced-over sky pulling a cartload

of *yŏnt'an* briquettes   most of that is fantasy   in reality,

some children, bent double, were rooted on a hill

like red-pepper plants left uncollected during harvest   in reality,
    my emasculated

friends disappeared singing current pop songs

but time did not fly away   it was sometimes found deeply asleep

inside a worn abandoned shoe,

and from time to time it plummeted upside down like a
    shotgunned bird

laughter burbled from my father   as I followed the river

of weariness, from time to time I rested

upon a bird's nest high up   most of that is fantasy too

3

time passed and nobody was able to come back

from the deep dark stinking hole

a letter was returned several times   answers were always to be
    found in the debris of questions, and friends would give out

like toy airplanes with spent rubber bands   when I was too tired

to even masturbate, the white roots of grass in a frozen swamp

swam before my eyes   time passed,

the prostitutes sang songs every day, and by the time they were
    twenty-three,

twenty-four, cigarettes had stained them yellow

and every night by eleven I caught the bus for home

and time passed   during the half hour the girls at the sewing
    factory ate lunch

the clothes irons stood cooling, and every half hour, in every
    wedding hall,

there was another bride and groom   time passed   in an infant's faded

hundredth-day photo, in a public graveyard for Chinese
    immigrants, in a cheap restaurant,

on a road where rainwater puddled, on leaves   time passed   on a
    street busy

with traffic a child pedaled along on a tricycle

some people were to be pitied, some who saw them

wept   nothing could come back

from the asphyxiating malodorous dizzying hole

4

my heart aches whenever I hear the word "time"

I was brought up as a treasured child, and nothing significant
    happened

to me other than my encountering in my path a few stones that I
    got easily past—middle school,

high school, the difficult period of learning, and then lust, and a
    desire to be heroic,

and feelings of shame   though there's nothing I need to forget,

time rises like a fog, like drunkenness

how   is   it   that   the   field   grows   so   wide

andhowisitthattherearesomanyredflowerswaveringonthehorizon?

                                                  that year
                                        snow fell often and
                                  the road turned quickly muddy
                                  I was night   I was on a train
                                  with you, passing a bare mountain

        the train from time to time stopped, something white
        flickered, and the train moved on again . . .   time passed

                              this also might have happened

                                        when I
                                turned round
                               and sank into
                           the rolling darkness
            stamping the ground
                            you began to break apart
              not a sound
                                        was heard

                                   (I loved you
              I was the two-*p'yŏng* room you were sleeping in
                several dolls with the same face sat next to each other
        and a bell tolled in the church inside a framed picture . . .
                                   I was your room
                     I was the grassy field you gazed at
        I was the stream that ran quietly alongside the grassy field
                             and I was nothing
                                   I was
                           a handful of air
                            like your heart
                 when of a sudden you bow your head)

whenever the word "time" comes upon me somewhere
I see the sky falling like an avalanche of snow, and something like
     an electric wire
vibrating   like others,
I several times failed at love   each time was only
a failure   I came to understand how touching pop songs
can be, and that neither the toyed with,
nor the toyers, are happy   time always
ran ahead of me, and over and over again I had to
pass through a narrow damp space between doors

that fall, though I didn't send anybody a letter

I got several from friends who'd gone off to do the obligatory
    military service they'd been postponing   all the trees in the
    world turned

yellow at the same time, as usual, and houses scaled the hillside
    right up to the sky, overwhelming the color of grass

that fall, a five-year-old Cheju Island pony bit somebody's private
    chauffeur

who was arguing with its owner, and a well-known writer serialized
    some travel pieces about his journey to South America

Dad, I didn't realize you were going to be here

that fall, the children playing house were more tedious even than
    Korean films, and the long-drawn-out yawns were heavier
    whenever we raised the flag or lowered it,

people were driven like posts into the ground, but the sound

of a hammer wasn't heard   that fall, when a dead young eel floated

to the surface of the stream in front of Moraenae, the stream, which
    had been dredged, also

floated, and a worker fell at the speed of a feather from the elevated
    expressway that was under construction   that fall, when dogs
    changed coats, the mother

of the children who'd died the previous summer after eating sautéed
    silkworm larvae bought from a sidewalk vendor,

hung out on dark street corners   a senile old man was abandoned
    at the Seoul train station,

as was a congenital idiot at the Ch'anggyŏng Palace   that fall, a
    Buddhist monk

returned as a mystic, playing a flute made of human bone, and
    when I asked

a woman for a date she spit and turned away

my father, who used to leave home in the early morning and come back in my dreams—

how would I have known he was buried here?
that fall, I decided to break my habit of talking as though there
    wasn't any fun in my life
but even that decision turned out to be no more than a joke
I picked up fallen ginkgo leaves and dead cicadas
and kept them in match boxes, and my sister and I locked our
    rooms
from inside   that fall, I realized that there was no fall that
    belonged
to any particular year, and I taught myself
not to debase things so as not to beautify them
Dad, Dad!   "am I your dad?"
that fall, I lived all the days I'd lived, and those I was going to
live   but I met another woman, who was like a drop of water
    clinging to a wall, and
I realized that not an eye in all the world would close
until she splattered, and so I understood why Gregor Samsa's family
prepared to go on an outing after burying him
Dad, Dad . . .   "you little fucker   you should be too ashamed to
    talk"
that fall, the face behind the mask was a mask

SOUTH SEA, SILK MOUNTAIN

a woman was immured in stone

for her love, I followed her into the stone

one summer it rained a lot

weeping, she left the stone

led by sun and moon she left

I'm alone now, by the edge of the blue sky above Silk Mountain at
the South Sea

alone I sink into the blue water of Silk Mountain at the South Sea

on a rainy day, in a car,
hearing music
I feel as though someone else is living
my life for me
I feel
it's not that the music
is so achingly far away,
but I feel
I've come too far
from where I ought to be
my life, that
does not need to be lived by me—
the lips, that do not belong to anyone—
there, I gently place
my own dry lips

EXCURSION

1

in a suburb of the city named "Pain" I saw dogs peeing
with one leg lifted   I saw a real helicopter, and a car factory,
and real stupidity   while on a train passing through
a suburb of the city named "Pain" I saw—a pregnant woman
carrying a shopping basket, a Negro soldier with a rifle on his
    shoulder

                                  playing choo-choo   playing
                         choo-choo   life is playing choo-choo
I saw—men dancing naked, a half-breed child
playing with marbles, filigreed television antennas

                                 is this desire?   is this desire?
      this thing that sometimes swells up and penetrates the roof
in a suburb of the city named "Pain" I watched a film,
ate a hot dog, and whistling whhhyy went to somewhere
Sodom, the calluses on the soles of feet, the moving castle

2

my godfather sky, today I went to the Neva River
I saw an endless line of shops and women
like dolls   I wanted to buy them to hold in my arms   my
    godfather
sky, today I scattered flower seeds in the hair
of passing children   one day, one day, the flowers will come
walking from all directions calling my name   my godfather sky,
today I mesmerized the tall keep-out walls, the foreign cars,
the doormen of the posh apartment blocks   the mesmerized Neva
    River
was beautiful   rumors grew in every street, and fresh flowers
gave off a rotten odor   the mesmerized Neva River was beautiful
the hostile glance of shapely lovers, chittering, and the sound

71

of their sucking lips   (my poor armpits.   how they tingle)   my

godfather sky, I grabbed a coach and went into a shop that made

soup for hangovers   I chewed on my memories like blood

   pudding dumplings, spit them out,

and had to run away across the roofs   I was running away, and

   dreaming,

and at the foot of the bridge the authorities checked my papers, and

   I came back, but without

my dream. . .

Heinz Insu Fenkl

O utside small circles of specialists, very little is generally
known about the DPRK. To many Americans, the
Democratic People's Republic of Korea is a mythic anti-Shangri-La
assembled from stereotypes, a police state modeled on images from
works like *1984* and any number of Hollywood films (which have
regularly used North Korea as an easy source of villainy after the
collapse of the Soviet Union). Meanwhile, Kim Jong-il has become
an icon more easily recognized than many American political
figures. High school students recognize the Dear Leader's trademark
hairstyle, they joke about his taste in films, and they turn him into
a caricature of evil—all without knowing anything significant about
North Korea or its history. North Korea periodically makes the TV
news for its nuclear threat, its lack of cooperation in peaceful efforts
at reunifying the Korean peninsula, and for its ongoing droughts
and famines. But despite the apparent coverage, the DPRK has been
the real "Hermit Kingdom" in modern times.

Recently, with the New York Philharmonic's visit, there has
been a dramatic turn in American media coverage of the DPRK.
The visit to Pyongyang not only made major headlines, but was
also the subject of a special documentary by Christiane Amanpour,
CNN's chief international correspondent, who was even permitted
a visit to the Youngbyun nuclear plant according to her strikingly

73

AZALEA

Inside

North

Korea:

Heinz

Insu

Fenkl

friendly special report. In early July of this year, George Bush announced his intention to take North Korea off the notorious "Axis of Evil" list and, eventually, to permit trade without the stigma of "doing business with the enemy." Such public gestures suggest a significant change in the U.S. attitude toward the DPRK.

When I began gathering materials for this special section of *Azalea*, I started by looking for materials on North Korea that were available to the general public outside academic and political circles. There was much more than I imagined, including numerous texts and films available on the Internet. My main challenge was in formulating a logic for selecting from wide-ranging sources in order to present a sort of North Korea collage. I wanted the materials to speak for themselves to specialists and nonspecialists alike, without any overt rhetoric on my part. I also wanted to present a spectrum of texts that would permit a reader to get a sense of the *texture* of what the DPRK must be like. I drew from both internal and external sources, that is to say, from texts by North Koreans as well as those from outside.

The following pages begin with an excerpt from Guy Delisle's comic book memoir, *Pyongyang*, which in its minimalist style presents a remarkably accurate sense of the bleak atmosphere of the city—far more successfully than any film or photographs I have seen. *Pyongyang* has unfortunately been relegated to comic book and graphic novel readers, but it deserves a wider audience for its unexpected and surprising glimpses into North Korean culture. The photographs in this section, which provide a real-life counterpoint to the comic book images, were taken by Peter Sobolev, a Russian computer engineer, during his visit to North Korea in May of 2004. A complete set of his photos, along with illuminating commentary from a non-American perspective, can be viewed at http://www. enlight.ru/camera/dprk/index_e.html.

The excerpt from Hyejin Kim's *Jia* describes, with understated vividness, the sense of North Korea as a nation perpetually at war. Although she has presented it as a novel, Kim's book draws incisively on many of the testimonies provided by North Korean refugees, and the narrative has the authenticity of a memoir or a foreign correspondent's report.

The children's comic book *Great General Mighty Wing*, written by Cho Pyŏng-kwŏn and illustrated by Rim Wal-yong, was excerpted from among several dozen examples of North Korean children's comics. (The entire contents of *Mighty Wing*, along with several other comic books and a wide variety of other texts, was once available to the general public for perusal on an educational website for North Korean citizens abroad, but many of the texts have since become accessible only by password.) The tone of many of the North Korean comics was familiar to me, since I had grown up in South Korea during the Park Chung Hee years. But among the typical stories of ever-vigilant youths who report suspicious activities, and heroic soldiers who fight against the Japanese or the Americans (depending on the historical era represented), I found *Mighty Wing* to be especially fascinating for its apparently innocuous artwork juxtaposed with pointed political slogans on every page. *Might Wing's* narrative is particularly relevant because it is also an allegory, for the drought and famine years, presented to children. Those who wish to read more of the text can find fifty pages online at www.geocities.com/gnoth7/mw/mightywing.htm.

Most of the poems in this section were taken from the poetry available on the same educational website that houses *Mighty Wing*. They were selected to reflect the sentiments toward nature and nurture found in this type of thematic poetry in both Koreas. The two works of prose fiction in this section are from different ends of the literary spectrum. Hong Sŏk-jung's *Hwang Chin-i,* excerpted here, won the prestigious Manhae Literary Prize in South Korea in 2004 (the first time for a North Korean work). The novel is not only well respected in North Korea (Hong's grandfather was Hong Myŏng-hi, author of the epic historical novel, *Im Kkŏk-jŏng*), but it was the basis for the 2007 film by South Korean director Jang Yoon-Hyeon (who was formerly best known for his horror thriller,

AZALEA

Inside

North

Korea:

Heinz

Insu

Fenkl

Tell Me Something). Ch'oe Ryŏn's short story "Make the Ocean Blue" provides an example of contemporary North Korean fiction by a promising new writer; the story's surprisingly wide range of concerns includes global warming.

Western readers tend to forget that the consequences of representation are radically different in the DPRK, and that there are severe constraints with which every publicly presented example of North Korean artistic and literary production must comply. Works must follow the guidelines prescribed by *Juche munhaknon,* the North Korean theory of literary production attributed to Kim Jong-il himself, but artists and writers exercise extra caution because their works are open to interpretation and criticism after publication. Although the North Korean works presented here have been translated into English and made available to a larger audience than originally intended, we hope the reader will keep the political and social realities of the DPRK in mind.

YOU'RE HERE FOR THE SEK?

IF THAT'S THE NAME OF THE ANIMATION STUDIO, YES...

OH! WELL, EVERYTHING IS ALL RIGHT THEN.

OUR APOLOGIES!

MISTER GUY?

I'M MR. KYU, YOUR GUIDE.

A PLEASURE.

THE DRIVER IS OUTSIDE.

3

I CAN BARELY MAKE OUT HIS FACE BECAUSE THERE'S NO LIGHT IN THE AIRPORT.

THE DRIVER HANDS ME FLOWERS THAT I KNOW AREN'T REALLY MEANT FOR ME.

TO HELP ME PREPARE FOR THIS TRIP, I WAS GIVEN A BOOKLET OF TRAVEL TIPS.

THANKS.

HOW NICE.

HYGIENE
Bring your own medication.
Do not drink the tap water.

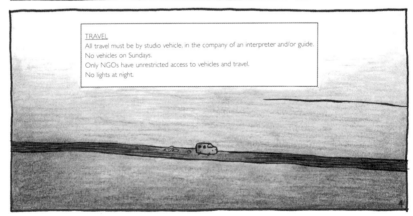

TRAVEL
All travel must be by studio vehicle, in the company of an interpreter and/or guide.
No vehicles on Sundays.
Only NGOs have unrestricted access to vehicles and travel.
No lights at night.

ALLOWED
Audio cassettes.
CD player and CDs.
Portable computer and printer.
Cameras and film, camcorder. Not everything can be photographed.
Food: mustard, ketchup, etc.
Books to give to interpreter at the end of the trip.

PROHIBITED
Mobile phone (confiscated at airport and returned on departure.)
Pornography.

MY GUIDE SUGGESTS WE VISIT THE HIGHEST POINT IN THE CITY TO ADMIRE THE VIEW BEFORE GOING TO THE HOTEL.

AN ELEGANT WAY OF TAKING ME ON A STOP THAT'S OBLIGATORY FOR NEWCOMERS WITHOUT BEING OBVIOUS.

6

82

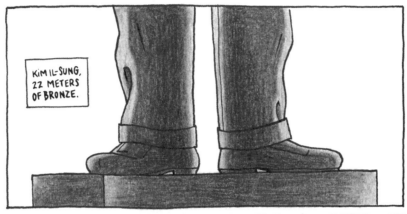

KIM IL-SUNG, 22 METERS OF BRONZE.

FOR VISITORS, IT'S A DISPROPORTIONATE ONE-ON-ONE WITH THE GIGANTIC FIGURE OF THE FATHER OF THE NATION.

WHO, DESPITE HIS DEATH (1912-1994), IS STILL PRESIDENT.

AZALEA

Guy
Delisle's
Pyongyang

PYONGYANG HAS THREE HOTELS FOR FOREIGNERS.

EACH HAS ITS ADVANTAGES.

THE POTONGGANG, WITH ITS CABLE TV (CNN).

THE KORYO, IN THE HEART OF TOWN.

THE YANGAKKDO, WHERE SANRINE AND I ARE STAYING.

IT'S A MASSIVE 50-STOREY TOWER WITH A REVOLVING RESTAURANT, BUILT IN THE 1980s BY A FRENCH FIRM.

THAT EXPLAINS THE FRENCH DESIGNER TOILETS.

AAAH! VIVE LA FRANCE.

ALL FOREIGNERS ARE ON THE 15th FLOOR, THE ONLY ONE THAT'S LIT.

I DON'T MEAN TO COMPLAIN, BUT THIS IS THE FILTHIEST TABLECLOTH I'VE EVER SEEN...

ARGH! AND IT'S WET, TOO! MY ELBOWS ARE SOAKING!

UGH! THIS STUFF IS SWIMMING IN OIL!

YOU'LL GET USED TO IT.

THERE'S A CAFÉ IN THE LOBBY. WE GO THERE FOR DESSERT. IT'S DRIER ON THE ELBOWS.

WHAT? THEY CALL THIS ICE CREAM?

WE MEET TWO TELECOM ENGINEERS FROM FRANCE.

THEY'RE HERE FOR A WEEK, LONG ENOUGH TO INSTALL A HIGH-DEFINITION TRANSMITTER...

FOREIGN ADMIRERS OF THE KIM REGIME WILL SOON BE ABLE TO WATCH THE DEAR LEADER'S HEROIC EXPLOITS IN HIGH-DEFINITION SPLENDOR WITH DOLBY SURROUND SOUND.

BEFORE (HERTZIAN)

AFTER (DIGITAL)

AN OBVIOUS PRIORITY FOR A COUNTRY GETTING THE MOST AID IN THE WORLD!

87

PYONGYANG: PHANTOM CITY IN A HERMIT NATION.

THE FEW DISMAL PICTURES YOU SEE IN THE WEST HAD ACTUALLY LED ME TO EXPECT WORSE.

TRAMWAYS, CARS, BUSES, TRUCKS... IT TURNS OUT THE STREETS AREN'T DESERTED AFTER ALL.

EVERYTHING IS VERY CLEAN. TOO CLEAN, IN FACT.

NO ONE LINGERS IN THE STREETS. EVERYONE HAS SOMEWHERE TO BE, SOMETHING TO DO.

NO LOITERING, NO OLD FOLKS CHATTING. TOTAL STERILITY.

IT'S ALL NEW.

DURING THE KOREAN WAR, BOMBS RAINED ON THE CITY FOR 3 YEARS, FLATTENING IT.

AFTERWARD, THE PARTY OBLITERATED ANYTHING RESEMBLING AN OPPOSITION...

AND SEALED OFF THE COUNTRY TO ALL SIDES.

THE CITY WAS ENTIRELY REBUILT ACCORDING TO THE GREAT LEADER'S PLANS.

IN EVERY ROOM, ON EVERY FLOOR, IN EVERY BUILDING THROUGHOUT NORTH KOREA, PORTRAITS OF PAPA KIM AND HIS SON HANG SIDE BY SIDE ON ONE WALL.

EXCEPT IN THE SHITTERS, OF COURSE.

AND SINCE "KIM IL SUNG IS KIM JONG-IL AND KIM JONG-IL IS KIM IL-SUNG", THEY'RE MADE TO LOOK ALIKE.

KIM SENIOR'S GRAY HAIR AND DEFORMING NECK TUMOR ARE GONE.

AS ARE KIM JUNIOR'S GLASSES AND EXCESS WEIGHT.

SAME SIZE, SAME AGE, SAME SUIT.

THAT WAY NOTHING EVER CHANGES – IT'S ALWAYS THE SAME HEAD AT THE HELM.

THE WORLD'S ONLY COMMUNIST DYNASTY.

HUH.

MY COFFEE BREAKS LEAD TO A FEW MORE OBSERVATIONS.

THE PORTRAITS, WHICH ARE HUNG HIGH ON THE WALLS, HAVE A WIDER EDGE ABOVE THAN BELOW.

THE ANGLE CUTS OUT ANY REFLECTIONS THAT COULD PREVENT YOU FROM CONTEMPLATING THE SUN OF THE 21ST CENTURY AND HIS VENERABLE FATHER. IT ALSO INTENSIFIES THE GAZE IN THIS FACE-TO-FACE ENCOUNTER.

THERE'S A DETAIL ORWELL WOULD HAVE LIKED.

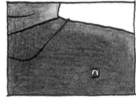

BOTH WEAR ONE OF THE OFFICIAL BADGES THAT INVARIABLY DEPICT KIM JUNIOR OR KIM SENIOR. YOU CAN'T TELL FROM THE PORTRAITS, BUT IT'S TEMPTING TO THINK THEY'RE WEARING EACH OTHER'S IMAGES, CREATING THE KIND OF SHORT CIRCUIT ANIMATORS LOVE...

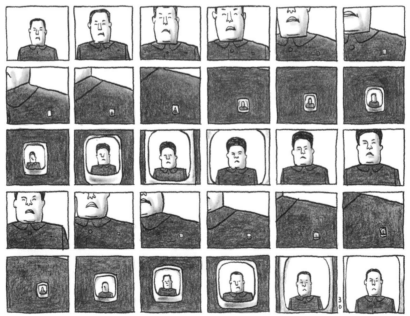

SCENE (117): When the character pulls on the ribbon, keep it tight as the bow unravels.

On else he looks like he's holding a snake and playing with it.

Hmpf.

MISTER GUY.

AFTER ASKING TWO DAYS AGO, I'M BEING TAKEN TO VISIT ONE OF THE PRIDES OF THE NATION...

THE PYONG-YANG SUBWAY.

BURIED 90 METERS UNDERGROUND, THE PYONGYANG SUBWAY CAN DOUBLE AS A BOMB SHELTER IN CASE OF NUCLEAR ATTACK. WHAT BETTER WAY TO CULTIVATE A CONSTANT SENSE OF THREAT?

THE

LONG

WAY

DOWN.

A REGULAR.

MARBLE FLOORS, CHANDELIERS, SCULPTED COLUMNS. IT'S A SUBTERRANEAN PALACE TO THE GLORY OF PUBLIC TRANSIT.

EVERYWHERE, GARISH MURALS TRANSFIGURE A REALITY THAT JUST SEEMS DRAB TO ME.

IN A CITY WITHOUT ENOUGH ELECTRICITY TO POWER ITS TRAFFIC LIGHTS, THE SUBWAY TUNNELS ARE LIT UP LIKE LAS VEGAS!

STRANGE... VERRRY STRANGE...

THE TOUR ENDS AT THE NEXT STATION. OUR DRIVER PICKS US UP AT THE EXIT.

I'VE NEVER MET ANYONE WHO'S SEEN MORE THAN TWO STATIONS.

Jia: A Novel of North Korea[1]

By Hyejin Kim

False Identity

Early the next morning, I tied the made-in-China lace-up shoes I had bought in the street market and set off for the Pyongyang train station. I was well layered in a thin white shirt and stockings, which I always wore for performances, two ivory sweaters, and thick brown pants. I wrapped my head in a dark-blue scarf and put on my oldest, worn-out coat. I tried to wear as much as possible, to keep my backpack light.

The streets were empty, and wind whistled through the alleys around my apartment. I got on my bicycle and rushed toward Ch'anggwang Street with my scarf pulled tight; I was afraid of being seen by anyone I knew. Crossing Taedong Bridge, Kaya Hotel and Pyongyang Station came into sight all at once. On any other day, I would have turned my bike to the right and headed for the hotel. But this wasn't any other day.

My head down, I made an abrupt left turn as the station grew larger, expanding beyond my field of vision. The Great Leader was smiling at me from the picture above the entrance, and my eyes

1. Copyright © 2007 by Hyejin Kim. Published in the United States by Midnight Editions, an imprint of Cleis Press Inc.

stayed fixed on him; the larger his face grew, the more convinced I became that he was not actually looking at me, but rather up and into the far distance. That comforted me.

The station was already crowded with anxious travelers pacing the terminal. A conductor said there would not be a train to Hamhŭng or Onsŏng that day due to an engine problem; some would-be travelers turned back while others decided to wait out the delay in the station. I was afraid that Sŭnggyu would catch me after discovering my escape, and I needed to get out of Pyongyang. Grabbing the conductor's arm tightly, I asked him if there was no other way to get to Onsŏng. If I hadn't held him I felt he would have flown away without giving me an answer.

"You can catch a car ride on the street—just ask the driver to take you on board."

"Where can I catch those cars?"

"Go to any big street, you'll see the trucks. Try to the west, crossing the Pot'ong River."

I made my way to Sŏsŏng Street. Pedaling furiously, I headed northwest and passed over Sŏsŏng Bridge. The layers of clothing stuck to my body and I felt heavier and heavier. On the other side of the Pot'ong River, several groups of people were gathered along Pulkŭn Street, on the side that would take them toward Pot'onggang Station. Each group had five or six people, all waiting to catch cars, and all carrying big bags. Some had mirrors, rice, and salt bags; others even had televisions.

Leaving the bicycle on the grass next to the road, I joined the closest group. Whenever cars passed, we waved our hands, but were ignored. Finally, one man took money from his jacket and waved it around. Soon enough, a military car stopped with a screech and a soldier asked us where we wanted to go. The car was going to Kowŏn, in the far east. I knew there was a station there with trains to Onsŏng, so I got in without hesitating, along with seven others. After checking our travel permits, the soldiers took 300 *won* from each of us, no matter where we were going. That was about three months' salary for a factory laborer. Some people on the street were left behind because they wanted to go in other directions or didn't have enough money.

The car was extremely cold, and after taking a seat, everyone took a big, crumpled plastic bag out of their packs and wrapped it around themselves. Clearly, they knew what to expect. I could hear my own teeth chattering from the cold.

The man who had waved the money looked at me sideways and gave me a grin that exposed his dark-yellow gums. "You didn't bring a plastic bag?" he asked. He proudly adjusted his bag so that it covered his whole body from the neck down. His bag, unlike the others, had special holes for the head and arms. It seemed that he had cut the bag specifically for this purpose.

"No," I said, avoiding his eyes.

"It's spring, but it's still cold, and it'll be much colder when we climb up. Protecting yourself is the most important thing."

"I didn't know that," I said, pulling my knees to my chest.

He smiled and said, "I'll share mine for 50 *won*. Come inside."

He opened one arm and made space, pointing at it with his eyes. I didn't want to get close to a male stranger, but it was getting colder. A middle-aged woman with a snub nose sitting in front of me was watching the exchange and snapped at him, "How dare you take her money? Be generous."

She turned her head to me and said, "Come here. Let's share mine, it's big enough for two."

I grabbed my backpack and slid in next to her; warm air from her body hung inside the plastic bag. The man glared at the woman, but said nothing.

"Is it your first time catching a car?" she asked. Her snub nose was noticeably redder than other parts of her face.

"Yes." I rubbed my hands and blew on my frozen fingers.

"What that guy said is right. You should prepare. Otherwise, it's a perfect day to die from the cold."

The car rocked from side to side, bumping my tailbone hard

against the seat, but eventually I fell asleep, letting go of the anxiety of the last few days. It was much better inside the plastic bag, sharing the heat of two bodies in that airtight space.

"Get up, Get up."

When I opened my eyes, the others were already out of the car.

"Are we already in Kowŏn?" I asked the snub-nosed woman, who had taken off the plastic bag and was folding it.

"No, we're at Majŏn. The car broke down with a fourth of the way left to Kowŏn. They'll fix it, but they aren't sure how long it will take."

"What are we supposed to do? We already gave them money." I stood up, holding my backpack.

"You can take another car or wait until they fix it. But don't even think about getting your money back."

"What will you do?"

She swung her backpack, which was much bigger than mine, onto her back and clutched a pumpkin-shaped knapsack and a small mirror under her arm. "There is a street market close by—I'll go there and sell my goods. You can have a meal there and wait until they fix the car." She headed off to the right with nothing more to say.

As the passengers scattered, I asked a soldier who was smoking outside when he thought we'd be moving again, and he answered gruffly, "We don't know, not long, but not before night. Come back after dinner." The group of soldiers headed to the street market, leaving one to fix the car. He looked not more than sixteen and seemed not to know what he was doing. I followed the group to the market.

So many smells emanated from the food stalls! My stomach gurgled at the smell of steamed sweet potatoes and egg breads and corn nuts fried in the pan. There were several groups of *kkotchebi* in the market. When they rushed past me, I had to breathe with my mouth, not my nose. I tried to find the people from the car. I saw the soldiers teasing a young woman in her food stall. She brought dishes to them with a coquettish smile, and some of them tried to touch her body. She didn't complain at all, but her face twisted as she got past them.

Two would be better than one, I thought, so I looked around the market for the middle-aged woman. I accidentally bumped into a man coming from the other direction.

"Watch out!" he spat. "Are your eyes just for decoration?" "Sorry," I muttered, lowering my head several times. He grabbed my right arm. "If I was hurt just now, what would you do?"

"Sorry, I didn't mean it."

"How do I know you didn't mean it? Are you trying to mess with me?" he demanded, eyeing me skeptically.

"Sir, I was looking for my friend, and I was distracted. Forgive me."

I was scared by his reaction, and tried to wriggle my arm out of his grasp. He said, "Be careful next time," and rushed off.

I met the eyes of an old female merchant who was selling underwear in different colors. She looked at me first and then her eyes deliberately followed the path of the man. When I followed her glance, I saw him walking away with several men. I removed my backpack and saw that the bottom was half-torn and some of my clothes were pushing out through the hole. I scrambled to look inside; the gray sock where I put my money was gone. I had hidden my money in two socks and sewed them into the bottom of the backpack. I grabbed the torn part and ran in the direction he had gone, crying, "Thief, thief! Catch him!"

I pushed people aside in my dash to catch him, but he was gone. I spun around, crying out for help, but no one even looked at me; I was the only stranger in that place.

I returned to the car and found the boy soldier groaning.

"Can you fix it today?" I asked him.

"I'm trying." His face and shirt were soaked with sweat, even on the chilly day. I crouched down next to him as he worked.

My thoughts raced. Did I have to go back? No! I couldn't. Where should I go? I had left Pyongyang and lost half of my money within a few hours. What worse luck was waiting for me? I was as miserable as the boy soldier.

Several hours later, the group of soldiers came back sluggishly, picking their teeth with toothpicks. When they saw that the boy soldier still hadn't figured out how to repair the car, they kicked him several times. "You good-for-nothing!" they yelled, throwing two loaves of bread to him. He picked them up from the ground nimbly and devoured them without even dusting them off.

One of the soldiers took the tools from the boy soldier's hands, and thirty minutes later the engine of the car made a tumultuous sound. Only half the passengers had returned, and the soldiers didn't wait for the rest. The snub-nosed woman didn't return, so, for five *won*, I shared another woman's plastic bag.

Friendship with Kkotchebi

On arrival at Kowŏn Station early the next morning, I saw many kinds of people, and more *kkotchebi* than you'd find in the Pyongyang Station and street market. They wandered around, begging for food from the crowds of people waiting for the train. Cigarette smoke and offensive smells greeted me everywhere. People with large bags grouped together—it made it easier to keep an eye on their belongings.

The railroad police patrolled the station wearing dark-green uniforms and expressionless faces, picking through people's bags with their fingers or with their thick, shiny truncheons. They looked about my age or a little older. Shifty-eyed men hung about like smoke in the air, stealing glances at people's bags. Young girls with worn-out clothes but thick makeup were everywhere, shouting, "Flower! Buy a flower!"

But none held flowers. They only approached well-dressed, young and middle-aged men. Everything was unfamiliar, and everyone looked suspicious to me.

I wandered through the station but couldn't find a place to sit down. I suddenly felt someone was watching me carefully, following my movements, and I turned my head to find a small boy, dressed in tatters. Like other *kkotchebi*, his face was covered with dust. Under his hat, his eyes were twinkling, and as soon as they met mine, he walked directly to me, with a slight limp. That was my first encounter with Sangwon.

When he was close enough, he smiled and asked, "Do you have some food to share with me?"

I looked down at him skeptically, and he didn't take his eyes off me. Of course, I didn't have food to share. Everyone knew no one had food to share; the only way hungry people could survive was to steal, so this boy was either really bold or not so smart.

Setting out on my journey, I had made a firm resolution that I wouldn't share food; my own survival came first. I had just one loaf of bread and an ear of corn, and I needed to save what little money I had left. But Sangwon's blunt eyes, so steady on mine, made me hesitate. Or perhaps it was his limping leg that changed my mind.

I said, "I just have one piece of bread and one ear of corn."

I would have felt better if he had pretended to cry or grab my leg, but he just pouted with his lower lip, shrugged his shoulders, and said, "Okay. If you think that isn't enough for two people, that's fine. Have a good trip."

He was funny. His way of watching me and withdrawing without a fuss compounded my guilt.

As he turned around to walk away, I called after him.

"Wait. . . . Maybe . . . we can make do with these for breakfast."

Sangwon turned back and smiled. "And then I might help you if it's your first time traveling," he said, winking. "I know where we can have a peaceful meal."

Like a gentleman escorting me, Sangwon gestured in the direction we should walk, strutting triumphantly, as though he had won something. His wiry body moved nimbly through the crowd.

He took me outside the station to an out-of-the-way corner that was chilly but still the perfect place for two people to sit side by side. Not too stinky either. He took his jacket off and shook it briefly. Laying it on the ground, he grinned, motioning for me to sit down. I felt the ground would be cleaner than his jacket, but I didn't rebuff the offer. Sangwon sat down next to me on the bare ground.

He smacked his lips as I took the food out of my bag, so I broke the bread in two and gave him the bigger half.

"I haven't seen bread for a long time. I eat watery gruel every day. That place only makes begging on the street look good." He stuffed himself with bread.

"Which place?" I asked.

"The nine-twenty-seven. I just got out of the nine-twenty-seven. Have you heard of it?" His big, round eyes turned to me; his cheeks bulged.

I had heard of the 927. The government tried to move beggars and people unable to make a living on their own to a specific place in each province, forcing them into abandoned buildings, usually former hotels. Because this system was instituted on September 27, 1997, it was called the 927. Supposedly it kept people from dying of hunger.

"Why didn't you stay there? At least you'd be fed regularly."

Sangwon's eyes bugged. "Are you kidding? Have you ever slept sitting up for several nights? That place doesn't protect people, it creates more problems. People die in there from diseases and hunger—we don't need that kind of protection." He ripped a piece of hard bread off with his teeth and ate it; he reminded me of a lion gnawing the meat off a bone.

"Why would you sleep sitting up?"

Sangwon stopped chewing and opened his mouth halfway. "You don't know anything. You're an alien, no wonder you stuck out."

He finished his bite and swallowed. "They put too many people in one small room. We all ate better on the outside."

When he spoke, he had to look up at me, and because his big hat covered his eyes, he took it off. His head was clean except for several scabs forming over his sores. He had no eyebrows or eyelashes; there was not one strand of hair on his face. He looked as if he had escaped from a Buddhist temple, not the 927.

"How long were you in there?" I asked, interrupting his eating again.

"Who knows? I gave up counting after seventeen days. Sitting in a corner, counting the days, made me more desperate. Anyway, I need to leave here as soon as possible. I don't want to end up back there."

"How did you run away?" I asked.

This time, he didn't raise his head to speak. "Through the window. I was stuck on the sixth floor. Some of the kids made a rope with our clothes and we ran away together. When the girl right after me was climbing down, the rope snapped. She fell and was dead on the spot. It could have been me."

I was shocked that such a small boy could talk about death with such a poker face.

Sangwon raised his head and his eyes fixed on my piece of bread. I hadn't started eating yet, so I handed it to him.

He shook his head. "I'm not going to eat my fill. I don't want to make my stomach expand." He patted his gut and smiled. "This guy is so sneaky. I give him enough food, but he always wants more. He's never completely satisfied, so I have to control him, or he'll control me. That's your share. I really appreciate what you gave me, but that's enough for today." He looked at me candidly, his eyes twinkling. Who could resist this face?

Sangwon pushed my hand back and urged me to eat the bread. I noticed that there were two stumps on his left hand where his fourth and fifth fingers should have been.

He saw me staring at his hand and raised both hands to show

me. "I was lucky. That time, I was using my left hand and not my right."

He had tried to steal some food from a market stall while the owner wasn't paying attention, but just as Sangwon's hand approached the food, the owner caught sight of him and grabbed his knife. He just wanted to scare him, but Sangwon's two fingers were lopped off in an instant. The owner was as surprised as Sangwon, and they wept loudly together. Sangwon got the food from the owner, but his fingers were lost.

Sangwon told this as if it was someone else's story. He must have been used to it—he spoke so well. He looked about six or seven years old, but I guessed he was eleven or twelve.

"Where are you going?" he asked.

I put a piece of bread in my mouth and chewed for a while. Could I trust this boy? Could I tell him I was running away? "I'm trying to get out of here," I said, almost to myself.

He watched me and kept his mouth shut for a while. At length, he said, "I got this disease when I was in the mountains."

Sangwon lifted one foot and removed his sock. All the toes were black from frostbite. He picked up a stone from the street, and before I could stop him, pounded the top of his foot with it. When I took the stone away from him, he smiled and said, "It's okay. I don't feel anything. They're completely dead. They aren't part of my body anymore." He put his sock back on.

"You should go see a doctor," I said, still staring at his foot.

"Oh, well. It's been a long time. I got it when I crossed the river. Not a big deal."

Sangwon had guessed my plan. Most people came here hoping to cross the border; their large bags gave them away. Wandering around with a small backpack certainly made me look like a novice.

"I ran into pickpockets in a street market," I explained. "I didn't expect it. An old woman let me know my backpack was torn; I didn't even realize I had been robbed."

"Don't trust anybody here—even old women or soldiers.

Oh, soldiers are the worst! They can do whatever they want. Don't even think about sitting next to them. Actually, you shouldn't have trusted me either."

He smiled as he said this, and I smiled back at him. How could I not trust this boy?

"This time of year is okay. In winter, it's easy to cross over because the river is frozen, but border control is much stricter. Summer is tougher—the water isn't as cold as in winter, but the river is high and the current is really fast, so border control isn't as strict. Young guys try in the summer. Spring is the best time, because the water is low and not too cold. Now is still a little bit early. The ice must have melted, but the water will still be chilly. You should be prepared."

Sangwon put his hat back on. The hat was big and was peppered with cigarette burn-holes, but it looked really warm. I helped him find the front of the hat, and he pressed it down hard and said, "If you'll trust me one more time, we can go together."

I raised my eyebrows.

"We should get out of here as soon as possible," he continued. "I was heading to the border too."

I nodded, and he reached out his hand, smiling, and motioned me to do the same. He slapped my palm twice. "Okay. So we're comrades from now on. Did you buy a ticket?"

"Not yet. I don't know if I have enough money."

"How much do you have?"

I showed my money to Sangwon, my comrade. He counted it and said, "It looks okay, if the station didn't raise the fares." He stared pointedly at the badge on my chest. "But there is one way to make money." He handed my money back to me and asked, "Do you have a travel permit?"

"Here." I showed it to him, but he barely looked at it.

"Okay. Then it's much easier. What's your destination?"

"I haven't decided yet. I can go as far as Onsŏng with this card."

"Then let's go to Hoeryŏng. That's closer to the place where I usually stay in China."

We rose and walked behind the station. I saw a line of eight or nine people sitting down with their backs against the wall. Some leaned their heads on the person next to them, their eyes closed tight, while others gazed blankly in front of them, never blinking. Their skin was black, but it was different from the foreigners with black skin I'd seen at the hotel. Black spots covered their faces.

"Sangwon, don't you think those people look weird?" I poked his forearm.

Sangwon pulled me to his side. "You'd better not look. They're dead."

"No!" I shouted, in spite of myself, gripping his hand tightly.

"They all died of starvation, waiting there."

I looked again. The dead sat naturally and seemed to watch people as they passed. I shuddered with fear.

Inside the station, Sangwon elbowed his way through the crowd and pulled me along. We came to a man wearing a neat blue coat, standing with a small bag at his feet. The man lit a cigarette.

Sangwon walked up to him and pulled at his coat lightly. "Hello, sir. Did you find good things to buy over there?"

He looked down at Sangwon with annoyance and snapped, "Go away. I don't have any food."

"No, sir. That's not my business with you today. I have a badge to sell—how about a hundred and fifty *won*?"

The man sneered, "Where? Show it first. If you're lying, I'm going to break both your legs."

"See, I'm not lying." Sangwon pointed at my chest. The man's eyes moved to the badge and then up to my face, then to Sangwon and back to me.

"Are you willing to sell it?" he asked.

Sangwon glanced at me quickly and whispered, "You won't need that over there." Then he grinned and replied, "She will, for a hundred and fifty *won*. It's a nice one, with two leaders' faces on one badge. You can sell it at a good price to foreign travelers if they know it's really from North Korea."

The badge showed the faces of both Kim Il Sung and Kim Jung-il. Working at the hotel, I had had to wear it at all times. I couldn't believe I was selling it now. My chest without the badge—I hadn't even considered that possible.

The man examined the badge for a moment. "This one has too many scratches. One hundred *won*."

Sangwon immediately grabbed my hand and said, "Let's go, we can do much better. A badge with the two leaders is worth more."

The man seized Sangwon's shoulder and grimaced. "This *kkotchebi*—you know this place too well. Okay, a hundred and thirty *won*. Don't even think about more."

"Okay," Sangwon said, unpinning the badge from my chest. "Here. Give me the money."

The man pointed at me with his chin. "Is she your sister?"

"No, she is my mom," Sangwon replied instantly.

The man sneered, looking at me, "Are you kidding? Doesn't she sell flowers here?"

Sangwon growled back, "I said she's my mom. Of course she doesn't sell flowers." He grabbed my hand firmly and started to walk away.

The man shouted after us, "Let me know if you need help. I like your deaf-mute sister."

"That dirty-mouthed—" Sangwon swore without looking back at him.

"Why did he buy the badge?" I asked.

"He can sell it to foreign travelers in China as a souvenir. It's one of the most popular items there, actually. In China, you'll see Chinese selling North Korean items to foreign travelers everywhere. Here the badge is sacred, but there it's like a toy."

I felt empty, as if I had lost a part of my body.

As though reading my mind, Sangwon said, "It's not as important as our lives. It's just a souvenir now—what we need is money and food. You would have to throw it away as soon as you crossed the border, anyway. Keeping it would be dangerous." He pressed the money into my hand.

"By the way, why did he ask me whether I sell flowers?" I asked. "I have seen so many women shouting that they're selling flowers, but with no flowers to sell."

"What he asked was whether you'd sell your body to him."

My face turned red with anger. I turned and saw the man still standing there, leering.

"People find ways to survive," Sangwon said, pulling me away toward the ticket booth.

People were shouting over each other for tickets, pushing and pulling like waves beating on the seashore. It was far too crowded.

"Wait here for a moment," Sangwon said. "I'll buy a ticket, just give me the money." I looked at him for a second. He was just a *kkotchebi*, looking for food and stealing from others, but for some reason, I was sure he would come back.

He took my money and was sucked into the crowd. A few minutes passed. Did I even give him my travel permit? I checked my pocket, growing anxious. I stood on tiptoe and scanned the crowd—it was impossible to see him.

I was about to move away to look for him when I felt a tap on my back. I wheeled around to find Sangwon's beaming face. "I got it!" he cried, holding up the ticket.

I was ashamed to have doubted him. Looking him up and down, I asked, "Are you okay? Didn't you get hurt?"

"Sometimes a kid has an advantage," he said, handing me the ticket and the rest of the money. "I even gave them less than the fare. They didn't notice—they're just trying to get rid of as many people as possible."

While we walked to the platform, Sangwon warned me, "Even though you have a ticket, some crazy people will try to take your seat, so never leave it. Go to the restroom before getting on the train."

The train didn't come for four days, and in all that time we never left the platform. People complained that the trains never ran on schedule; the railway employees said fuel had run out. No one knew when the train might arrive. "Pretty soon," the train employees said, but they didn't know. Some people left to sleep in nearby inns. Women, young and old, walked around shouting, "Clean, warm house while you wait." I wouldn't go; I was afraid of missing the train. I bought food with the rest of my money, and we tried to eat as little as possible. Sangwon had a fever from the infection in his feet and was limping harder.

When the train finally arrived, it was as if war broke out. The distant whistle sounded and people jumped up and grabbed their bags, screaming and shouting; suddenly the whole place was alive with noise. The railroad police made us stand in one line, and a policeman made an announcement about civic morality. People who didn't follow the rules would be punished severely. Nobody listened.

As the policeman was finishing his announcement, a dozen men rushed the platform and scaled the gate. Hundreds of people pushed madly after them, and the railroad police were overwhelmed. Some thieves made the most of the opportunity, cutting the bottom of one unsuspecting man's bag with a knife and catching the corn that ran out in their own bag. A flock of *kkotchebi* rushed to get their share. Finally the man realized what was going on and bawled, "Damn these hoodlums," kicking the *kkotchebi*. They didn't budge until they had collected all the corn.

Railroad inspectors tried to check each passenger's ticket and travel permit, but it was useless. They beat anyone they found without proper documents, but the crowd pushed past them. They shouted, "You can't get on the train without a ticket and a card. We'll inspect you sons of bitches again on the train!"

People dashed for it anyway, some dropping off the train like falling leaves. Those who didn't have tickets or permits climbed up on the roof. The inspectors didn't care about them, saying they would all die of cold or electric shock.

Sangwon and I rushed to find a seat. Finding one, he said, "Sit here and don't move. Put your bag next to you. If people swear at you about having your backpack like that, don't listen. And don't be scared. If they scream, you yell at them too. Okay? I'll be right back."

I grabbed at his coat. "Where are you going?"

"I don't have a travel permit. I'll be back after the ticket inspectors pass this compartment."

I looked at him anxiously, but he winked and said, "Don't worry about me. I'm a professional. Be careful, some people seize this chance and steal other people's things. Don't take your eyes off the bag."

Sangwon slipped through the crowd and disappeared. His tiny body could fit anywhere.

The train gave several long whistles and the employees shouted, "The train is leaving." Those stuck on the platform tried to climb in through broken windows. The train started moving, and when I looked through the window, I saw a man running alongside. He threw his bag inside first and put his hand on the windowsill. His face distorted with pain for an instant from the shards of glass in the sill, but he didn't give up. When half his body was through the window, a railroad policeman outside harshly grabbed him from behind and yanked him down. I stuck my face out of the window to see if he was okay, and he looked at me and shouted, "My bag! My bag! Throw it back to me."

When I turned to find his bag, it wasn't his bag anymore. Passengers in the train were fighting over it. A big soldier stood up and pushed away the others. He seized the bag with a threatening look.

Nobody resisted as the soldier took the bag to his seat and opened it. It was filled with bundles of clothes. I saw some tattered gray pants tangled up with yellowish underwear.

110

The soldier angrily sifted through the bundles. "What are these stinky things?" Then, opening a bundle, he found machine parts. The soldier's companions grabbed the bag and began rummaging through the clothes. Several more machine parts came out. Then a rice ball, some fried tofu, and bean sprouts—the owner's lunch.

The soldier said, "They are still hot. Let's take care of these for him." Looking around intimidatingly, he and his companions ate the food on the spot.

I was worried about Sangwon. The inspectors were harsh to people who didn't have tickets, and I doubted his age would make much difference.

Finally, a good while after the ticket inspectors had passed by, Sangwon reappeared, and we shared the seat. He fit in the space where my bag was, so I held my bag to my chest.

"Where did you hide?"

His hands were black with dust. He crowed, "Those people who work here aren't thorough enough to search between compartments. They don't care about *kkotchebi* anyway—we don't have anything for them. If we don't make trouble, they ignore us."

As we rode, Sangwon spoke about how he had lost his family. It's a common story in North Korea, and the reasons are always death by starvation or punishment by the government. He was an absolute orphan, but he smiled and said, "It's better this way; I don't have any pressure to take care of my family. Many *kkotchebi* have to beg for food for their parents or grandparents."

As an only son, Sangwon was adored by his hardworking parents. Both worked in a fertilizer factory in Hungnam, north of Kowŏn, and Sangwon remembered the chimneys shooting fat plumes of gray smoke up into the sky. The floods of 1995 and 1996 hit his hometown hard, and the polluted water brought disease and death. All the factories closed, and starving people started pillaging them for machine parts to sell on the black market or in China.

continued page 145

Excerpt from Cho Pyŏng-kwŏn's

동화만화

Great General Mighty Wing

T R A N S L A T E D   A N D   L E T T E R D   B Y   H E I N Z   I N S U   F E N K L

대장이 된

억쇤날개

조병권지음
림왈용그림

금성청년출판사 1994

Great
General
Mighty
Wing

IN OUR HOMELAND, EVERY SPRING IS MEDICINAL; EVERY CLUMP OF DIRT IS GOLD.

117

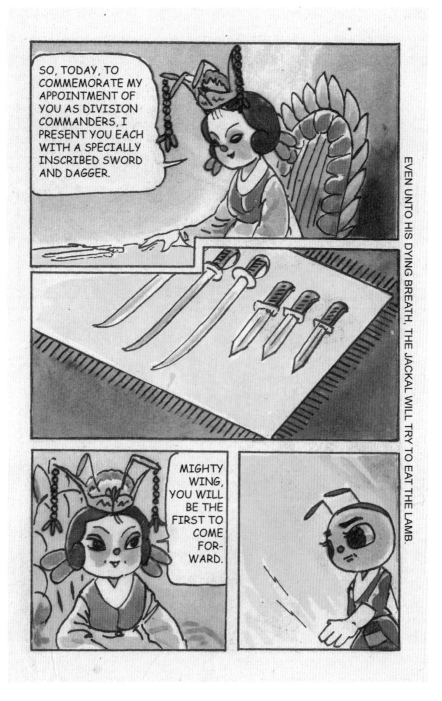

Great

General

Mighty

Wing

ONE'S HONOR IS HARDER TO KEEP THAN IT IS TO EARN.

ALL THINGS SEEM DANGEROUS IN THE MIND OF A COWARD.

AN OLD ENEMY IS STILL AN ENEMY.

NEVER THINK OF THE ENEMY AS A LAMB--ALWAYS CONSIDER HIM A JACKAL.

A HUNDRED ALLIES ARE NEVER ENOUGH; YET A SINGLE ENEMY IS ALWAYS TOO MUCH.

YOUR MAJESTY! I COME TO YOU IN GREAT HUMILITY. I HAVE FAILED YOU IN MY DUTY AS YOUR GENERAL, AND NOW YOU LIE HERE A **WRETCHED CORPSE** BEFORE ME. PLEASE, YOUR MAJESTY, I BEG YOUR FORGIVENESS!

I PROMISE TO FULFILL FOR YOU THE GREATEST WISH YOU HAD WHILE YOU LIVED. I WILL DEFEAT THE DAMNED HONEYBEES ONCE AND FOR ALL, AND THE GARDEN OF 1,000 FLOWERS SHALL BE IN OUR HANDS. AND I SWEAR TO YOU THAT NEXT YEAR, ON THE ANNIVERSARY OF YOUR DEATH, WE SHALL...

...HOLD THE MOST LAVISH MEMORIAL SERVICE FOR YOU. OH, YOUR MAJESTY, TAKE YOUR PLACE IN HEAVEN WITH AN EASY MIND! **YOUR MAJESTY!**

WHEN THE ENEMY SHARPENS HIS SWORD, WE MUST ALSO SHARPEN OURS.

NEVER LET DOWN YOUR GUARD IN THE PRESENCE OF THE ENEMY.

Photos by Peter Sobolev

139

AZALEA

AZALEA

Sangwon's parents were no exception. When they left him at home to travel to the border to sell some parts, their bus tumbled into a bloated waterway and was swallowed up. Sangwon heard the news of their deaths, but their bodies were never found.

Jia, continued from page 111

Sangwon found himself alone in his house, with no idea what to do. For the first time he could play outside with abandon; nobody controlled him, and he didn't have to hear his mother's nagging. It was starvation, however, that came to control him. Soon he stopped going out. A neighbor said the government would take care of him, so he waited for them. When the government finally did pay Sangwon a visit, they said they would take his house, that it belonged to them. The only place he could go was the orphanage or a camp for children in similar situations.

The day before he was to depart for the orphanage, Sangwon heard there would be a public execution. A family was accused of eating human flesh. The family had been hungry for a long time, and they decided to sell their house and use the money to buy pork for soup. They went to a butcher's shop, bought the pork, made the soup, and ate well. Shortly thereafter, the police stormed into their house and arrested the entire family. The butcher had been selling human flesh, and they were all charged with murder, along with the butcher.

Out of curiosity, Sangwon walked to the public execution grounds. He found the street market completely closed. A crowd had gathered around the accused family and the butcher. A judge announced the charges as the crowd stood hushed in anticipation; only the family's sobbing could be heard. The judge asked the accused whether they acknowledged their crime, and a middle-aged man, who appeared to be the father, said they really didn't know what they had eaten, and begged for forgiveness. The judge declared they would not be excused for their crime. The youngest in the family, a boy, looked no older than six or seven, but the police said that he was sixteen—the minimum age to receive the death penalty. No one believed the police, but they dared not argue that he was

145

only a boy. Perhaps they thought it would be better for the family to leave this world together.

Sangwon knew the boy was younger than he was. Their eyes locked for the briefest moment, and he watched as the boy's eyes filled with fear. Policemen fastened the family members and the butcher to several long stakes and covered their mouths and eyes with towels. The family sobbed and pleaded for mercy. Moments later, the sound of simultaneous gunshots. The sobbing stopped at once.

People turned away and returned quietly to their houses. Some gathered in the street market to sell and buy goods again. Sangwon stood there for a while before heading home and packing his things in haste. He vowed never to feel fear such as he saw in the boy's eyes.

This was how Sangwon's journey began. By the time I met him, he had already crossed the border three times and been arrested three times in China. On the first occasion, the Chinese police caught him on the street and handed him over to North Korea. After the North Korean authorities interrogated him, they simply warned him not to cross the border again and let him go. The second episode was the same. But, the third time, he ran into the same investigator and was taken to the 927.

Sangwon looked at me and giggled. "You know, when some people are arrested and have to be interrogated, they put their money inside their bodies so it won't be taken away by the investigators. Women put money wrapped in plastic bags in their . . . down there," he said, pointing between his legs. He continued, "Some people eat their bags of money or put it up their butts. If the police suspect them, they force people to eat food that causes diarrhea and then follow them to the restroom. Then the policemen search their shit to see if there is any money or valuables, like gold or silver rings and necklaces."

Sangwon taught me a song describing the *kkotchebi*'s life. He said he learned it in the street market and that all the *kkotchebi* knew it. The lyrics were a dialogue between an old man and a *kkotchebi*.

146

Old man: *What is your name?*

Kkotchebi: *My name is chebi (swallow)*

O: *It sounds pretty*

K: *But, it is kkot–chebi (flower-swallow: beggar)*

O: *What do you eat?*

K: *I eat ori (duck)*

O: *You must be rich*

K: *But, I eat guksu-ori (noodle-duck: low quality noodles)*

O: *Where do you live?*

K: *I live in sudo (the capital)*

O: *You live in a nice place*

K: *But, it is ha-sudo (sewer)*

The train was pandemonium—slow and cold pandemonium. An icy wind came through broken windows, and in the dark before dawn, I saw a black lump drop from the sky and past my window.

I shook Sangwon. "Did you see that?" I asked, pointing outside. He was drowsy and said nothing.

A middle-aged woman in front of me spoke. "It's a dead person. Someone must have fallen asleep on top of the train and rolled off, or he died of electric shock up there and others pushed him off." I was stunned. Sangwon closed his eyes again, indifferent to her explanation. She continued, "That's not so bad compared to other things that happen on this train. If you see these scenes as often as we have, you won't care anymore either."

I fell asleep hugging Sangwon. Sleeping on the train was brutal; the seat was so hard it hurt, and fleas and bedbugs bit me all over. Though vendors sold food at each station, I was afraid I would have to go to the restroom, so I ate only a little. Even the restroom was filled with people, and passengers gave up using the toilet in the restroom, doing their business between compartments instead.

Shyness and shame no longer existed. Nobody cared. Nobody blamed others. People joked whenever someone relieved himself, saying, "That looks like it was a great meal!"

The train often stopped due to engine trouble; we were stuck at one station for a day and a half. The ticket inspectors came to check tickets at some stations, and passengers who didn't have tickets or travel permits sneaked out between the compartments and climbed to the top of the train. When the inspectors got to me, I stroked Sangwon's hair as he lay on my lap and told them he was my ill cousin and I was taking him to his mother in Hoeryŏng. Sangwon showed his spindly leg to the inspectors. They grimaced and turned their heads, then went on to check other people.

As the days passed, it seemed as if walking would have been faster than taking the train. I thought the journey would never end. Patience was a struggle. But, looking back, the train trip turned out to be the easiest leg of my journey.

Two Poems by O Yŏng-jae

Translated by Chae-Pyong Song

OH, MY MOTHER

—Upon hearing after 40 years that
my mother lives in the South

Alive,

Still alive,

And almost eighty

Even today Mother is still alive.

A sun suddenly rises

In the middle of a black night

A heavy shower of joy at once fills,

Overflows, and gushes out of my heart.

A heavy joy crushes me.

Collapsed, I cry,

This son wails.

On my knees, my senses . . . gone,

I bow over and over again.

What has kept Mother going

Till today,

Is not the grace of God,

Nor Time's sympathy.
It is Mother's faith
That kept her head high up to the world,
Because she will not close her eyes
Till she embraces this son once more.
To her faith,
I bow on my knees.
Mother, thank you.
Oh, Mother, thank you.

Oh, My Mother—Her Voice

Los Angeles and Taejon,

The Pacific in between.

The phone conversation between Mother and Chairman Yŏng-hŭi

Graciously sent to me;

Unwinding the cassette tape

I listen to Mother's voice.

The voice is not familiar,

Foreign to my ears,

So I listen . . . over and over.

The sound revives far-gone days,

And Mother's voice

That echoed that day;

The voice

That sang lullabies in a low tune,

When by the window on a snowy day, she,

Walking to and fro, piggybacked me;

The voice that searched for me on the other side of darkness

When I walked a long night's walk back home alone.

After setting a birthday table,

With the scent of steamed rice-cake filling the air,

The voice that woke me:

"Young-Jae, honey, time to wake up."

This same voice echoes,

Breaking through the veil of distant years.

The sound that floats over

My childhood and boyhood

Days gone by, so far away.

Those familiar sounds she made, opening and closing the gate at
    home;

The sound of her grinding barley in a mortar jar in the morning
    and the evening.

The sound that carries me

The tears she squeezed out

Sitting in front of the smoky kitchen fire hole

And the camellia oil.

The voice familiar to Mother's ears

That I finally found

After fumbling efforts,

The sound I can't erase in one lifetime.

Let us not live, divided apart, any more.

Mother's voice

Crying out for me, choked.

Come hurry on, to Mother's arms,

Come hurry on, to Mother's arms,

With the sun of harmony in your chest.

It calls me,

Ah, Mother's voice!

Hwang Chin-i: Introduction

Bruce Fulton

It is commonly agreed that there are virtually no historical records confirming the existence of a sixteenth-century *kisaeng* named Hwang Chin-i. And yet from the slenderest historical fabric a myth has been woven that has engaged several of modern Korea's most accomplished fiction writers. Modern fictional representations of Hwang Chin-i range from Yi T'ae-jun's novel written during the colonial period (1936), to postwar works by Pak Chong-hwa (1955) and Chŏng Han-suk (1955), to Ch'oe In-ho's two eponymous stories (1972), to novels by contemporary writers Kim T'ak-hwan (2002) and Chŏn Kyŏng-nin (2004)—not to mention half a dozen film treatments.

Hong Sŏk-chung's three part novel *Hwang Chin-i*, Part I, Section 25 of which is translated here, is notable for several reasons. First, the author is a North Korean writer (and the grandson of Hong Myŏng-hŭi, author of the ten-volume historical novel *Im Kkŏkchŏng* [1940], one of the finest examples of storytelling in modern Korean literature). Second, in 2004, two years after it was first published in North Korea, the novel was honored with the Manhae Literature Prize, named after the great colonial period poet and activist Han Yong-un; this marked the first time that a North Korean literary work had been recognized with a major South Korean literary award. Third, and not surprisingly, Hong's novel focuses not on Chin-i's celebrated liaisons with *yangban* worthies but rather on her relationship with Nomi, a commoner.

Part I, Section 25 of Hong's novel depicts the well-known scene of the funeral procession of Chin-i's heartbroken young admirer passing by her home. It comes at a crucial point in the novel, with Chin-i's engagement to a young man of Hanyang (Seoul) having recently been broken off and Chin-i herself having been reduced in status. At the same time, Chin-i must contend with Nomi's developing interest in her. The writing indicates that Hong Sŏk-chung has inherited his illustrious grandfather's storytelling skill. The narrative is colloquial, at times colorful, the author has an eye for detail and an ear for dialogue, and Chin-i appears before us not as stereotype or icon but as a complex young woman faced with the challenges posed by her beauty and her anomalous status as the offspring of a low-level official and a servant woman who becomes a *kisaeng*.

Hwang Chin-i

by Hong Sŏk-chung

Translated by Bruce and Ju-Chan Fulton

It was a day of cloud and wind, the time of year when summer begins to give way to autumn, and already a few leaves were dropping from branches to be sent whirling into the sky. From South Gate a flock of dusky sparrows took flight, looping about the slate-gray sky above Pujung before scattering like a shower of dark hail among the paddies and dry fields beyond the city wall to feast upon the nearly ripened grain. Overhead a lone crow uttered an eerie caw, drawing looks of displeasure from passersby who then answered this ill-omened bird by spitting over their shoulders. There was a desolate feel to the day.

Since early morning, would-be spectators had been gathering along the gully between the foot of Chanam Mountain and the wall behind Hwang Chinsa's dwelling in anticipation of the funeral procession for young Ttobok of Granary Row. Word had gotten out that the pallbearers would likely be passing this way, for the lane that ran along the gully was filled before the morning sun had crested the ridges, and the mountainside as far as Prominence Rock now wore a snowy blanket of onlookers garbed in their traditional white attire.

For days now the dwellings of Pujung—the quarters of the menfolk, the womenfolk, and the hired help alike—had been abuzz with talk of Chin-i and Ttobok of Granary Row. Ears perked up at the story of how this son of a minor official had fallen for the only daughter of a *yangban* family, of how his heart had finally broken when his love went unanswered, of how he was now a wandering ghost, but what really drew the attention of listeners was the news that in a single morning the engagement of the *yangban*'s daughter had been broken off by the family of student Yun of Hanyang and that her status had suddenly fallen to the level of a slave girl's. Herein lay the reason for the burst of activity displayed by the people of Pujung from the first light of dawn, even those sluggards loath to stir from home, once it was known that the young man's bier would pass by the young lady's house.

The previous night Old Granny had lingered outside the paper-paneled sliding door to Chin-i's room, worry creasing her face, before finally venturing across the threshold.

"I know I shouldn't be bothering you at a time like this, but I don't know what else I can do. It's just that I'm afraid Nomi will get to fussing and fighting and make a big scene. And when I mention this to him, he's not about to listen."

"What do you mean?"

"Well, if you can believe it, people are already staking out a place for themselves out back to watch tomorrow morning when they come by with the body of the Granary Row boy. That's made Nomi as mad as a snake, and he's hissing that he's going to round up the tough guys from the *kisaeng* quarters, tear the onlookers limb from limb, and chase them away. I don't know, I'm just afraid that if he gets away with beating up those people and driving them off, well, you might be able to avoid humiliation tomorrow, but by and by the storm will break when we least expect it, and there goes your reputation—what then?"

When Chin-i didn't answer, Old Granny continued: "Young lady, at this point you're the only one who can rein Nomi in. If we don't move smartly we'll have an awful mess on our hands, and for you, young lady, an awful mess means a spectacular disgrace. Just now I was out to the servants' quarters and I can tell you that Nomi had the bloodwrath look about him—worse than She-Who-Beat-Her-Daughter-in-Law-to-Death. There he was with the head thug of Pujung—you know, the one that everyone calls Monster—and the way they were muttering and palavering made my skin crawl. *Egu!* There's no reasoning with Monster."

"Bring Nomi here."

Ever since that day when Nomi had encountered Chin-i's ill mother at Prominence Rock on Chanam Mountain, he had hovered about Chin-i, a constant and protective presence. And when Nomi had come to Chin-i's rescue in the hills, she had offered him a heartfelt if formal word of thanks, but thereafter had remained aloof while still keeping a watchful eye on him. At the odd moments when their eyes met, it would be Nomi who turned away, recoiling like a hand from a hot stove, while Chin-i was left with the sensation that in his gaze was something that hadn't been there before, but she never openly betrayed this feeling. Whatever might happen, until such time as Nomi might prove useful when Chin-i finally had to accept her downgraded status, in his presence she gave no thought to abandoning her superior position. Indeed, there were occasions when she was more stiff and haughty than usual.

Nomi arrived from the servants' quarters and after he had offered his respects with a deep bow, Chin-i gave him a frosty look and addressed him in a tone as quiet and yet lucid as the sound of a pearl rolling on jade.

"I would not want any disturbance, no fussing or fighting, when the funeral procession for the Granary Row boy passes our way."

Nomi remained silent.

"I would not have you harm those who have gathered along the way."

Chin-i allowed these words to sink in.

"Have I made myself clear?"

"Yes."

Chin-i did not know that her words had left Nomi feeling contrary. She did know that Nomi was incapable of outwardly refusing her instructions.

As soon as Nomi had withdrawn, Old Granny approached. Her concerned expression had not changed.

"As they used to say," she murmured, "fight fire with fire, and if you spread your legs to a man, he won't notice your harelip. When the pallbearers come parading by and start in with that damned curse hex, you'd better have the fabric ready for them."

It was this curse hex that on the one hand accounted for Old Granny's worries, and on the other hand gave the spectators high hopes of feasting their eyes on something thrilling and exciting. For when the pallbearers come to a stop outside a house and the call-and-response begins, the calls from the head pallbearer are like messages from the dead conveyed by a spirit-possessed shaman in a *kimil* exorcism. When a call-and-response is directed toward a family, it's in their best interest to offer up a bolt of fine cotton fabric to the head pallbearer, who is the speaker for the departed, lest out of his mouth like jumping frogs come all manner of shameful and hidden facts, and if the family is the least bit slow in presenting the fabric, in an instant their good name is dragged through the mud.

It was with indifferent silence that Chin-i the previous night had met Old Granny's worries about the curse hex. For this reason Old Granny could not bring herself to repeat her concerns that morning, but at the same time she could not conceal her uneasy expression, which seemed to say "What now?"

Onlookers continued to throng beyond the wall, while inside the house dead silence reigned. Chin-i's mother had not set foot outside her room since the day she had explained her origins to Chin-i, and Chin-i's brother had disappeared without a trace after his brutal attack on Igŭmi the servant girl. It being early morning, the outer quarters of the home should have been bustling, but the servants in both the inner and outer quarters, buoyed by curiosity, must have joined the spectators outside, for the house was dead-rat still.

What a coldhearted world! thought Chin-i. It's one thing to take pleasure in viewing the celebrations and happy events of others, but if you have to satisfy your curiosity by witnessing the pain and sorrow of others, then your goodness of heart has left you. Indeed, she asked herself, what was the use of even thinking in terms of good and bad if people were heartless and ignorant enough to pack a lunchbox and journey from distant hamlets to see a prisoner lose his head in the marketplace outside Ojŏng Gate?

Chin-i listened attentively to the voices from beyond the back wall—voices calling out in search of others, foul-mouthed voices saying "I was here first!," voices erupting in belly laughter. . . . All of them titillated by the prospect of witnessing her pain and sorrow, her embarrassment and humiliation.

All right, then, I'd best make sure to show them what they want to see.

And with that, Chin-i opened her mother-of-pearl chest and retrieved the wedding finery she had stored deep inside.

It was the *sashi* hour, midmorning, when the funeral procession came into sight around the corner outside the wall. Appearing first was the guardian, clad in crimson jacket and black skirt, wearing a gourd mask draped with bells, brandishing a lance and shield, followed in turn by the bearers of the red banner inscribed with the name and title of the deceased, the silk spirit-banner, the elegy banner, and the pole-mounted hempen cloth, and finally the coffin-laden frame itself, the head pallbearer jingling his hand-bell as he sang a plaintive dirge, to which the eight pallbearers, headbands low on their brows, carrying poles across their shoulders, responded with a dismal refrain.

The time had come for the spectacle all were awaiting. When the head of the procession arrived at Hwang Chinsa's back gate, the pallbearers came to a stop and began marching in place, signaling the call-and-response that precedes the casting of the spirit hex.

The call of the head pallbearer and the response of the other pallbearers were as piteous as the weeping of a resentful ghost:

Farewell, mountains and streams; farewell, flowers and trees
I begin my journey to the yellow heavens
Pass over now, oh yes.

But once did I see her, and how lovely she was,
The only daughter of Hwang Chinsa
Pass over now, oh yes.

A goose on the wing without a mate, my love unrequited,
I'm a lonely ghost
Pass over now, oh yes.

The funeral procession resembled a trembling line, the marchers taking one step forward then two steps back, one step back then two steps forward, their dirge blending with the ringing of the bells.

Chin-i clutched the ring handle of the back gate and steeled herself. She could sense the gazes of the assembled onlookers directed toward the gate. She would have to present herself before these people at just the right time, not too soon and not too late.

Behind her stood Old Granny and Igŭmi, gripping tension showing on their fear-blanched faces as they observed their mistress. Meanwhile, in the attached quarters, sequestered at his mistress's command, Nomi paced the yard like a caged tiger, his body racked with fever.

The head pallbearer's recitation was gradually closing in on its target:

Heartbreaking it is that a body, once gone,
Can never come back
Pass over now, oh yes.

Arrived we are at the home of Hwang Chinsa,

Here we shall stay until. . . .

Pass over now, oh yes.

It was then that Chin-i opened the gate. The instant she appeared, the eyes of all assembled fixed themselves upon her like spear points. The murmuring of the crowd built until finally it muffled the dirge.

The onlookers were in a state of shock. Instead of fleeing to the farthest reaches of the kingdom in fear of being cursed by the deceased, instead of locking herself up and hiding beneath a quilt, Chin-i had dared to appear before them in the flesh. None of them could have imagined this in his wildest dreams.

Chin-i approached the bier as it swayed on its framework of carrying poles. The call-and-response came to a stop. The pallbearers lowered their burden to the ground; the ringing of the bells ceased and the head pallbearer fell silent.

Chin-i faced the young man's casket. With a flourish she spread wide the folds of her long crimson skirt with its flower pattern and draped it over the casket.

Dead silence fell over the lane. It was as if the throng had been doused with cold water.

Chin-i's lips began to move, as if she were whispering to someone visible before her. And amazingly enough, there arose with unmistakable clarity the face of the young man who had gazed at her in thrall beneath the moon of the Yudu festival.

"Please hear my words. Though I know you not, apart from a single glance that night, through your death I have learned of your ardor for me. Now that our paths have diverged, it is not possible for me to return your love in all its sincerity. But if perchance we were to meet again in the other world"—and here Chin-i paused—"surely I would offer you recompense for your love that went unrequited in this world. As a token of my promise to you, I bestow on this your altar my wedding finery—understand me and receive it. Though human life be entwined with heaven's will, how can the heart not be wrenched by such as this? The living are forever separated from the dead, but with this pledge between us in the next life, may it please you now to depart. . . ."

Chin-i's voice broke and she could not finish. Tears streamed from her eyes.

The assemblage was frozen in place. You could have heard a pin drop.

And then Chin-i withdrew from the bier. A leaden silence remained in the lane until she had disappeared through the gate.

Chin-i returned to the detached quarters and went inside and sat. She had just pledged her love to a dead person's soul, in front of all those people.

Was it the right thing to do?

It was not that Chin-i feared the inevitable and endless posturing over the rights and wrongs of what she had done, nor was she fazed by the prospect of her name being bandied about on the tongues of numerous gossips. Rather, it was perfectly clear to her that her action was not a matter of rashness or whim; instead, and most important, she had just bestowed upon this dead person's soul every last ounce of love in her possession, and so until her life in this world was spent, she would be like stone or wood, absent this emotion that was love.

Such was Chin-i's earnest wish at that moment, a desire that infused her entire being, and to this end did she entreat the Seven Star deity.

Two Poems by Li Chong-dŏk

Translated by Chae-Pyong Song

If I Truly Meet Mother Unexpectedly

Truly
When the day comes, the unification comes,
If I meet Mother
Unexpectedly

Ah, ah, so choked up,
I would forget all the words that I etched for many decades,
The bursting sound—of the heart and the soul—
Resonates only with "Ŏmma" [Mamma].

The voice to which I ran, as if falling on my face, to be embraced
Even when she came back late from the market;
The voice to which I played the baby
When we met again even after one day's separation.

The mother who left me, saying
She would be back after three nights' stay at grandma's,
The three nights—during which I waited so long—passed by
thousand and ten thousand times, and I am waiting still. . . .

She must be over seventy, all gray-haired,
Yet in my memories
She has all black hair, neatly parted,
Gleaming with castor oil

Mother, Mother,
I cannot age another day without meeting Mother.
You, Mother, cannot close your eyes
Till you see this son.

Love melts iron, they say.
Not just love between this son and Mother but,
If all the nation's love unites,
Can it topple this concrete dividing wall?

On the Unification Street of a construction site
Where one more story has risen again,
With a new day
I resolutely engrave this into my heart.

If I meet Mother this time,
I will forget all the ages and times,
Go back to the moment we became separated,
And, a child again, I will be embraced by the folds of her skirt.

Truly, when the day of unification comes,
Like a dammed stream burst open,
The sound of our race and our nation unified
Will shake all of the peninsula, three thousand *li* long.

Oh, oh, the cry for unification, hotter than the subterranean heat,
Neither on earth, nor in heaven, but within my heart,
Will burst into "Ŏmma"
And shake up the whole earth.

DANDELIONS

On a green rice field footpath
As if strewn about
Dandelions bloom in yellow
How lovely they are!

I pluck one blossom and put it to my mouth
It reminds me
Of the spring aroma of
the lunch Mother carried out when I was young

On an evening walk back home from school
When I blew them *hoooo* on the palm
Your seeds scattered like parachutes
In the end, they rooted in the hometown fields.

Ah, dandelions, dandelions
Also bloom in my heart of love and destiny;
The lovely flowers of my hometown
Rooted in this soil!

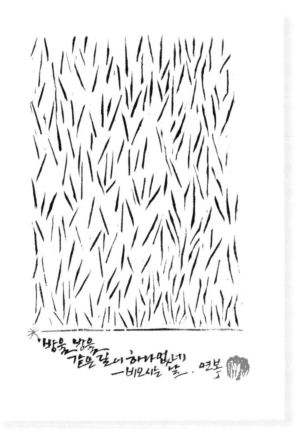

Make the Ocean Blue

by Ch'oe Ryŏn

Translated by Heinz Insu Fenkl

"Look, Daddy! The ocean's so blue, but how come this didn't get blue?"

The young captain was barely a day back from fishing in the deep ocean; he looked at the white cloth his daughter was thrusting at him after she had dipped it in the sea.

"What are you saying?" he asked, confused.

The six-year-old girl squatting in the sand sighed loudly. "Daddy, look at this! It's so blue over there, but the water here isn't blue at all. Why, Daddy?"

When he realized what his daughter was asking, the young captain laughed out loud toward the sea. "Ha ha—You mean it's blue out there but clear right here, right?" He laughed again but quickly stopped when he saw the annoyance in his daughter's eyes.

"Well, you know, seawater looks blue because it's transparent," he said. "When the sun shines on the water. . . ."

He was about to spout terms like "light absorption" and "reflection," but stopped himself short and fumbled for words that were easier to understand. In the end, he gave up, thrust out a hand and lifted his lovely daughter up into his arms.

"Hae-song, let's forget it. We'll take Daddy's boat out to the middle of the ocean and have a look to see if the water's really blue."

"That's great!"

AZALEA

Make the
Ocean
Blue:
Ch'oe
Ryŏn

Hearing her father say a thing she had only chased in dreams until now, she clapped her hands and shouted with joy; but something crossed her mind, and she looked her father straight in the eye and asked, with a serious expression, "But when, Daddy?"

"When you've grown just this much more," he said, holding his broad palm less than a hand's breadth above her head. To her eyes it seemed she could grow that much after only ten nights' sleep—no, just a week.

"All right," she said. "I really want to go out there. The water will be really blue there." Full of confidence, she looked out at the horizon. The sea, still full of its secrets, shimmered intensely blue in her eyes so full of dreams and thirsty for knowledge.

Hae-song couldn't quite understand why this memory, now twenty years in the past, surfaced at this particular moment. Was she dwelling on her childhood because of some mental weakness? Try as she might, she could not figure out how this childhood memory was connected to her nervousness about the meeting she was about to have.

When she noticed the room number of the office she was looking for, Hae-song sighed—*Whew*—and cautiously knocked on the door.

"Hello," she said in greeting.

She made a polite bow and froze as she looked up again. The apparent owner of the room—who was on the phone at his desk facing her—was a handsome young man. He couldn't have been more than thirty. Hae-song was about to turn around, thinking she might have the wrong room, when the young man, still holding the phone, motioned with his free hand for her to wait a moment. It was a smooth, practiced gesture.

"That's right. She's been living apart from her family for about a year. Please do everything you can. So she can have a nice meal with them when she gets home. . . . Ah, I'm asking because I trust you, not because I doubt your. . . . Think what you will of that. Well then, thank you for your hard work." He replaced the receiver and paused, staring down at the corner of his desk. Hae-song did not miss the warmth that shone for a moment from his eyes.

Suddenly, he looked up at her.

"I'm here to see Pak Shin-ch'ŏl, the Comrade who came down from the State to be in charge of site management," said Hae-song.

He looked her over—she was dressed in a purple summer suit rarely seen in this coastal area—and indicated a green chair.

"That would be me," he said. "Have a seat."

Hae-song hesitated. She hadn't expected to be meeting with such a young man. Which was probably why she had the uneasy feeling that what she had come to discuss would not go as planned.

She became aware of the young man's gaze as she collected her thoughts. "I'm Yun Hae-song, doing research in marine biology. I have a question for you."

The young man's eyes grew serious, as if he were anticipating what she was about to say. With sweaty hands, Hae-song clutched the strap of the handbag she was resting on her knees.

"I heard at the mine that a surveying team was sent down by the State to do a feasibility study for a pilot chemical plant here on the coast of Ryŏnp'o. Is that true?"

"Yes, it is. And?"

"I know that to manufacture those chemicals you will have to harvest hundreds and thousands of tons of the seaweed that grows along the coast. If that happens. . . ."

" . . . "

When Hae-song saw the dubious expression on the young man's face, the words she needed to say came rushing out. "If that were to happen . . . the coastal sea would be devastated in a matter of decades."

"The sea would be devastated?"

She repeated her words, as if he had not understood what she had said the first time. "Yes, that's true. The seaweed itself and the microorganisms that live in it aren't just a source of food for the

AZALEA

Make the

Ocean

Blue:

Ch'oe

Ryŏn

fish, they also provide shelter and a place for the fish eggs to hatch. If the seaweed were to disappear, the fish would lose their habitat and the entire marine ecosystem would collapse."

Shin-ch'ŏl regarded the confident and yet anxious young woman, the light shining from her eyes beneath her pronounced forehead. "And so?" he asked, his voice full of curiosity.

Hae-song stood up. "You must not build the chemical plant here."

Shin-ch'ŏl gave a sidelong glance toward a wall map labeled "Ryŏnp'o Coastal Currents" before he replied. "So, Comrade, as someone who studies marine plants, you're saying that you have a responsibility to protect them."

He nodded slightly and continued. "Your feelings are understandable, Comrade. But this enterprise has national significance. That is to say, the chemicals produced here will increase the yield in the mining of rare minerals, and that will be of immense benefit to the nation. I hardly need to explain that they are vital to national defense. And the quantity of seaweed that will be used in production isn't all that much if you compare it to how much is currently growing in the coastal waters. We believe this is the most reasonable use of marine resources."

The color drained from Hae-song's face.

"How could that possibly be the most reasonable use of marine resources?" she asked. "Once the work begins, they'll want to increase production, and then the seaweed harvest won't be enough. If we all just keep exploiting the ocean for its raw materials, what will happen to it in the end?"

A strange expression appeared on the young man's face. It was imbued with anxiety about how to handle this beautiful young woman who had appeared so suddenly, speaking such explosive words.

"If this issue can't be settled here, then I'll bring it up with the Nature Conservation League," said Hae-song. "Please have an answer for me by tomorrow morning."

She hoped that her short, clipped tone would have the cold resonance of a legal decree. But when she noticed the expression in Shin-ch'ŏl's glance, she realized her assumption was far off the mark. It was obvious what his eyes said—he was looking at a brave and admirable girl.

"Do what you have to do," he said. "But to be realistic, the situation requires more thought than that. To repeat myself, this enterprise will be of great benefit to the entire nation. We've already had our proposal approved by the Ministry."

His voice resonated, soft and kind.

∾

The sea was quietly rising and falling. At one end of the far horizon the blue sky met the ocean in a soft layer of fog and it was impossible to tell where one ended and the other began. Waves came rushing from that distant horizon, raising white spray as they collapsed onto the sand, as if they had come to plead some secret sorrow of the heart only to throw themselves exhausted onto the shore; and the white sand softly embraced them all in its bosom, taking to heart all of their feelings and frustrations.

Hae-song wanted to cry. It wasn't the cold treatment—of course, she could take that—but it was the look in his eyes, like he was dealing with a naïve little girl. She found that far more humiliating than the most vehement rejection would have been.

No, you must not give up.

Hae-song gathered her wits and toughened her resolve. She slowly walked around the curve of the shore.

A shrill voice, its source invisible, came flying on the wind. "Not this one! It's mine!"

As she came around the bend Hae-song saw a boy, who appeared to be about six or seven years old, and a woman. The two of them were sitting close together on the white sand, facing each other like old friends.

Azalea

Make the

Ocean

Blue:

Ch'oe

Ryŏn

"Why not?" the woman asked, sounding rather displeased.

The boy, wearing pants with suspenders, his sun-bronzed arm outstretched, was clutching something protectively in his fist. "But this is the best one," he said.

The woman did not want to back down. "Give me a nice one, too. It's for a present—for a kid about your age. He's turning seven."

The boy had been staring blankly at the woman's pleading expression, but now he produced his precious seashells one by one from where he had them bundled inside his shirt.

The woman laughed happily. "Thanks. So that makes a total of seven for me." She stood up.

Hae-song's gaze shifted unconsciously to the woman's clothes. She was wearing a navy blue outfit embroidered with many wildflowers whose names Hae-song did not know, blooming in reds, grays, and browns, exuding such vitality and freshness that each flower seemed alive. Hae-song was drawn in by some mysterious force, but she knew immediately that the woman's grace and elegance did not come from the way she was dressed.

When the woman felt compelled to look up at Hae-song, the radiant joy in her eyes shone on Hae-song's heart like the sun on a frozen ice pond. She greeted her with a look and spoke without hesitation.

"The boy gave me the shells he collected. He found only the prettiest ones—it's enough to make you wonder. I tried to find some myself, but it's as if my eyes just couldn't spot them. Maybe the pretty ones are only visible to children."

The woman opened her hand to show off the shells. They shimmered all the colors of the rainbow, each with its own strange and unique shape. A clear and innocent joy rippled across her face as she looked at them.

"I'm going now," said the boy.

The woman watched him run off somewhere, arms spread like he was flying, and laughed happily once again. "It's my first time seeing the ocean," she said. "That must be why I'm so happy. Like a child."

Hae-song examined the woman as she carefully wrapped the shells in her handkerchief. She must have been about thirty. She wasn't someone you would call beautiful, but she had a distinctive quality that grabbed your attention. It wasn't the straight, elegant line of her nose or the gracefully curved eyebrows that made her attractive—it was her eyes, the light emanating from them was as beautiful as sunlight sparkling in a stream. Was she here at the shore on vacation?

Hae-song felt even more desolate now. There was such a great abyss stretching between this woman's joy and her own loneliness. "Everyone who comes to the coast here is charmed by the beauty of the ocean," she said. "But not many people realize that it will all eventually be destroyed."

The woman gave her a searching look, her eyes shining with curiosity. "What are you saying?"

Hae-song looked up at the empty sky for a while. A seagull, which had been suspended in the air, flapping its wings and crying shrilly, suddenly pierced the surface of the water like an arrow, having spotted something. There was a splash of white, but then the water's surface resumed its calm rising and falling as if nothing had happened.

"There's going to be a factory here. A chemical plant. They're going to use the seaweed to manufacture chemicals."

"A chemical plant?"

"That's right. To produce some sort of reagent. But a few decades from now, when they run out of raw materials on this coast, they'll have to expand the facilities more and more. The rate of growth of the seaweed won't keep up, and the fish that use the seaweed as shelter will have to move somewhere. . . . The seagulls, too. And then what will be left of the ocean? What sort of ocean would it be without fish, seaweed, and seagulls?"

Hae-song, after this sad exclamation, gnawed on her lip, feeling sorry for herself. This woman she had just met by chance, wrapped up in her boundless happiness—what need did she have for Hae-song's outpouring of anger? Hae-song looked away.

Azalea

Make the
Ocean
Blue:
Ch'oe
Ryŏn

The woman was silent for a while. Strands of hair that had fallen across her face fluttered in the wind.

Hae-song quickly glanced back; her words must have had a great impact on this woman.

Brushing the hair out of her face, the woman asked quietly, "Do you live here, Comrade?"

"I'm from Pyongyang," said Hae-song. "Until just a few years ago, I lived here in a village by the sea. I collected seashells, harvested kelp with the girls at the food factory, and sang songs watching the sun go down. The people of my village love the sea a lot. Even during The March of Tribulations we took care of the sea, though it was a great ordeal for us. But . . ."

Hae-song turned to gaze at the distant horizon. "I know that factory is necessary and the amount of seaweed they harvest can be limited. . . . But fifty or a hundred years from now—I mean, is it naïve and childish of me to be caring about the sea?" Hae-song paused for a moment and spoke again, still looking away. "I truly thought I could delay construction of the factory by pleading with the people. But it turns out that those people have their own agenda."

"So you gave up?"

"No. I've made up my mind to stand up to them. But. . . . I don't know if I have it in me."

A warm and gentle light momentarily rippled across the woman's face. "You'll win, Comrade. I'm sure of it."

Hae-song looked at the woman in surprise. How in the world could she be so sure?

When she entered Pak Shin-ch'ŏl's office the next morning, her face pale, she was in for a shock. The woman she had met at the shore yesterday was sitting across from him. She stood up with a warm smile.

"Please come in," she said.

For some reason, Shin-ch'ŏl had a gloomy look about him; he glanced at Hae-song and turned to look out the window.

"I didn't introduce myself properly before," said the woman. "I'm Yŏn-kyŏng." She led Hae-song to a long bench and sat down beside her. "You said you were Comrade Hae-song?" The woman held Hae-song with kind and gentle eyes. "Comrade Hae-song, I am the researcher who developed that catalyzing agent."

"What?" Hae-song immediately sprang to her feet.

The woman was no longer smiling. The look in her eyes was serious and guarded. Hae-song could tell at once from her expression that what she said was true. In the time it took to confirm this, Hae-song became confused, with no room to maneuver. The woman guided Hae-song back into her seat.

"I might have made a big mistake if it weren't for you, Comrade. I could only see that the seaweed contained the minerals I needed. I wasn't looking ahead to the future of the sea. Thank you."

Hae-song had no idea how to respond. But she could sense that Yŏn-kyŏng was expressing something heartfelt from the warmth of her hand.

"Comrade Researcher," Shin-ch'ŏl's voice range out, breaking the silence he had maintained until then. "Let me repeat myself. This is not such a simple matter."

Picking up the notebook she had left on top of the desk, Yŏn-kyŏng said calmly, "I've made up my mind about the matter. The most important thing is that now we know why we have to stop construction of the facility."

Shin-ch'ŏl looked away from Yŏn-kyŏng. Even from his profile it was clear that he was having great difficulty suppressing his anger.

"I'm afraid I have to leave now because I have a phone appointment with the Research Institute." Yŏn-kyŏng stood up and took Hae-song's hand once again. "I'm in Room 204 of the Hae-an Hotel. Would you come for a visit tonight?"

Looking into Yŏn-kyŏng's eyes, Hae-song nodded unconsciously.

"Then I'll be expecting you."

When Yŏn-kyŏng left, the room was filled with thick silence. Shin-ch'ŏl simply stood facing the window. Hae-song felt like she

Azalea

Make the
Ocean
Blue:
Ch'oe
Ryŏn

was sitting on a bed of nails. She got up from her seat, took a few steps toward the door, but froze when she heard a sharp voice.

"Stop!" Shin-ch'ŏl turned around to face her. "Let's be clear about this. The final authority regarding the construction of the chemical plant lies with me."

Hae-song looked at him coldly. "Since you are a representative of the State, I hope you will see this issue with the future of our nation in mind."

"That's right," said Shin-ch'ŏl. "I am speaking in the best interests of the State. In this case, I think to highlight the important creation of an individual is precisely in the best interests of the State." He rushed past her and went outside first. *Bang!*

Hae-song shuddered when she heard the door slam. . . .

When Hae-song stepped into the hotel room, Yŏn-kyŏng was reading something. A bright smile blossomed on her face when she saw Hae-song awkwardly hesitating in the doorway.

"Please come in. I was just thinking you might not come."

The room was clean and neatly appointed. On top of a small desk in the middle of the room, the seven shells Hae-song had seen the previous day were arranged in a circle.

Yŏn-kyŏng offered a plate of red tomatoes, which she had prepared earlier. "Please have some," she said. "To tell you the truth, when I came here I used to think that I could leave things like site checking, design, and execution to other people. But now that I'm here, I see it's a very good thing I came. I got to see the ocean and meet good people there. . . ." Looking directly at Hae-song, she asked suddenly, "So did you have an argument with Comrade Shin-ch'ŏl?"

"Excuse me?" Hae-song was taken aback by the unexpected question.

Yŏn-kyŏng smiled as if she were happy. "Don't think badly of Comrade Shin-ch'ŏl. He's actually a good comrade. I know him well since he's a classmate of my husband's. He volunteered for this assignment just so he could help me. He's younger than Ung-i's

176

father, but he's got a lot of clout in the State. Of course, he's very stubborn. It's a flaw if you see it that way, but if you see it as a man's confidence in his own beliefs, then you can consider it a strength, right?"

In the red light of the setting sun that streamed in through the window, her face was enchantingly beautiful. The fact that this kind and attractive woman happened to be "The Inventor of the Chemical That Laid Waste to the Sea" vanished from Hae-song's mind. She was like an older sister: someone with whom Hae-song could talk as a woman, a sensitive woman, a normal woman who loved life. Hae-song put the tomato Yŏn-kyŏng had given her back on the plate.

"Sister, there's something I want to ask you," Hae-song said. "To give up your creation—that can't possibly be a casual thing for you. Tell me the truth. You're upset now, aren't you? I . . . did some research. I heard that your research took nearly a year of working in fits and starts, sweating blood while you left your husband and dear son behind at home. . . . And so. . . ."

Feeling her voice tremble, Hae-song lowered her eyes. Her next words resonated like a whisper. "Sister, I want to know everything there is to know about you."

Yŏn-kyŏng quietly grasped Hae-song's hand. "Yes, Hae-song. . . . I am upset. . . ." She let go and fondled the shells on the desk one by one. To Hae-song, the clattering sound they made as they touched was heartbreaking.

"The reason I'm upset—it's not because I have to start my research over. My own hardship doesn't matter to me. But my husband and my son, Ung-i . . . they're waiting for me. When I think of how disappointed they'll be when they hear I have to start all over, it makes me heartsick."

Yŏn-kyŏng lifted her head, which had been ever more downcast, and looked toward something outside the window. "A few days before I left the mine, I got a letter from my husband saying Ung-i had drawn a red circle around May third. That's my

AZALEA

Make the
Ocean
Blue:
Ch'oe
Ryŏn

son's birthday. And he'd said, 'Dad, this time Mom, me, and you will all be together inside this circle, right?' That's what he said."

Yŏn-kyŏng squinted, as if she were drawing a mental picture of her son. "I really wanted Ung-i to be happy this time. I wasn't able to have a proper birthday celebration for him for three or four years. Strange, isn't it? The things you plan for and wait for most eagerly—it's those things that don't go as planned. Whenever Ung-i's birthday came around, I would have some amazing plan and I tried one way or other to make sure I got time off just for that day. But it would never happen. Do you think it's fate playing games? Last year, too, the only time I could take time off to come home was on his birthday. The train was delayed, and when I finally got home it was late at night. My husband was sitting in the kitchen smoking and Ung-i was asleep with his toy machine gun flung by his side. I knew everything right away. Ung-i was crying, waiting for me, and my husband tried to comfort him with the toy he got him for a present. . . . But he still couldn't get rid of Ung-i's sadness—that emotion was still etched on his sleeping face. His father was exhausted playing mother. . . . My heart felt like it would burst. I took Ung-i in my arms and cried. What kind of a wife and mother am I? I. . . ."

Clear tears welled up in Yŏn-kyŏng's eyes, ready to spill over.

Hae-song couldn't help her own stinging tears that suddenly welled up. The seven shells on the desk glittered even more beautifully in the dying light of the sunset.

A little later, Yŏn-kyŏng spoke again. "I really can't get used to this pain. . . . The work my husband does in planning takes so much concentration. I know that, and yet I leave him to take care of Ung-i. . . . He suffers like that because he met a woman like me."

"Sister." Hae-song, sitting all the while, her face wet with tears, suddenly raised her head. "Please forgive me. I've caused you a great deal of trouble for nothing. Can't you reconsider your decision to shut down the chemical plant? The truth is . . . I'm not a marine botanist."

The seashells dropped from Yŏn-kyŏng's hand. "What? What did you say?"

Hae-song answered without hesitation in a voice whose clarity even shocked herself. "I'm actually a mechanical engineer. I came down here because they needed help with installing hydraulics in the heavy machines factory and I met the local villagers and talked to them. . . ."

Yŏn-kyŏng took a breath. Her face grew pale for a moment as if she were severely stressed. She got up and went to the window. Only after a long while did the color return to her face.

"Thanks. I actually envy your courage. It doesn't matter. The fact that you're not a marine botanist doesn't change anything, Hae-song. I mean, what sort of ocean would you want me to leave for my son?"

"Then what are you going to do?"

Yŏn-kyŏng was staring at the shells as if they contained the answer to Hae-song's question, as if they could give her some mysterious wisdom and strength. "I have to leave in two days," she said. On her face appeared the light that one sees on someone who has overcome great suffering.

"Where? To Pyongyang?"

"I have to go to Samhŭng. I notified the Institute about my decision today. To develop a new chemical reagent."

There was a knock on the door, and the woman from the reception desk downstairs appeared. "Is Ch'ae Yŏn-kyŏng the researcher here? There's a phone call for you from Pyongyang."

"From Pyongyang?"

Yŏn-kyŏng gave Hae-song a quick look over her shoulder as she left. It was momentary, but from her eyes Hae-song could sense that the phone call was something out of the ordinary. With an uneasy feeling, she looked steadily at the door through which Yŏn-kyŏng had exited.

⁓

Yŏn-kyŏng returned more quickly than expected. But Hae-song could not help but be shocked—it was like looking at an

Azalea

Make the
Ocean
Blue:
Ch'oe
Ryŏn

entirely different person. Yŏn-kyŏng had lost her confidence; her eyes, which had gleamed with determination even while her face was pale with grief, were wavering. "He . . . It was my husband . . . ," she said. "He asked me when I was leaving to come home."

"What did you tell him?"

"I couldn't answer him. I think . . . he seemed angry." Her voice sounded as if all the strength had drained from her body. Putting her hand to her forehead, which was clammy with sweat, she collapsed onto the floor. "Hae-song, please let me be alone. Let's meet again in two days. There's something I need to do in the meantime."

Hae-song left Yŏn-kyŏng's room. The lonely sliver of the moon floated dimly in the night sky as if it were gathering together every bit of its remaining strength and spewing its last light. It was so sad that tears suddenly welled up in Hae-song's eyes.

"Twice the burden," she said to herself.

Why should this great woman, doing all the same work as a man, have to take on yet another responsibility? A heavier and harder burden. About the failure of the research and her worries, Yŏn-kyŏng didn't say a word. . . . Yes, that was because everything else was trifling compared to the suffering in her heart. What is happiness, anyway? If a woman like Yŏn-kyŏng was drowning in sorrow and suffering, then who deserved to be happy?

With a tightness in her chest, Hae-song reached out and clutched the branch of a willow that draped down over the road.

∾

When Hae-song went to meet her two days later as promised, Yŏn-kyŏng was nowhere to be seen. The dorm manager said she had left an hour earlier after asking for a box lunch she could eat on the first morning train. The office door was locked, too. Hae-song was walking out, crestfallen, when she saw Shin-ch'ŏl coming into the main entrance of the building.

"I . . . ," Hae-song went toward him without thinking, happy to see him.

But Shin-ch'ŏl walked past, ignoring her. Hae-song bit her lip. This young man was not going to forgive her. But she followed him for a few steps and asked, "Where is Yŏn-kyŏng?"

At her words, Shin-ch'ŏl turned his head stiffly. "Yŏn-kyŏng? I wouldn't know." He answered curtly and walked toward his office.

Hae-song felt insulted, but quietly turned around to leave.

"Just a moment!" Shin-ch'ŏl approached her. "Why are you still following her and causing her grief? Let me give you a word of warning. Stop following her around. Things have all turned out the way you wanted, Comrade."

Hae-song's face grew pale. "What sort of villain do you take me for? I don't believe I'm guilty of antisocial behavior."

"So you think you're being humanitarian?" Something flared in Shin-ch'ŏl's eyes. "Of course, you believe you're acting rationally. With logic like two plus three equals five. The ocean will be damaged, so that woman must put aside her work. No matter how many tears she shed, no matter how much she suffered, it doesn't matter. Even if she's endangering her own life with those new experiments, it means nothing to you. Am I right? Absolutely flawless in theory. That's why she went back to extracting chemicals from waste oil, a process the Institute stopped because it was too dangerous."

Hae-song's face grew hot with resentment, but she could not refute him. Instead, she felt new waves of concern. "Where is she now?"

Before he turned away, Shin-ch'ŏl reluctantly threw out some words to the effect that she should go and check the beach at Hae-an Park.

Yŏn-kyŏng looked like a picture, sitting on a rock on the curve in the shoreline where they had met a few days ago. She did not flinch though each incoming wave sprayed into the air. She was so lost in thought she didn't notice Hae-song at first.

AZALEA

Make the

Ocean

Blue:

Ch'oe

Ryŏn

"Sister, what are you thinking about?"

Yŏn-kyŏng glanced at Hae-song with a blank expression and went back to looking down at the waves. When Hae-song came and sat by her side, she took a small bundle wrapped in a handkerchief and untied it. It was the shells. She put them down one by one in a line.

"My husband is here now."

"Here? In Ryŏnp'o?" asked Hae-song.

"Comrade Shin-ch'ŏl said he arrived today. But he doesn't want to see me. Why, do you suppose? Why, Hae-song?"

"He said he doesn't want to see you? How could he not want to see you?"

"Oh, I know why. He's mad at me. He has a right to be angry." She carefully picked up the shells.

"That can't be," said Hae-song. "Something must have come up. He'll come soon, right?"

Yŏn-kyŏng slowly turned around. She straightened Hae-song's collar for her. "Do you really think he will?"

"Of course."

Yŏn-kyŏng's expression seemed to brighten for a moment, but then she seemed to recall something and it grew dark again. "But I didn't know he was here, and I made an appointment to go to the chemical plant in Yŏngp'yŏng. To get some chemicals. The plant manager there is a classmate of mine, you know."

"Can't you go later?"

"It's almost time for the train."

Hae-song realized that she could not change Yŏn-kyŏng's course. The more she understood this, the more it pained her heart. Yŏn-kyŏng forced a smile, sensing her thoughts. "Don't worry. Each person has his own path to follow, right? I'm going because that's the path I've chosen. It's the one I have to follow."

"Oh, sister!" Hae-song gently buried her face in Yŏn-kyŏng's shoulder. "Don't be too late. I'll wait for you."

"Thanks, Hae-song. I'll be back tonight."

They came down from the flat rock arm in arm.

~

It seemed to Hae-song that this was the hardest wait of her entire life. One hour . . . two hours. . . . When she realized it was time for Yŏn-kyŏng to return, she couldn't control her nervousness; she finally came out and sat on a small bench in the park in front of the dormitory. Here and there, fiery red sweetbriers bloomed, wafting their distinct fragrance. Where was Yŏn-kyŏng by now. . . ?

Suddenly, she heard a gravelly voice calling from behind her, "Are you Comrade Yun Hae-song?"

Her first impression was that a rather dangerous man was standing behind her. She turned around. "Yes. And you are. . . ." She had no memory of ever having seen this man, who knew her name, so she asked again.

"My name is Lim Hyŏng-jun," he said. "I came to see Ung-i's mother. I heard about you from Comrade Shin-ch'ŏl."

So this was Ung-i's father.

Hae-song was shocked. For some reason she had expected Yŏn-kyŏng's husband to be kind and generous, but the man standing before her was intimidating, sharp and cold as steel.

"Oh. . . . Yŏn-kyŏng will be here soon. She went to Yŏngp'yŏng, but it's about time she got back."

"Yes? That must be why she wasn't in her room." He scrutinized her. His sharp expression made Hae-song involuntarily blush and turn away. "I was told you were a marine botanist," he said. "Now that we've met, could you tell me a little about the kinds of seaweed that live in the ocean around here? The research I read said there was a lot of *kulch'i* and *kuwŏlp'ul*, but if you listen to what the locals say, that doesn't seem to be the case."

Hae-song answered with her eyes downcast. "Yes, actually, *kulch'i* and *kuwŏlp'ul* are sea plants that generally thrive where it's cold. But since the currents in this area have gotten warmer, seaweeds like *ttŭmbugi* and *p'urunji* have also started to proliferate."

"I see. My wife was hoping to extract the minerals in

AZALEA

Make the

Ocean

Blue:

Ch'oe

Ryŏn

those seaweeds. *Ttŭmbugi, ch'ŏng'gak, p'urunji*—the ones full of phosphorus. She was basically correct. That same mineral helps expel heavy metals like cadmium, lead, and zinc from the human body. But that's not the only reason seaweed is important. It's a major purifier of the sea and plays an important role in counteracting global warming. The ocean absorbs tens of times more CO_2 than the land, and most of that is done by seaweed. That vitally important seaweed must be protected to prevent the desertification of the seabed. It takes a marine ecosystem many decades to come back to life once it's been destroyed."

Hae-song's eyes grew wider and wider. It wasn't because she was surprised by his knowledge. It was because she realized that he was explaining all of this at length because he feared what contradicted his own understanding. He did not want to interrupt himself. The more she sensed this with her woman's intuition, the less she had the courage to look him in the eye.

"I'm sorry. It's because of me that Yŏn-kyŏng. . . ."

"You don't have to console me."

"I'm not trying to. I only wanted to say that there's a possibility that all the research Yŏn-kyŏng paid so dearly for may have a useful application."

Hyŏng-jun looked at Hae-song anew, as if struck by something unexpected. He spoke again, in a deflated voice: "In any case, our happy illusion is shattered. But to glue it back together like a broken pot is hypocritical. Neither I nor my wife want that kind of hypocrisy."

Sparks flashed in Hae-song's eyes. Slowly, her face flushed red. "Then why haven't you seen her yet?" she asked. "Do you know how upset she was when she left? She needs to be strong now."

Shocked by her dagger-like words Hyŏng-jun glanced up. He turned to the side, dodging her sharp glance. "I don't think I have it in me now. But thank you anyway. . . ."

"No, she's going to be here any moment. You have to wait."

Hae-song spoke more forcefully than she intended.

Hyŏng-jun shook his head. "No, I think that what both of us need now is not to see each other."

There was a sudden fierce storm in Hae-song's chest. "So it's true." She lifted her head, marshalling her strength. "Why are you avoiding her? Do you really not know how big a blow this is to Yŏn-kyŏng? Why can't you even say something reassuring to her? Is this the appropriate thing to do? Are you saying you can appreciate her as an exemplary human being but not as a wife and mother?"

Hae-song suddenly felt cold. She couldn't understand how she could be shouting like this. But it was at that moment when everything coiled up inside her, thread by thread, had exploded all at once.

Hyŏng-jun's thick eyebrows wavered. As he looked at her, a blue flame flashed in his eyes. Hae-song thought he would spit words like balls of fire, but he suddenly turned and walked away, his shoulders sagging. Tears flowed from Hae-song's eyes. He took a few unsteady steps. She couldn't even remember what she had said. But she saw that the preceding moment was one of the most important and critical moments in her entire life; and in that moment, whether right or wrong, she had acted with conviction.

Hae-song walked along the park path in the dark blue night that had descended. She heard footsteps hurrying toward her, and when she heard panting close behind, she turned instinctively. It was Shin-ch'ŏl. An uneasy chill ran down her spine as she saw the helpless rage in his eyes.

"What do you think you are, Comrade? What did you say to Comrade Hyŏng-jun? I asked you, what did you say to him!" His voice was rough and rang out like a shot.

Hae-song struggled to answer calmly. "I told him he was small-minded. If all husbands were like him, I said I'd give up on the idea of becoming a scientist."

"What?" Shin-ch'ŏl's eyes burned fiercely enough to burn right through her. "Small-minded? What do you know, Comrade? Do you even know why he's avoiding her? He brought his boy with him.

AZALEA

Make the

Ocean

Blue:

Ch'oe

Ryŏn

Do you have any inkling of a father's pain, how painful it would be for him to take his son away from his mother again? Do you even know—when he resolved to support his wife who would have to leave her family behind again—how terribly his resolve was tested? What? How will you ever be a scientist with such a small heart?" He scoffed, turned sharply, and walked away.

Hae-song staggered, as if she had been caught on the point of a spear. Shin-ch'ŏl's words pierced her heart. She could not deny the truth behind his harsh words. No—I can't give in so easily. Hae-song resumed walking with firm resolve.

Hyŏng-jun was sitting on a long bench facing the sea, which was lost in blue-black darkness. A light flickered from a boat floating far away in the middle of the ocean.

Though Hae-song stood beside him, Hyŏng-jun spoke quietly as if he were talking to himself. "Why I brought Ung-i with me, I don't know myself. He doesn't know his mother is here. If Yŏn-kyŏng knew Ung-i came . . . she wouldn't be able to bear it. She'd just fall apart. No matter how strong she is, she's still a woman."

He stopped mumbling to himself and looked at Hae-song with sympathy in his eyes. "A little while ago, you said something about 'a wife and a mother.' Yes, women have a duty to their families. I, too, thought Yŏn-kyŏng had to perform her duty to the family. So there were times when she got behind in her research."

A wistful smile appeared on his face. He gazed for a long time at the light that twinkled like a star far out in the ocean. He continued, "But each time, I realized that Yŏn-kyŏng, whom I have loved all this time, wasn't the kind of woman to stay at home to take care of a child. To be so absorbed in creation that she forgot herself—the happiness, the joy, the pride—all those things combined to form my image of Yŏn-kyŏng. I mean, together with the anguish and tears when she failed. If you take all that away, then she becomes just an ordinary woman. That scared me. I even wondered if I had lost her. It might be strange to hear this, but I couldn't get used to the idea that someday the image of the young Yŏn-kyŏng would disappear. I just wanted to see her forever, laughing, happy and sad like when she was young. That's why I put her back on the path."

Hyŏng-jun glanced back at Hae-song. "When I did that, the fire that burned in her again was so strong it surprised even me. To tell you the truth, that heat and light was many times more precious and beautiful to me than my authority as a husband. I know Yŏn-kyŏng is like a ball of fire. A fire that entirely consumes itself. I want to stare at that fire forever. If you think happiness is a loving, devoted wife and a happy household, maybe that fire burns up her happiness—and mine as well. But I'd be sad if that fire went out."

It was already dark. The only thing visible to Hae-song was the horizon, dyed red, but she was seeing the blue and joyful waves undulating in the ocean. It was not the ocean she had known, it was whispering sublime knowledge that she hadn't quite understood until now. . . .

Yŏn-kyŏng returned to her hotel only after 9 P.M., drenched in sweat. On her back she carried a large pack that looked rather heavy.

"It must have been rough. But what is this?" Hae-song said, taking the pack from her.

"Oh, it's some things I need for my research."

So this passionate woman had already begun her new research project. Hae-song led Yŏn-kyŏng to the table. "Come and eat."

"I ate before I left." Yŏn-kyŏng looked evenly at Hae-song, with an affectionate smile. "By the way, I've decided to take some time off. I'm going to stop at home first on my way to Samhŭng." She walked gracefully to the clothes cabinet seeming sufficiently revived.

"Sister . . . your husband was here."

When those words struck her as she changed her clothes, her shoulders stiffened. She turned quickly around. "When?" Anxiety, tension, and uneasiness were all tangled together on Yŏn-kyŏng's face. She grabbed Hae-song's hands and shook her. "What's going on? Tell me! I need to see him. Right now."

Azalea

Make the
Ocean
Blue:
Ch'oe
Ryŏn

Hae-song, avoiding her fiery eyes, said quietly, "Your husband said there was somewhere he had to be. He said he would see you off on the first train tomorrow morning. He said to tell you . . . that he understands everything."

In the uneasy silence that filled the room, Yŏn-kyŏng slowly crumbled into her seat. She cried out, heatedly to herself, "What? . . . What does he understand? You can't do this to me. Why won't you try to stop me. . . ." She leaned limply against the pack, completely exhausted.

"Sister, please calm down and try to get some sleep. Please." Hae-song helped her to her bed. Yŏn-kyŏng, her face pale, lay down like a child and Hae-song tucked her in.

The night was long, but sleep did not come to Hae-song. She knew that Yŏn-kyŏng, lying next to her, also could not sleep. She whispered quietly, "Sister?"

"What is it?" Yŏn-kyŏng's voice was thin, without a trace of sleepiness.

Hae-song fumbled to find her hand and held it. "You know, Sister, I wrote to my mother. I asked her to take care of Ung-i. . . ."

Surprised, Yŏn-kyŏng lifted her head and tried to sit up.

"Lie down, Sister. Hear me out. Ung-i's father also does important work, but because of Ung-i, it must be hard for him. Before my mother retired, she was director of a nursery school for twenty years. She'll take good care of Ung-i. Now you don't have to worry about him."

Yŏn-kyŏng squeezed Hae-song's hand tightly. "Thanks, Hae-song."

"And I want to go with you to Samhŭng to help you out. I can go on to Pyongyang from there. Will you let me?"

"You don't have to do all that, Hae-song. You really shouldn't."

"No. Please let me. I have some things to take care of up there. And I want to go with you."

Yŏn-kyŏng did not answer.

The dawn became a brighter and brighter blue. All things hidden in the darkness slowly revealed their shapes.

Yŏn-kyŏng stood anxiously on the platform. Standing by her side, Hae-song also looked nervously toward the gate.

There weren't many people on the platform. Standing huddled in the early morning air with faces that hadn't yet shaken off sleep, they became suddenly agitated as the green signal light, visible far down the track, lit up. The sound of the whistle came flying. The train was coming.

Hae-song looked at Yŏn-kyŏng, distressed. Her face was bluish, and all she could do was stare intently at the spot where she believed Hyŏng-jun would appear. But the man who appeared, pushing people out of the way, was Park Shin-ch'ŏl. He came out through the gate, looked all around and, spotting Yŏn-kyŏng, came running straight to them.

"Comrade Yŏn-kyŏng!" Gasping for breath, Shin-ch'ŏl pushed the bundle he was carrying right into Yŏn-kyŏng's arms. "This was sent by your husband."

"What?" Yŏn-kyŏng looked at the bundle as if she had been given an electric shock. It was a familiar deep red cloth. "Where is he?"

Shin-ch'ŏl avoided her questioning look. Just then a long, sharp whistle sounded. "Please get on the train."

But Yŏn-kyŏng was going toward the gate.

"I have to see him," she said.

Shin-ch'ŏl answered hesitantly, "Actually, he came to me an hour ago. I wanted to tell you, but he wouldn't let me on my life. He said he would rather not see you because he thought he might just grab your ankles and never let go. He said he'd rather go out to see the ocean."

Yŏn-kyŏng hugged the bundle to her body. The whistle sounded. As if she had made up her mind, she turned and went up the steps onto the train. Hae-song followed her up, too.

Shin-ch'ŏl's eyes followed Hae-song. "Comrade," he called.

AZALEA

Make the

Ocean

Blue:

Ch'oe

Ryŏn

Hae-song just looked coolly at Shin-ch'ŏl, who suddenly lost his balance and staggered. Shin-ch'ŏl thrust his hand sharply downward to keep his balance, as if he had lost his equilibrium because of that look. "Whatever happens, let's meet again," he said.

Hae-song turned away, pretending she hadn't noticed the fiery look in his eyes. Even in the great rush, a light smile shone on Yŏn-kyŏng's face. Shin-ch'ŏl said "Goodbye" but no one heard.

The train pulled out. Hae-song felt a gentle pain creep up on her as Shin-ch'ŏl's waving form disappeared in the morning fog. People were still not awake from their sweet sleep. Even if they had been, not one of them could know the pain in the heart of this woman researcher traveling with her. Not many would know how far she would have to go, how hard it would be. They couldn't be blamed for not knowing, and yet. . . . And yet. . . .

Yŏn-kyŏng had not even thought to go inside the car; she was still in the outer compartment by the door. Her hair flew in the fierce wind. Suddenly, she unwrapped the bundle. There were packages of wrapped clothes and toiletries inside, and on top of those was tucked a small folded paper. Yŏn-kyŏng quickly unfolded it. It was graph paper, the kind used in elementary school composition books. On it were letters written painstakingly in pencil; even at a glance she could see that the words were all carefully printed in order to stay inside the boxes.

"Dear Mom, Dad told me that you're giving me the ocean for my birthday present. Dad said it's a really wide and blue ocean."

It was Ung-i's voice, the voice of the son she loved, the one she always embraced in her dreams. Yŏn-kyŏng hugged the letter to her breast. She looked sublimely happy, as if she could evoke the smell of his skin, the warmth of his body to her heart's content from this single sheet of paper.

"Ung-i!"

Yŏn-kyŏng had no doubt that her beloved son and husband were hearing her voice. She was sure of it—boundless love transcends time and space.

The vista opened, and a rosy light enveloped the train. It was the ocean, just before sunrise, rising and falling majestically. The sun was still below the horizon, and yet its red light tinted the entire ocean. The golden rays, full of the joy of the new day, jostled each other, finding a space to push forward toward the train. Illuminated by joy, Yŏn-kyŏng's face burned more brightly than the light of dawn, more beautiful than ever.

"Hyŏng-jun!"

Hae-song did not hear Yŏn-kyŏng's whisper, but she felt it resonate through her entire body. She was right. Hyŏng-jun was standing like a picture on the white sand by the sea. He was waving at the train, his clothes blowing in the early morning wind. Though his features were not visible, his form, standing with the red sea as the background, gleamed like a statue poured from bronze. At his side crouched a small shadow moving to the side, then forward, playing in the sand.

"Ung-i!"

She was crying. The tears that coursed down her cheeks sparkled beautifully in the light of dawn. Effortless tears, tears helpless with joy. Happiness—a human being cannot live without it. Whatever hardship and pain they suffer, great hearts—inspired by joy and the thrill of a challenge, energized by boundless love—seek happiness. Hae-song felt herself crying, too. She shouted inwardly. The valleys and gorges that this simple and vulnerable woman must still traverse are deep. But with a loving husband and son standing at the summit, how can she give up mid-way? No. This isn't darkness and suffering, it's light and passion and joy.

It seemed to Hae-song that she was finally seeing the "light" Hyŏng-jun had described.

Shouting and cheering joyfully, trembling and churning, the ocean was seeing the women off.

Falling Persimmons

by Chŏn Pyŏng-gu

Translated by Chae-Pyong Song

On the hill of Kwansan port, overgrown with weeds,
Where the dividing line crosses,
Hoo-doo-dook, Hoo-doo-dook,
Falling Persimmons.

Where only the house remains, its owner gone,
A persimmon tree already for many years
Has been solely ripening persimmons,
And dropping them without sympathy.

If I reach out a hand, I could quickly pick
one red, juicy persimmon,
But the barbed wire that pierces the heart
Blocks even one step.

The piteous persimmon tree,
You too suffer the pain of division.
When will you summon the owner?
When will the day come when he, riding on your branches, will
Pick out persimmons with pleasure?

With the wedding celebration table

Neatly piled with those appealing persimmons

This village's lasses, they say,

Went to P'aju, across the Imjin River, to their grooms;

Their faces, red like persimmons,

Must be deeply wrinkled by now.

Where are the brides of those days?

Though I search beyond the river, I can't see them.

The red persimmons that I could embrace only in dreams,

Hoo-doo-dook, Hoo-doo-dook.

They strike this heart;

They strike this peninsula,

Crying for the owner, crying for unification.

Hoo-doo-dook, Hoo-doo-dook. Ah, the falling persimmons.

Five Poems by Chong Hyon-jong

Translated by Wolhee Choe

SPLENDOR—BUDS

Through you
I am true, my love.
Through you
all things breathe
dance
shine
and smile.
Luminosity about to burst—
the light genesis nonpareil, you
propagate;
(in other words)
all space is budding to bloom.

Through you
all is reborn, my love
is there anything left out?
Oh the womb of dawn.

In that splendor
dreams and hearts are budding,
expanding universe.
Through you
I am true, my love.

My Mind's Ruin

1

Nested in me, this ruin began
rippling even before
distant ancestral froth stirred
its sign deepened
with things past
with vanishings.
Oh gestures and embraces
tears, smiles
time's wind-blown waves.

2

On this fallen temple
aesthetic aspirations alone bestow dignity
some of which may throb
in songs built in the void
of my desires' ruined columns.

This Time without Bottom or End

Time's aspect:
nothing to gain
everything to lose.
Neither maledictory nor recriminatory
I say time is sorrow.
Its depth is without bottom or end,
clueless, why argue, really
no bottom, no end.
Even if coal and gold,
even the axis of the earth were dug out,
boundless sorrow
with desire,
without bottom or end,
spreads necessity in the world,
the necessity neither a flower
nor a gaze in the void can
actually change.

O time, desire's covering
even deception and metamorphic magic
are of necessity rags of pain.
While living, letting go
of all cannot be, not
before you lose time.

At Dawn

Not switching on the light
I watch
to catch the light of dawn
to merge with the boundless light
wishing to be drenched. . . .

Oh, body in blue,
mind of dawn.

The more days and years endured
the tenderer my mind becomes;
August's passing is unbearable.
September and October
unbearable.
I cannot bear
things flowing away,
cannot bear
human affairs,
changes and pains,
cannot bear
being become nothing,
the visible become the invisible.
I cannot bear time
any trace of time,
shadows of time
I cannot bear.
All the traces are wounds,
all the flux and change
pain and the painful.

Beauty Looks Down on Me

by Eun Hee Kyung

Translated by Sora Kim-Russell

Spring Snow

I cannot forget the day I first saw Botticelli's *The Birth of Venus*. A late spring snow was fluttering down. As I followed my father into the carpeted Italian restaurant, I realized it was a world apart from any place I had ever known. Small flower vases and candlesticks were set on the tables, and the air in the room was quietly stirred by the subdued conversations of affluent, refined-looking people skilfully handling Western-style silverware. Father and I were shown to a reserved table beside a window. A waiter took my father's elegant overcoat and my old, clumpy parka and hung them on a coat stand.

From the moment I sat facing him, I directed my gaze at a large painting dimly lit by a spotlight on the wall behind him. I couldn't look him in the face. The air inside was warm and sweat soon began to ooze along the folds on my neck. *Now that you're a middle school student, you must do more for your mother.* I nodded almost imperceptibly in response to Father's words. *And you can call me whenever you want.* That sounded a bit like a lie. As soon as the food arrived, I lowered my eyes and pretended to be absorbed in eating. Transferring a shrimp to my plate after dipping it in sauce, Father spoke again. *You have a healthy appetite. Don't worry. When you grow up, the fat will melt off on its own. Why, when I was your age, my nickname was Pork Bun.* I thought that sounded like a lie too.

Azalea

Beauty

Looks

Down

on Me:

Eun Hee

Kyung

Once all the food was eaten and the plates cleared away, I had nowhere to focus my eyes, so I looked up at the painting again. Following my gaze, Father turned to see where I was looking. A superior smile rose to his lips. *That's Venus. The scene where she's born out of the sea foam.* Why did I feel so sad the moment I heard those words? Was it because of the smooth, beautiful face like that of a porcelain doll, milky-hued with a touch of green? Or the long, blond hair wrapped around her slender, naked body and fluttering in the breeze, or the defenseless-looking, bare, white feet poised on a great gaping shell? Or was it because of the mysterious sorrow deep in her eyes that were gazing up into the empty air? *I'm sorry,* Father said mournfully, sighing deeply, when he saw that my eyes were brimming with tears.

Looking back, as I followed my father around that day, I was constantly tormented by the question of why I was born. Every time my footsteps lagged behind, he would stop and stand waiting for me, probably thinking, just as other people did, that it was on account of my size. I was already used to that kind of misunderstanding. Having been a fat kid, I always looked crabby or unhappy, when in fact I was merely shy. On the days I met Father, I always went home feeling sad because I was convinced I could never please him. He seemed especially displeased with the fact that I was fat. Had he been with a bright, innocent child, he could have been the tragic hero, but a fat kid who looks stupid or crabby could never amount to any more than someone who reminded him of his own mistake, his one moment of folly.

Venus

Once I was old enough to be able to buy things I liked with my own money, I hung a picture of Botticelli's Venus on the wall of my room. Since it had a naked woman in it, my friends thought it was a different style of pornographic poster. B said that fat people are obsessed with the classics as a form of psychological compensation to try to prove how refined and sensitive they are. But neither the sensuous Venus welcoming her lover Mars into her bed, nor the pure, innocent Venus standing with Eros holding his bow, were the focus of my attention. To my eyes, even the *Venus de Milo* with her elegant symmetry, as if nothing better could even be imagined, merely looked like a model for an art class. The only Venus in my book was Botticelli's Venus.

That day, my friends and I went to B's house to pilfer some whiskey his parents had bought on a trip to Europe. Throughout the house were bottles of ginseng wine and other kinds of liquor that we had previously topped off with water. But that day, we could only lower the level in the new bottle a little bit, as B warned us several times that it was expensive stuff. We decided to drink just a drop more of the whiskey that B's father kept in his study, and I went to get the bottle. His father's study was a place I liked—the dust-covered books, the secret solitude, and the faint, fatherly scent hanging in the air. Of all that B had, it was perhaps what I liked the most. I took the bottle from the bookcase, and, on my way out, stole a glance at the book on the desk. I was always curious as to what book B's father was reading. A museum catalogue that looked like it had been bought at his latest travel destination was lying open on top of the desk.

It was a statue of an immensely obese woman. The sagging roll of flesh around her middle made her look as if she was carrying a baby on her back, wrapped tightly round with a thick cotton quilt. Her upper body, leaning forward to buttress breasts the size of stone mortars, was securely supported by a belly like a clay jar and short legs as thick as pillars. There could be no distinguishing legs and arms, or neck and waist, and her face as well had nothing that might be termed features. It was as if an elephant's legs were attached to a haphazardly rolled snowman. The woman's name was "The Venus of Willendorf." The caption said it was a stone Venus made about

AZALEA

Beauty

Looks

Down

on Me:

Eun Hee

Kyung

20,000 years ago during the Ice Age, preserved in a museum in Vienna, Austria.

I gazed at her for a while, almost like someone possessed. At last, I set the bottle down on one side of the desk and began carefully tearing the page out of the catalogue. After I folded it a couple of times, it fit neatly into my trouser pocket. Even now, I don't understand exactly why I did it. Was it because I had sensed something for the first time, however slightly, about a twenty-thousand-year span of time? You might say, tritely, that I sensed a primitive age inside my body, but in truth, it wasn't without some traces of mockery or cynicism.

These feelings, though, were immediately forgotten when my friends shouted joyfully at seeing the bottle in my hands. Only when I was changing my trousers after returning home did I recall the woman's picture in my pocket. Feeling drowsy from the alcohol, I carelessly slipped the picture between the pages of the first book I grabbed from the bookshelf, then went straight to bed. As I threw myself onto the bed, it uttered a groan as if it were being tortured.

My weight was probably at its peak around then. Those painful physical education classes still appear in my dreams sometimes. I had almost forgotten about the woman whose picture I stole, the first time I'd ever stolen anything in my life. But when I stood on the scale in the public bath on Sunday mornings when no one else was around, she would sometimes come to mind. Each time, I would get down from the scale, muttering, "Venus, please, don't bless me. Take from me your bounty and fertility." I didn't remember her so often as to feel an urge to ransack all the books in my bookcase looking for that photo, inserted between the pages of some book or other. I don't know why, but after I became a college student, I tied together almost all of the books I had read in the order in which they had been stuck on the shelves and sold them to a secondhand bookstore. The ever more faded picture of Botticelli's Venus disappeared during the move.

When I started high school, Father took me out to another fancy restaurant, but once I was in college, I never heard from him again. Mother had a habit of telling me that the older I got, the more I resembled him. Of course, she said that when she was unhappy with me. She stopped talking about him after I started college. It was as though, now that I was grown up, she had come to terms with the fact that Father had left. Though she seemed much freer than before, it was no guarantee of her immediate happiness. It had taken too long for her to reach that point. *Now that you are a college student, you have to do more for your mother.* Had I met Father then, that's certainly what he would have said. It was really the only thing he could have done for her.

Phone Call on a Sunday

My thirty-fifth birthday fell on a Sunday. Upon returning from church, Mother prepared the traditional birthday soup made with dried seaweed, which she had soaked in water the night before. Watching television with her after she finished washing the dishes, I declared that I was going on a diet to commemorate my birthday. My mother stared at me dubiously, as if she had just heard those words spoken by a bear preparing to hibernate. I had lived as a fat person since infancy, and that was no short period of time. It's true that it had been uncomfortable, but human narcissism can adapt to any condition, no matter how bad, and find ways to rationalize it. Seeing that Mother had thought for the past thirty years that I accepted my obesity quite naturally, her long searching stare wasn't at all unreasonable. But she didn't seem to have picked up on the reason why I had suddenly decided to go on some kind of a diet. She replied briefly in a reluctant tone: *It'll be nice to have some space on the drying rack.* Mother had always complained that there wasn't enough space to hang the clothes, even though there were only two of us, because my clothes were all large. It never occurred to her that it might be because she didn't do laundry often enough. *Let's see . . . will we have more room around the house once you shrink?* A tired, blank expression hardened by many years of life came to Mother's face as she turned her head to survey the interior of our house.

AZALEA

Beauty

Looks

Down

on Me:

Eun Hee

Kyung

A talk show rerun was on cable. As the faces of the program guests appeared on the screen, Mother moved closer to the TV set. Two attractive young men dressed like twins in identical white clothing appeared, shaking their long, feathered hair and smiling brightly as if they hoped to fill the screen with sweetness. Mother had never even heard their songs. Yet they had recently become her favorite celebrities. Each time the two appeared, Mother would invariably ask me, *Hey, which one is Hyŏnjŏng, and which is Hyŏngjun?* Mother couldn't tell whether I was right or wrong, but she could always detect an uncertain reply. It wasn't that she really expected a sincere response from me. She had long ago got into the habit of talking to herself as if we were having a conversation, having realized that despite her complaints, there would be no change in my taciturn character. *If there were three of them, it would be much easier to tell one from another, but it's harder because there are only two. Just like telling a left turn from a right turn.* That spring Mother had given up on trying to get a driver's license after she had failed the written test for the eighth time. She must have been thinking that once she gave up on trying to tell Hyŏnjŏng from Hyŏngjun, she may as well have to start giving up on more and more things in her old age.

After attending a two-hour lecture to the effect that growing old was a matter of learning the composure needed to accept and resign oneself to senility, Mother stopped going to the Senior Citizen's Welfare Center. Although she had been forced to give up many things in the course of her life, what Mother hated most was resignation and any pressure in that direction. In actual fact, call it resignation if you like, Mother had almost never made any choices for herself. It was no different when she held me to her breast as a newborn baby.

As soon as the program ended, Mother sat back from the TV. *How many kilograms are you going to lose?* she asked. When I said I planned to lose twenty, she cocked her head and nodded again. *Are you planning on seeing someone?* she muttered behind my back as I went into my room. Contrary to Mother's complaints that I was impossible to figure out, I sometimes thought there was nothing she didn't know about me; this was one of those times.

Of course, it wasn't that I had had absolutely no interest in diets until now. You can't ignore what's going on in the world. Nowadays, fat people aren't simply looked at in an insensitive and apathetic way. They are also treated like lazy good-for-nothings who lack self-control and don't take care of themselves. I know that the many potential brides I'd been introduced to, and undoubtedly my own mother as well, probably thought at some point that my sexual ability would leave a lot to be desired. B joked that if my weight went over a hundred kilograms, I would have to start counting it in tons. *The number 0.1 longs for something and looks better than 100. To be honest, if you weren't so heavy, you would have been far too ordinary in every way.* But whether what B said about me being heavy was true and I therefore couldn't be swayed that easily, or whether it wasn't true that I was so ordinary, I especially hated being manipulated by conformist values. What could change me was not the general majority but certain people who were important to me.

That afternoon, I took the bus and went to a large bookstore in Kwanghwamun. After carefully looking through dozens of books for about two hours, I bought three diet books that I thought were theoretically more persuasive than the others. B's company, which closed on Saturdays and opened on Sundays instead, was ten minutes away. B answered his phone immediately. I told him I'd come out to buy some books, and he assured me he would be there in the bookstore before I'd even read two pages. However, it was two hours before he showed up. A newspaper reporter is like a husband who drinks heavily; he always offers an excessively logical excuse for being late, and never forgets to add that he's going to have to quit. While talking to me, he read the titles of the books next to me, simultaneously going over the day's lead stories in his head.

Azalea

Beauty
Looks
Down
on Me:
Eun Hee
Kyung

According to B, it would be as if I was living a new life. I would never again suffer the indignity of having someone in a crowded elevator that was on the point of leaving hit the "close" button as I came rushing up gasping and was about to set one foot inside. And I would be freed from getting red in the face whenever I tied my shoes, worrying that I might unwittingly strain too hard and let out a fart, as if I were sitting on the toilet. I would leave behind the anguish of having to conceal my wounded pride whenever a waitress delivered a meal I'd ordered to some ugly, sloppy fat guy, since all fat people look alike, and having to call her over in a loud voice. *That's the way to think. All of us, including you, are finally going to get a look at the real you, the you that's been wrapped up inside those rolls of flesh.* B considered it entirely my fault that his old car had lost its muffler. *Don't you realize that the bottom of the car sinks so low when you're in it, it can hardly get over the speed bumps? From now on you won't have to worry, when you get on an airplane, a boat, or a playground ride, or whatever, whether the person next to you is wondering if it's going to tip to your side.* Ordering one last bottle of soju, B asked, *Why did you decide to lose weight all of a sudden, anyway? Trying to sleep with some girl?*

That had come up during a get-together of high school friends whom I hadn't seen for a long time. One of the guys bragged about how he used his company's corporate card to enjoy unlimited one-night stands, hitting the hottest spots in Kangnam. Married friends responded nonchalantly to his bragging, but the unmarried ones gradually leaned in closer to him. When his entertaining tales of adventures with women at company expense ended, someone sitting in a corner sighed deeply. *You know, I haven't slept with a woman for 11 months, 3 weeks, and 2 days. What? No way!* An exaggerated chorus of sighs arose all around, as if they were a paid audience filling the studio seats for a television talk show. I confided to B alone, on our way home, that it had been two years more for me than for that friend. 11 months, 3 weeks, and 2 days! I had brought it up for fun, meaning to suggest that he must have been keeping a daily tab since he even remembered the number of days, but B interpreted my words differently. *Honestly, I don't think it's a problem that will be solved by dieting*, B advised me, a serious look on his face. *It's a matter of how assertive you are. Have you ever tried approaching a woman and striking up a conversation?* Despite having known each other a long time, there were still a lot of things B didn't know about me. It was just that the conditions under which I lived meant that I always had to first consider, even before I ardently desired something, whether it was okay for me to desire it; it wasn't that I was passive about wanting things. Besides, even without B spelling it out plainly, I wasn't so stupid as to not know that, when it came to sleeping with women, there were many simple solutions that didn't entail going on a diet.

By the time we came out of the bar, night had already fallen and was waiting for us. *How's your mother doing?* B walked with me to the bus stop after he'd phoned for someone to drive him home. *Hasn't she been complaining of boredom since she gave up the restaurant? Relieved, more like it. I think she still goes there sometimes to eat. She taught the new owner, so the food tastes okay.* Actually that was a pretext. She was surely bored to death after twenty years of the same food, always in the same place, but apart from there, Mother had nowhere else to go. *Is she still going to the same church? No, she switched to the Full Gospel Church.* I explained why. *She said she couldn't stand the sight of those rich Kangnam wives singing hymns so affectedly with their mouths moving like goldfish, so she switched churches because she wanted to bawl out hymns at the top of her lungs. Your mother is always so feisty.* B laughed loudly, as if he found it funny.

Since it was Sunday evening, there were not many people on the bus. As I placed my books on the empty seat next to me, B's words came to mind. It was true that every time I took a seat on a bus, I was careful not to touch the person sitting next to me. Several times I had been unable to bear the misunderstanding of some young woman and had gotten off the bus halfway. I smiled

AZALEA

Beauty
Looks
Down
on Me:
Eun Hee
Kyung

wryly. B was different from me in every way; I was unnecessarily complicated and sensitive. He was simple, cheerful and devoid of malice, as befitting a son lovingly brought up in a good environment. I didn't know him as a child, but he must have been a bright, earnest-looking boy.

I slowly turned my face toward the window. The road outside was darker than usual. Perhaps because there were not many cars, the streetlights created patterns here and there on the dark, deserted road. Mother had always led a dull life, and though she desired change, there was nothing she could do about it. The only thing she could change was the church she attended. She had never been a feisty person. If Mother had answered that phone call, she might well have replied flatly that it was the wrong number, that the person they were looking for didn't live there. But then, not only would her hands have been shaking too hard for her to prepare lunch, she would have been unable to look me in the face when I asked about the phone call; she would have ended up wrapping herself in her quilt and curling up on her side.

I'd received the phone call a week before, in the morning, while Mother was at church. It was a young man's voice. He said he got the number from the restaurant, and asked whether he was correct in assuming that I was the son. Then he mentioned Father's name and told me the name of the hospital and the room number. It was a short conversation. It was thanks to a kindly nurse on duty at the hospital that I learned the name of his disease and the date of the operation. *Are you family? Yes, I am,* I answered in a dry voice, like the young man who had phoned. A week went by after, and the only thing I did was to call up the restaurant to tell them that if they gave out our number to strangers, Mother would be put in a tight spot, and requested that they not even tell her someone had asked for our number. I tried to remember what Father looked like, but my mind was blank. Instead, what came to mind was a fat kid, lost in some sad thoughts and hurrying after his father for fear of losing him.

210

Our Daily Bread

Dr. Robert Atkins, a cardiologist, discovered an interesting
fact while performing autopsies on deceased soldiers during the
Vietnam War. Thick chunks of fat were attached to their internal
organs. How could such accumulated fat, a common pattern among
older people who eat a lot of meat and get little exercise, be found
in young soldiers on the battlefront? It was due to carbohydrates,
the staple of their diet. The human body is a big chemical factory.
Excess carbohydrates in the body turn to fat; but fat, no matter how
much is consumed, cannot be stored without carbohydrates. That's
where the theory of the Atkins Diet comes from—eat all the fat you
want but no carbohydrates.

Mother, who had run a small restaurant that served rice
soup for over twenty years, naturally held the opposite theory.
When I told her that I would lose weight by eating fatty pork,
she pretended to be puzzled, asking where all that grease would
go. I tried telling her that once food enters the body, it turns into
completely different substances, but it was no use. She adopted an
especially firm attitude when I said that I would completely cut
out carbohydrates like rice, bread, noodles, and rice cakes. She was
unyielding in her argument that rice is healthy food, homegrown
produce eaten by generation after generation of ancestors, and
that noodles have only half the calories of rice, while buckwheat
noodles are widely known as a diet food. Mother had been
watching morning TV programs almost without fail. When it
came to the rule that fruit or juice should be avoided, she retorted:
*Even sugar-free juice? But fruit itself contains a lot of sugar. And
don't buy potatoes, either. Starch immediately breaks down into
carbohydrates.* Mother's eyebrows rose high, full of confidence.
Can you name one food that is as nutritious as potatoes? I know, I
hurriedly replied as if to cut her off, since I was not accustomed
to explaining things to Mother. Everyone knows how much sugar
and potatoes have contributed to human history. The problem is
that this is no longer an era of nutritional deficiency when people

need to generate energy at low cost. On the contrary, in the U.S. alone they pour billions of dollars a year into dieting and keeping in shape.

Azalea

Beauty
Looks
Down
on Me:
Eun Hee
Kyung

The scale I had ordered through the Internet arrived the following day. People imagine the difficulties fat people face to be simply a matter of having a hard time walking up stairs, or spending a lot on food, but it's not so. What is far more uncomfortable is the way we can't do anything without attracting people's attention. One of the major advantages of Internet shopping is that, just as a bachelor can quietly purchase a "real doll," a fat person can choose things like large-size clothes or a scale without feeling that everyone's staring at them. Standing on the first scale I had ever owned in my life, I gazed down at the needle as it sped blithely over the figures.

On my way home, I bought a small spring-bound notebook with pages ruled in blue from the stationery store next to the bus stop. The notebook was held closed by a fabric-covered rubber band and contained fifty pages. Leaving forty-two pages, I tore out the rest then wrote one day's date on each of the pages with a thick pen. The preparations were pretty much complete.

The Second Week

As soon as I opened my eyes, I started the day by recording my weight.

For breakfast I ate vegetables with eggs or tofu. I had to change my entire cooking method to be able to eat without getting bored. For vegetables, I alternated between things like tomatoes, cucumbers, and bell peppers. Dinner was meat and fish. I ate slices of grilled pork one day and sushi the next, followed by grilled fish, fried bacon, boiled chicken, grilled sirloin, and so on. From anyone's point of view, they were decent meals to be sure, but it took more patience than I thought to eat the same food every day. It was a particular struggle to eat all of these things without rice. Until now, I had chosen my meals based on the main items and thought of rice as something that automatically came with them. Now it was completely different. My appetite demanded only rice, and my body went crazy with excitement at just the thought of warm, glossy rice. That wasn't just because of appetite. Fat can only be stored if it's consumed with carbohydrates. Thus, my body's instinct was to plead and clamor for carbohydrates.

Lunch was the most difficult. I offended the restaurant owner by only eating side dishes and not even touching the rice. On the plate of dumplings I had finished eating, only the peeled dumpling skins were left untouched with the stuffing taken out. When I ate *bibimbap*, I first skimmed off the hot pepper sauce, which was made with sweet rice and mixed with sugar, then carefully removed and ate the vegetables that were set on top of the rice.

When I went to restaurants with my coworkers, they would talk until the end of the meal about the fact that I had started dieting, the incomprehensible aspects of the diet I had chosen, and common knowledge regarding the terrible things that might happen if someone as fat as me did not go on a diet. A friend who joined the company the same year as me made the most scathing comments regarding the side effects of dieting and the yo-yo syndrome, using our friendship as an excuse. The only one among them who didn't speak was the new female employee, but I could sense that she was using her chopsticks quietly so she wouldn't miss a word of the conversation. It was all outward encouragement. However, since other people's problems are a matter of common curiosity anyway, I didn't enjoy being made its subject. Eventually, I started eating out alone. I pushed all my dinner appointments back six weeks.

Changes began to appear in my body after three days. I felt dizzy, as if suffering from anemia, and began to lose my concentration. Whenever I saw a chair, I sank into it even if only for a short while. I lost enthusiasm for everything, and even my daily routine at the office became difficult for me to handle. When

AZALEA

Beauty

Looks

Down

on Me:

Eun Hee

Kyung

the new female employee overtook me as I was walking slowly up the stairs holding onto the handrail, she even carried my files for me as she couldn't just stand by and watch. *Are you okay? You look pale.* Though I hated the fact that I was drawing attention to myself, I pointed at my head and smiled wryly. *My brain is angry with me. What? What about your brain?* Since I didn't have the energy to explain further, her wide, innocent-looking eyes began to get on my nerves. The brain, the most sophisticated part of our body, doesn't bother with tedious tasks. Instead of producing energy for its own use, it gets its supply of glucose from carbohydrates; but now it had been getting none. Dr. Atkins said you shouldn't satisfy your brain's demands. Over time, the brain cannot help but adapt to the new system. However, you clearly risk a certain degree of danger by not feeding your brain, even for a short time.

Mother could not help noticing. On the fifth day, ginseng chicken soup was on the table for supper. *Chicken's okay, isn't it?* Mother sounded glib, as if to suggest that she couldn't possibly be expected to know anything about the stuffing of sweet rice hidden inside the breast. I was speechless, unable to do anything but stare blankly at the chicken that was giving off hot steam with the savory scent of rice. Meat was okay, but the instant I chased it with cold noodles or rice and stew, I would start gaining weight—this explanation was so obvious that it refused to leave my lips. Instead, my mouth quickly began to fill with saliva. While I hesitated, my selfish, greedy body had already tucked in the napkin, and was sitting there holding a knife and fork, looking at me with an expression that said: Come on, hurry up.

Everyone has to eat grain to stay healthy. Staring fixedly at me, Mother uttered terribly tempting words. There was nothing wrong with what she said. You only had to think of a farmer's rice bowl mounded high like a grave to realize it: next to sugar, grains are most easily converted into energy. But in my state, forced to burn up all my surplus reserves, I absolutely had to avoid consuming any more food.

After a light meal of canned tuna and tofu for dinner, I had an unpleasant taste in my mouth, so Mother brought me fragrant honeyed water in a clear glass with ice cubes floating in it. *It's the only way. Listening to your body is the key to health.* Her words, as sweet as the honeyed water, were also true. The body, like a baseball trainer, sends us all kinds of signals to control the game called "survival." The problem is that when it comes to fat, there is a complete difference between the satisfaction my body craves and the health I desire. As for my brain, it was increasingly not on my side. It was the brain that was ordering the viscera to stock up on glucose in order to secure energy for itself, regardless of what the other organs might suffer. Frantic to go on storing more, the brain is always three minutes late in telling the body that the stomach is full. Even as I reluctantly waved away the honeyed water, I could feel at the same time that someone inside my body was struggling desperately to rush out, without stopping to put their shoes on, and grab the glass.

Grilled mackerel and pan-fried tofu, which I had requested, were served for dinner the next day. But there was also a bowl of glossy rice and fried squid with noodles on top, which I had not asked for. Everything was in very small portions. Mother declared that everyone knows it's a bad habit to eat an unbalanced diet, and she ordered me to eat a variety of foods but to reduce my intake by half, just as the morning program on TV advised. I ignored her, so she changed her tactics again the next day. In addition to salt and pepper, she used a sweetly scented marinade on the meat, and she even added sugar, which was pure carbohydrates, to spicy chicken soup and fried squid. The less I was able to overcome temptation, the bigger my discontent with her grew. Eventually, I started losing my temper at the table.

It began with me shouting that she had to throw out her old, outdated beliefs about food and other things. I grumbled that she should let me handle my problems my own way, especially when it came to my own body. But the grumbling grew into nervous

Azalea

Beauty

Looks

Down

on Me:

Eun Hee

Kyung

criticism. I even told her bluntly that I would never be able to get married, as she so desired, if I failed this diet, and would therefore certainly not produce any fat children. I implied that her current, hopeless life was fate's inevitable revenge for her one immoral act. I knew exactly how to hurt her. But Mother had enough dignity to despise those who hurt her. Whenever she couldn't get her way, she reminded me of her absolute authority and self-sacrifice on my behalf when I was just a helpless, wretchedly abandoned fetus, and she did so with enough vigor to stuff me back into her womb like a boa constrictor swallowing an elephant. *Why did you give birth to me? Why did I have a son like you?* Had we been a chicken and an egg, we still would have growled at each other like this.

The diet was difficult because I had to struggle against the millennia-old system of survival instincts installed in my body. The human body comes programmed with a system, dating back to the age of stone axes, that intensively stores fat. But today's standards of beauty and health call for burning off all of one's body fat. Dieting creates a dilemma between our primitive body and modern culture. I was confronted with dilemmas daily, through different trials in every aspect of my life. One day, upon returning from the archives, I found a paper plate with a slice of mousse cake topped with sweetened whipped cream and a red strawberry waiting for me. A glass of cola sat beside it. With whipped cream already stuck to the corners of his mouth, my coworker waved a fork as he told me it was the new female employee's birthday. I sensed my coworkers all watching the plate and me, as if they had placed bets.

Have mine, too. I moved the plate of cake to my colleague's desk. Looking at me with an intrigued expression as I handed him the glass of cola as well, he quizzed me as if playing a game. *Why is cola bad for you? When you eat concentrated sugar along with fat, the body has a tendency to store fat.* I continued talking in a slow, cool voice. *If you wonder why bad things taste so good, it's because you have the body of a millennia-old primitive man who goes crazy at the mere mention of fat.*

216

I called the other person living inside my body Primitive Man. I gradually began to feel a sense of hostility toward the animal instinct for survival and the systems in my body that were attached to it. Human beings don't have sex anymore just to preserve the species. My birth was proof enough of that. And yet, my body persists in asserting that I am still an animal no different from Ice Age man. Why do pleasure-seeking humans, having resisted the instinct to preserve the species, still submit to the pleasurable instinct to store fat? Is it because the dominant human gene is to seek out pleasure?

I lost weight little by little each day. There were days when I weighed the same as before, but even on those days, my body definitely felt lighter. My watch hung loose on my wrist, and I had to tighten my belt by three holes. Fastening the collar button on my shirt, I realized my weight loss had started primarily in my neck. When I looked at my reflection in the mirror while taking a shower, it seemed as though there was more space in the mirror, and when I met someone in a narrow hallway, I only had to turn slightly to get past without touching the wall. It was easier to catch a cab, too, presumably because there were fewer cabdrivers that didn't want to take me. There were more and more instances in which the new female employee, who had previously been so hesitant to respond whenever I pointed something out, smiled and replied promptly. Once I had lost eight kilograms, I became convinced that this diet was proof that modern humanity represented a new stage of existence, having abandoned the natural choices made by animals for the choices of enlightened civilization. But more importantly, I found satisfaction in the thought that I was resisting my genetic inheritance. In the meantime, three weeks had passed.

Things You Can Choose and Things You Can't

B paid a visit to my workplace one lunch hour. *Anything goes, so long as you stay away from the carbohydrates? That shouldn't be too difficult?* But B and I had to keep passing by restaurants. Ox

AZALEA

Beauty
Looks
Down
on Me:
Eun Hee
Kyung

bone soup or hangover soup, sushi, fried rice, and curry rice are all dishes that can't be imagined without rice. Even light lunch items such as cold buckwheat noodles and udon are packed full of carbohydrates. Pasta is no different. B stopped in front of a Chinese restaurant. *Meat's okay? Yes, but most Chinese dishes contain starch.* Standing on the pavement and looking at the signboards of restaurants around him, his gaze settled without much hope on a sandwich shop across the street. *No good, of course? Bread is bread, but there's also sugar in the mayonnaise. I don't care if you eat or not, I need to have lunch.* Complaining that he'd lost his appetite, B finally hauled me into the nearest fast food place.

B ordered fried chicken, a cola, and a biscuit, and I ordered a hamburger without sauce. *Won't it cause a nutritional imbalance if you keep not eating rice like that? After all, isn't the principle of a diet that you should keep eating just one type of food and lose weight through malnutrition?* Since every person talking to me over the past few weeks had questioned me about diet methods, I was sick of the subject, but I tried explaining that dieting is more a matter of metabolism than calories. Though lions only eat meat, they don't have problems with their nutritional balance because carbohydrates are synthesized inside their bodies. On the contrary, even though cows only eat grass, they have a lot of fat in their bodies. Though camels hold fat in their humps, they are able to cross the desert because fat converts into water when it burns. And so on. B snickered. *Wow, you're nearly on automatic! A stuck channel.*

A boy who appeared to be waiting for his mother who had gone to order was sitting by himself across from me and staring at me with a piercing gaze. I don't like fast food places, and it's not just because whenever a fat person appears, people immediately think of the lawsuit against McDonald's. It's also because they can see up close what others are eating, and because those places are usually full of children. Young children, being candid, stare openly whenever something catches their eye, and most parents only recognize their children's right to innocence, failing to teach them about the self-respect of people who don't want to be stared at like that. If they see me eating just a salad, the parents will whisper to their child, *He has to eat just a little like that because he's fat. But he's still fat even though he eats so little; don't you feel sorry for him?* But even if a fat person is eating French fries, a double hamburger, and a coke, they don't ignore him just because what he's eating matches his size. They exchange looks that say, "He's fat because he eats like that," while suppressing their laughter, then look away quickly when they sense my gaze. It's not because fat people are large that they are so readily noticed. People stare at fat people because they feel there's something different about them. I saw the boy watch closely as I ate only the insides of the burger and tossed the buns onto a tray.

B pointed at the chicken. *Want some? You said you can eat fatty food. Unbreaded chicken is okay, but that looks like it dove into the oil wearing a cheap coat.* B raised his eyebrows, a bitter look on his face. *You're really having a hard time of it. Yeah, I envy bears the most, because they lose all their weight just by sleeping through the winter. They lose weight by sleeping? That's the first I've heard of bears getting liposuction. No kidding, they've got money, too.* But B didn't look like he was enjoying joking around as usual. I could hear the ice rattling as B absentmindedly shook his cup. I changed the topic. *Do you know why human beings overeat?*

During the Ice Age, our ancestors starved on a regular basis. Many died because they couldn't make it through the times when there were no plants to gather or animals to hunt. Therefore, if they found something to eat after a long period of waiting, they would always throw a big feast and overeat. The purpose of the feast was to store fat, and the purpose of storing fat was to be able to survive the next cold spell, drought, or other time of need. If children don't eat properly for even a week, their limbs stop growing. According to researchers who study the bones and teeth of prehistoric humans, there is a clear difference in density between the parts that stopped developing due to starvation and the parts that developed actively after a round of heavy eating. The ability to survive didn't depend

AZALEA

Beauty

Looks

Down

on Me:

Eun Hee

Kyung

simply on eating but on overeating. Therefore, even fat people, whose bodies have ample fat stored up for emergencies, get hungry regularly and enjoy the taste of food. Overeating is a genetic flaw built into the human body.

So all you have to do is blame everything on your ancestors. B interrupted me. Strangely, his expression as he scrutinized my face was just like that of the kid sitting opposite. It was the first time B had ever looked at me like he was looking at a fat person. It was like he was telling me that while I'm aware of and struggling against my inner fat guy, the fat guy becomes my true identity. B added, still wearing the expression of a stranger, *What you're saying is, it's not your fault because you were born the wrong way. Am I right?*

I put the empty cup and dirty napkins on my plate without saying anything. He went on. *You seem to really hate the guy you call "Primitive Man," but aren't you that guy inside, crying out for fat? You think you're a highly rational self that commands the being called you, while he's a primitive person living off of you like a parasite? What are you talking about? He existed before you got the current shell called your "body." He is you. Isn't that right?* I picked up the tray and stood up without responding. Clever, innocent children don't know the reason fat kids who look grouchy and stupid don't play ball with the others and instead watch them from the classroom window while greedily licking the chocolate in their hands, or the pleasure and stimulating animosity of the sweetness that taints the mouth. Shit, who cares whose genes are inside my body?

At the Dinner Table

That evening, I returned home and ate grilled pork with half a bottle of soju. I chose soju, according to Dr. Atkins' advice, instead of the beer I usually drank. Mother had the remaining half. The TV was on behind the chair where I was sitting. Her eyes glued to Hyŏnjŏng and Hyŏngjun, Mother spoke. *Tell me the truth. Why are you so crazy about losing weight? What's going on?* I looked down at the sliced pork sizzling on the electric frying pan. The piece of fat left on the pan, which Mother had separated from the lean meat, was sizzling especially loudly. Holding the last glass of soju, I stared blankly at the wall behind Mother as usual. There was nothing hanging on it.

As two weeks had passed since the date of the operation, I thought he might have been discharged from the hospital. However, the patient was still in his hospital room, waiting for a second operation. I wanted to ask how he was doing but hung up the phone instead. I didn't want to let even the nurse know that I was wondering about his condition. Things went that way because I was determined to suppress my desire to know if the patient wanted to see me. It was the same in regard to the pain his body must be undergoing. It wasn't that I was unconcerned, but too much relentless time had built up between us, like fatty dregs that thicken the blood, for me to naturally feel pity for him.

I had opened the notebook that was sitting on one side of the table and was checking the dates when Mother suddenly shrieked. *Hey, your body's not completely blocking the TV screen any more. It's only Hyŏnjŏng on TV today, isn't it?* I moved aside so she could see the rest of the screen. Mother often joked around when she got tipsy. On TV the pretty boys were grimacing and eating rice cakes stuffed with wasabi as a penalty for losing a game. *Pretty people even look pretty when they're eating.* Mother began talking to herself. *They say that when you get old, you look gross when you eat. Who wants to look at something gross? That's when it's time to take a person's food away. It's time for them to die. They say that's what happens when you stop caring about someone. When love fades, there's nothing worse than seeing that person eat. Wanting to take food away from someone, doesn't that mean you want them to die? There's nothing more shameful than eating. It's said that liking starts with eating together and love grows at the table.* I remarked cynically, *If you look pretty when you eat, you'll turn into a pig.*

Mother stopped wiping the grease from the frying pan and heaved a deep sigh. *Why don't you go out and buy another bottle of*

AZALEA

Beauty

Looks

Down

on Me:

Eun Hee

Kyung

soju. You say you're losing weight but you don't exercise. And don't treat rice like it's some deadly enemy. Mother suddenly flung the greasy paper towel down roughly and started nagging at me. The more Mother drank, the more her jokes turned into lectures and nitpicking, which would then be followed by sob stories about her unhappy life. *You shouldn't do that. It wasn't that long ago that people went hungry because they didn't have anything to eat. Don't forget the spring famine. After all, back in those days, people did whatever it took to avoid starvation. Do you know how many families in our neighborhood sent their daughters to work in bars? It's not like that anymore,* I interrupted. *People don't starve to death nowadays, so you . . .* I gulped down what I wanted to say next because she was glaring at me. Even after I stopped talking, Mother kept staring hard at me. She looked both mystified and dubious. *What's wrong?* I asked bluntly, and Mother laughed feebly and replied, *Nothing, you just reminded me of someone.*

The Final Week

My body seemed to have completely shifted from synthesizing fat to burning fat. I regained the usual rhythm of my life and the change in my body was apparent from the astonished looks of everyone who knew me. If a client I had not seen for a while dropped by and commented in flattering tones that he hardly recognized me, the new female employee would chime in, saying how remarkable it was. Then she would add, turning toward me, *You have such big, pretty eyes.* Whenever I took a few steps, I could tell that my butt had grown smaller. My footsteps felt as if they rang far more lightly. It was also easier for me to nod since my double chin was gone. *So, this is how you become a cheerful person,* I murmured in front of the mirror.

My colleague congratulated me on the change in my belly. He even asked me whether his potbelly had anything to do with the fact that whenever he went mountain climbing, he would grab wildly at trees and rocks rather than tighten his stomach muscles. I explained that since the stomach is the fat storehouse that the body defends to the end, the fat around the belly was the last to go. The new female employee asked me why sweet foods were fattening. The easiest way that the body obtains energy is from a glucose injection. Next come sweet foods. Since it only takes a single step to convert them into glucose, the body naturally seeks sweets when it's tired. Because it's born with a fondness for sweetness, a newborn baby seeks out its mother's milk, which contains sugar, and is thus able to survive. Children, who need a lot of calories in order to grow, also can't help but like sweets. The reason old people are addicted to sweets is a little different. Mother, who could finish off a bowl of sweet and sour pork by herself, used to rationalize her gluttony by saying, as if it were a tried and true proverb, that growing old was like reverting to childhood. But, it's not because old people need a lot of calories like children do. Instead it's a strategy for obtaining energy easily, as the aged body, which has grown weak, doesn't want to work hard.

My physical changes were not the only thing. Fat people's larger frames tend to make their feet look disproportionately small and sad, but now I felt like my silhouette had come alive. My suit jackets that used to strain against my arms and back to the point of tearing were now much looser. It just so happened that all the department stores were having sales then. I bought two suits and a brightly colored spring shirt. I felt lighthearted, as if I had just finished preparing for a long-awaited outing.

I called the hospital for the third time. My hand was in a rush to dial the number. The second operation had ended in failure. The nurse, speaking in the same kindly voice, told me I should contact the hospital's funeral parlor. I dialed again with a trembling hand. The funeral was the next day.

I returned home and hung the new suits in the closet. They were different from the other clothes that had been hanging in the closet for so long. They had an air of politeness and dignity, their shoulders bowed forward slightly like they were entering someone else's house. Exuding all the luster and sense of vigor that new

AZALEA

Beauty

Looks

Down

on Me:

Eun Hee

Kyung

things should, like newly appointed replacements with innovative plans, the suits were dispelling the air of gloom that had settled in the long unchanging wardrobe. My gaze stopped at the sight of my old jacket hanging in the far corner. Unlike the new suits, the arms of the limp jacket were sagging like my old flabby shell, and the large space created by the back and chest looked empty, as if nothing could ever fill it. I took the jacket out and slowly removed the dust with a clothes brush. It was the only black suit I owned. I could hear Mother talking to herself in the kitchen as she set the table for dinner. She was probably grumbling about the dishes I had requested. As I listened, I felt a sadness more excruciating than any I had ever felt in my life.

Children Born by Mistake

When we were kids, B always used to joke that his birth was a mistake. *If my father hadn't had 5,000* won *for a motel or 50,000* won *for an operation, one of the two, I wouldn't have been born.* But B's story changed each time he told it. *Actually, my father did give my mother the money for the operation. But on the way to the hospital, she was passing in front of a shopping center and saw a beaded handbag that she really liked in a store window. My mother immediately used the operation money to buy the handbag. My mom always says, worry about the consequences later. That's her style. If not, I would never have been created. Anyway, as a result, I was born. I competed against a beaded handbag and lost and that's how my life began.* On some days, B changed his story from a beaded handbag to a pleated skirt or a pearl ring. The way he joked about how he was born was something I had envied in B.

We were about thirty years old when I heard the true story from B. *Actually, I had an older sister.* B's parents had one son and one daughter, so I knew he had a sister who was three years older. *I don't mean that sister; I mean the one who was born a year before me. After all, even if she died four months after she was born, she's still my older sister.* B's father was the only son born in his family for

224

two generations, and he was therefore responsible for continuing the family line. From the day the first daughter arrived, the family elders started pressuring him to have a son. When his wife got pregnant again after two years, B's grandfather, who did not even consider the other possibility, prepared five possible names for boys based on the family's generation names. But the baby was born a girl this time as well. Each time B's father came home from work, his wife would be crying under the blanket and hugging the baby. When the hundredth day had passed and her postpartum recovery was nearing its end, she went to visit the next-door neighbor with her eldest daughter walking beside her, after putting the baby to bed. When she returned home, the baby was dead, lying on her stomach with her little nose and mouth buried in the padded quilt. B's father fell into utter despair because he had secretly had a vasectomy the day before. He had thought that was the best solution, since he didn't want to impose the family's irrational value system, which was unacceptable even to himself, on his wife when she was so depressed after her second pregnancy. But his decision had been to raise two daughters; he had not intended to take the risk of raising only one child. When he went back to the hospital, the doctor told him there might be some live sperm remaining in his body, so fertilization could still occur though the possibility was low. As soon as they had buried the dead baby, the couple jumped into bed. Surprisingly, she conceived again and gave birth to a baby the following year. This time it was a son.

B said he would never forget the shock of hearing his grandfather, who loved him exclusively and believed that girls had no souls, describe it as the time the family narrowly escaped disaster. It wasn't until much later that he was struck with amazement by the remarkably determined sperm bearing his name that had remained alive in his father's scrotum for four days before emerging into the world and succeeding in its task. The way his newborn older sister had made the entire family happy by breathing her last feeble breath just a hundred days after her birth; the selfish,

AZALEA

Beauty

Looks

Down

on Me:

Eun Hee

Kyung

merciless human family instinct that, in the end, whether they had intended it or not, had conspired to commit murder; the bargain to quickly exchange death for life—all of that had made him sick. His parents had been just like chimpanzees, the female lewdly shaking her swollen red genitals and the male running after her and grunting with nose aquiver. Had his mother really lingered so long in their neighbor's house with no ulterior motive? He felt misgivings about all these things, yet what troubled B the most in his adolescence was disillusionment about his father's desire. How had his father been capable of shuddering in sexual pleasure on the very blanket where the newborn baby's corpse had lain? The only way B could endure it was by cracking jokes about his birth.

I still clearly remembered B's last words that day. *But I think I've come to terms with it now. Life goes on mean and dirty like that, and we learn about the world from within our fathers' hypocrisy. Maybe,* I replied coolly. *You and I are different. Your father went behind a curtain briefly in order to have you, but my father never wanted me at all.*

Venus

I didn't have the courage to go in and pay my respects before my father's photo. I formally presented my condolence money at the entrance then took a step back behind other funeral guests who were arriving just then before retreating to the hallway. A young man dressed in black came up to me with a friendly look on his face. I reluctantly let him lead me into the crowded room where people were eating. No one took any notice of me. Of course, it wasn't the sort of place where people show curiosity toward others, but then I realized that I was no longer so fat as to be conspicuous. I thought I would just sit near the entrance briefly and leave right away, but the young man in charge of the funeral arrangements politely asked me to sit further inside. There was an empty seat in the corner. I sat and stared blankly for a moment at the liquor bottles and food that were set out on the table.

A middle-aged woman with a white pin in her hair came to me carrying a bowl of rice soup on a tray. She set the bowl in front of me and gave me a friendly look; the whites of her eyes were bloodshot. She seemed to be a relative of the deceased. *Have a bowl of rice soup. It'll warm you up.* The spicy smell pricked at my nose, while the white grains of rice floating in the oily red broth already had me excited. However, instead of picking up a spoon, I quickly opened a soju bottle so that the grief-stricken woman with her kindly air wouldn't feel embarrassed. Other guests kept coming in, making it hard to get up, so I just went on drinking soju. The soup quickly cooled off. Almost all of the seats were filled, except for the table I sitting at. As luck would have it, it seemed to be reserved for relatives. All my life, I had had almost no relatives. Ever since I was young, my mother didn't like outings with her family, where they got together and attacked each other with unwanted advice. My father's relatives greeted each other warmly, remarking on how long it had been, and after briefly shedding tears, set about sharing food and drink while talking loudly about all kinds of things. I had always imagined the people of my father's world. All the adults would be dignified and warmhearted, and the children would be innocent and clever. But these people who were gathered to mourn Father were the same as those I had always seen. Their wrinkles expressed both joys and sorrows, and while they seemed wearied by life, they apparently led ordinary lives, comforted by small things or putting on a brave front. There were also quite a few fat people. That was one more reason I hadn't thought of as to why no one looked my way. It didn't matter. They didn't know me, and I didn't know them.

Oh, why didn't you eat? It's all cold now. The same woman returned and brought me fresh soup even though I told her it was okay. Judging from the way relatives were addressing her, she must have been a sister of the deceased. A young man sitting next to me offered me a drink. *Excuse me, but I'm not sure who you are.* . . . Instead of giving an answer, I quickly emptied the glass and

AZALEA

Beauty

Looks

Down

on Me:

Eun Hee

Kyung

returned it to him, thinking it was time to get out of there. The man didn't ask me any more questions. Instead, he pointed to the steaming hot bowl of rice soup. *It's okay. Please, go ahead and eat.* The reason he kept stubbornly pressuring me to eat was probably because it's a given that an unknown person drinking alone in a place like a funeral hall, where friends and family gather together, has some kind of problem, and to anyone looking, I was drinking too fast. As I didn't have the heart to shake off the blameless demands of the man, who even went so far as to put a spoon in my hand, I finally began eating.

Once I had chewed the grains of rice, they slid smoothly down my throat. I could feel my body cheering madly. My stomach squirmed like it was dancing while my insides grew warm with pleasure. Here are those carbohydrates you've been wanting so much. The spoon's movements grew ever quicker. I had a strange feeling while I was shovelling in the rice soup. More than the affection of a father feeding his starving children, I felt like a messiah saving a suffering body. Feelings of despair and a self-destructive, impulsive spite accelerated the movement of my arm. In a flash I had completely emptied the bowl at a voracious speed, even dribbling some of the soup from the sides of my mouth, as befitting an uninvited guest at a feast. As soon I swallowed the last drop of the soup and set down the bowl, the woman in the white mourning dress approached me and asked, as if she had been watching me: *Would you like another bowl? You had so much to drink.* Her kindness might have sprung from a wish to avoid having an unknown drunkard make trouble at the wake, but I happily replied yes to the sister of the deceased, like a child eager for praise. I started gulping down the second serving at an excessive speed, slurping exaggeratedly.

In the age of stone axes, human beings were always hungry. So they diligently stored up fat whenever they got the chance. The human body has been unable to adjust to the present, where there is a surplus of fat. But we will eventually evolve. After all, isn't it typical of humans to keep pushing a rock up a hill even though they know it's bound to roll back down again the moment they reach the top? That's right. There's no hurry. It took tens of thousands of years to discover a technique for sharpening stone axes. That's one way of looking at it. Sometimes in life people are shipwrecked, suffer citywide power outages, or are cut off by blizzards and forced to starve; how are they going to cope with such disasters if they have no fat stored in their bodies? So, it's still an effective system. Truly, there is no machine as honest and obedient as the body. I nodded deeply. After all, hadn't I lost twelve kilograms by not eating any carbohydrates for a whole month? My body had kicked and struggled, determined not to submit to my will, but in the end it was bound to yield results according to my design. It turned out that my body really did belong to me. Okay, then. Now, the primitive man inside my body is having a party on hearing that rice is on the way. If I eat rice soup like this, my body will immediately start to accumulate fat again. Then Mother and I will sit together again at a peaceful, loving meal table.

As I raised my head from the bowl of soup that I was devouring, someone addressed me in a loud voice. *Hey, you must be the third son!* He had half risen to his feet, while I sat bewildered. *When did you get back from the States? You're starting to look more and more like Uncle. No.* Dribbling soup, I dropped the spoon and staggered to my feet. At that moment the thought suddenly came to me that everyone there knew about me. I was gasping and my face turned red. I felt queasy, as if I were about to vomit. Pushing my way through the crowd I came out into the hallway and collapsed into one of the plastic chairs neatly lined up side by side. Through an open door, I glimpsed the room where the photo of the deceased was enshrined; it was completely empty. They must have been eating, because neither the chief mourner nor any other family members were to be seen. Far off I could dimly see Father's picture. Staggering slightly, I began to move forward to see what Father had looked like once he was really old.

AZALEA

Beauty

Looks

Down

on Me:

Eun Hee

Kyung

Perhaps I had kept looking at Botticelli's Venus to avoid looking at something else. Whenever things I didn't want to see rose again and again before my eyes, Venus intercepted them and took me to another door. Then she told me the story of her birth. The youngest son of Uranus, the god of the sky, hid in his mother's genitals to cut his father's penis in half when it entered, and threw it into the sea. White froth gathered around his father's penis as it drifted in the sea, and soon after, a beautiful maiden was born in the foam—a goddess who would bring abundance and beauty to the world. But she couldn't free me from everything. In the end, the image remained of myself standing in front of a door that was always closed. In front of the door that wouldn't admit him, the fat boy took the clumpy parka, which looked even shabbier for being the only one left on the coat stand, while outside the snow fluttered down.

Ever since some point in my adolescence, another figure had sometimes appeared and disappeared behind that picture. It was a naked women standing firmly on elephantine legs, her entire body wrapped in fat like a pelt. She was another goddess: the Venus of the Ice Age. Anthropologists say that a woman as fat as that couldn't have existed in those days. Such a woman existed only in the mind of the artist who created that Venus. The artist of the Ice Age had imagined the most beautiful and voluptuous woman in the world, and she was the very picture of divine food.

I saw the oldest son of the deceased walk into the room, preceded by two children in black. When our eyes met, he bowed his head slightly to greet me as if I were someone he had been waiting for. With his hands on the shoulders of his two fat sons, he looked at me for a moment with a superior glint in his eye, like my father had when he was younger. Father's portrait hung behind him. Scowling at him, I walked resolutely towards the portrait. Just as I had seen a world that differed from my own at that Italian restaurant, Father should also have seen a son who differed from what he knew. But he left with the memory of a fat boy. As I looked at Venus, I thought that all of the beautiful things in the world were looking down on me. I bowed slowly before Father's portrait, rose, and turned my face to spit a grain of rice out of my mouth. The queasiness, as if I were about to vomit, rose up in my throat once more. At that moment, the eldest son took a large picture frame that had been leaning against the wall from behind the funeral wreaths and handed it to me. The frame was meticulously covered in newspaper, as if it had been wrapped at home. It had been a long time, but the dimensions of the frame looked familiar. I did not ask what it was.

AZALEA

My Purple Sofa

by Jo Kyung Ran
Translated by Theresa Joo

I'm still not sure how that coat of mine caught fire in the first place. One thing you ought to know, though, that house I was invited to was unusually cold inside. While the others were drinking beer, reheating stir-fried octopus, frying more oyster and scallion cakes, and playing poker, I was practically hugging the kerosene heater in the middle of the living room. Since we are in a new year now, it must have happened at the end of last year.

I went all out trying to look my best, so I wore the black three-season dress with the scooped neckline underneath the coat, and a velvet scarf to fill in the scoop—and that's all it took. It was a dinner get-together, and the couple who hosted it were the only people I recognized. The moment I took my coat off I felt goose bumps on my arms, and even where the scarf covered me. The husband draped a cardigan over my shoulders. Imagine: a worn-out brown cardigan with a black dress—they simply do not go together. And so the cardigan ended up over my knees and I made do the best I could. There were all sorts of people there—a man who sells china wholesale at Namdaemun, someone who's been a screenwriter for various theaters for years—oh, and even a lawyer, supposedly a fellow alumnus of the husband. I don't imagine I'll ever have the opportunity to meet those sorts of people again. What's more, all the guests were unmarried. Now you see why in spite of the bone-chilling cold I didn't put on the cardigan.

It was past two when the party broke up. Some people said they were going to a karaoke bar, but I wasn't in the mood. Well, let's be honest; there was also the fact that I didn't get an invite from the wholesaler, the screenwriter, or the lawyer—nonetheless, I just wanted to go home and throw my frozen body on the heated floor. I do remember that I put on my coat, but before I slipped into my shoes to leave, I had to cozy up to the heater one last time. I've got a pretty sharp nose, and I can't believe I couldn't smell my coat burning. I said goodbye, went home, and fell asleep without washing my face.

It was 9:15 in the morning two days later when I discovered the burn marks. At the bottom of my coat there was a hole the size of a handkerchief. I had finished my breakfast and I was about to leave for the bank and the supermarket. I absolutely loved that coat—I guess that's why I still remember these details down to the exact minute. It's also the only winter coat I have, but the main thing is, the moment I saw that coat I was like, oh my god, this is so made for me. You know what I mean; coats, jeans, skirts. . . . Even without putting them on, you know they'll feel just right on you—it was like that for me with my coat. I rarely shop for clothes at the department store, but this coat—it's black, with a nylon and polyester weave—I snatched right off the hanger the minute I saw it. To pay so much for a single article of clothing—well, I guess there's a first time for everything. The coat was pinched in at the waist and wrapped me nice and snug all the way down to my ankles. Whenever I put it on and went out, I felt good about myself—I'm all skin and bones, you know. And sometimes, every once in a while, I even got complimented on how pretty I'd gotten! There are clothes like this that make a person look good, right? And this was the coat I managed to burn. You can imagine how bummed I was.

And now this coat of mine looks like it was kissed by a flame-spouting beast. It reminded me of a fight I had with my little sister once. It started out as an argument and developed into a scrap. I was about to yank her hair when she tackled me and ran her fingernails down my face. It hurt me inside whenever I looked at my face in the mirror after that. And the sight of my scorched coat eats me up even more. I can't just throw it away, but I can't wear it the way it is now either. And so it's still hanging at the very front of my closet. Well, I guess I should at least pretend to be thankful that it hasn't been too cold so far this winter. Every time my eyes drift toward that coat I try to just look away; but still, it unsettles me no end. It's like the way I feel when I look at my sick turtle. What about you: how many coats do you have to get you through this long winter?

It's five in the afternoon and I guess all the weariness got to me, because I'm sprawled out on my stomach on the sofa, relaxed as can be, like a cat that lazily stretches but stays put. You might think a cat like that is asleep—but it's always ready, 24/7, to spring up, wherever, even on the deck of a huge fishing vessel powering along through an ocean thousands of meters deep. Actually, I don't know anything about cats. But as far as I know, cats are the best when it comes to solid understanding and keen judgment. So I'm having second thoughts about my sick turtle—should I keep it? Why can't it just put itself out of its misery like a cat?

Did I mention last time that I've been killing time knitting? How many letters have I written to you anyway? My memory is a bit hazy. What number is this one—thirty-seven? Fifty-six? I think I told you that I quit my job at the bookstore downtown? There's practically nothing I haven't told you about. Have you ever heard of something called the bedtime ritual? It's like you can't go to sleep unless you do certain things in a certain order—it's a kind of obsession. For me, writing to you every night is almost like that. Maybe this repetition is why you seem to have a photographic memory when it comes to everything about me. Every time I get one of your letters I'm amazed at some of the things you remember. Well, you're probably like that with everything under the sun and not just me.

Right now I'm working on a child's sweater of green cotton yarn, weaving in a leaf pattern as the background. I've been knitting for years now, but this is the first time for the leaf pattern. I had to learn it from scratch from the yarn shop woman. I've even knitted things as large as a floor cushion to get my hands used to various gauge sizes. But knitting is not so much about training your hands, it's more about focus and sticking to the job. If your mind wanders even briefly, guess what, your patterns get all messed up—where you were supposed to do an inside stitch you've done an outside stitch, and so on. To be honest, knitting isn't as easy as you might think—skip just one little stitch or make one tiny mistake, it will stand out right away and then you have to start all over again.

It seems the yarn shop woman has been keeping an eye on my knitting. Sweaters, wool hats, shawls and such that I've knitted have gone out to the Tongdaemun shops and the Namdaemun markets for sale. I think the yarn shop woman and the yarn wholesaler might have some connection. She told me my things will go to those shops and markets, but who knows; they might be stocked in department stores too. All of which is to say that I'm pretty darned good at knitting. I can tell you for a fact that there is not one close friend of mine who hasn't received one of my handmade sweaters as a gift—well, not like I have lots of friends anyway, right? And if I did, I probably wouldn't have all this time to be writing to you. That reminds me, I don't think I've knitted anything for you yet.

So there's my skill at knitting, and besides, it's not like I have another job right now—if I work flat out for four days or so I can complete a child's sweater. If I set myself to it I can knit three or four sweaters a month, which means that for the time being I shouldn't have to worry about getting by—and I can always knock out a muffler or a wool hat in one sitting. Besides, as far as the money she gives me, the yarn shop woman could be a lot worse. And finally, there's the little bit of savings I've been putting aside until now. But I guess I can't very well knit my life away. Knitting's a winter thing. And it's my good luck this particular winter that knitted sweaters, hats, and so on are trendy. The reason I started knitting as soon as autumn came was because the yarn shop woman's offer wasn't half bad—though I didn't plan on making a career out of it. Then again, I'd been spending the whole day doing nothing in particular, and that gets really boring and tedious. And you know I'm not into reading books or watching videos like the typical woman.

The women who gather every afternoon at the yarn shop are a pretty mixed bunch, right down to their looks. They're mostly middle-aged, but with a sprinkling of newlyweds. The shop sells yarn and knitting needles, and when you see a sample of something you like, the woman shows you how to make it. But from what I can see, it's pretty much a social gathering. For entertainment you can't beat gossiping grandmas. Anything you want to know, they'll tell you. Spousal relationships? You bet; they even know whose husband had a hemorrhoidectomy and on which day too! When such topics come up, the yarn shop woman shushes them, saying, *Mind you, we've got an unmarried woman here too*—and then she gives me a look.

What with quilts, yarn, and suchlike on display we don't have much floor space and so we sit contentedly across from each other, one knee bent to the side, one knee up, while we do our knitting. Someone might bring steamy stuffed sausage to share, and on the odd occasion, someone gets into an argument and throws balls of yarn or sharp knitting needles around. "I'm going to get you where it hurts!"—when the foul language comes out everyone except the combatants buries her face in her kitting and bursts out laughing. The Yellow Woman, who is practically glued to the yarn shop the whole day long, won't leave until six o'clock and then it's to go to a dance class. We call her the Yellow Woman because she eats so many mandarin oranges that her fingernails are a yellowy orange. I've heard she's almost like family to the yarn shop woman. The Yellow Woman actually looks pretty cool, curled up in the corner, whether she's knitting a sweater for her elder son who's completing his military service, or blowing out streams of smoke while she tries to keep her permed, dyed-brown hair out of her face. Every time she talks about her son her teary eyes get this faraway look. My own mother probably did the same at some point, her head bent to the task as she knitted a sweater for her little girl, insensible to the pain in the tips of her fingers.

I'd like to have something warm this afternoon, like prawn tempura and rice.

By the way, I hope I'm not boring you with this letter.

I can never forget the street that connects the Kwanghwamun intersection and the YMCA. You mentioned some time ago that you like to walk that street. Even on a weekday afternoon it's thronged with people and littered with flyers and garbage, but it's still a street I've grown quite fond of—not only because I worked at the D bookstore in that area for a good six months, but because even before that I liked to wander that street, or else take it in from one of the fast-food places while I chewed on cold French fries and watched the people go by. Speaking of which, I wonder if you were among those who passed by outside. Or maybe you were one of the people I made business cards for.

I could have hung onto that job a little longer if scanners and fancy computers hadn't become so popular. You remember, don't you, that D bookstore was just outside one of the Chongno pedestrian underpasses. I used to sit at a small desk in a corner with a computer, a scanner, and a printer, making business cards on demand all day long. They weren't regular business cards, but ones with fancy designs that young women liked. What I did was very simple—the customer would pick out a card from the twenty-four designs on display and I'd add a requested line or name, and print it out. If they had a photo they wanted, I could scan it and add that to the card too. There were twenty-six cards to the page, so I'd take my ruler and cut them out, and that was that. It took about twenty minutes to make one set. During those twenty minutes the customer would take a look at the children's books in the next section or drop by the stationery shop along the commercial strip near the subway before returning to pick up her cards. I thought it was a simple and uncomplicated job, and just right for me.

Perhaps you might remember me back then. The woman tucked away all day long between the children's books and literature sections, making business cards, or gazing at people browsing through books—me, the woman with the long wavy hair. The bookstore was always busy right from when it opened. Some days a woman who looked like Yang Hǔi-ǔn would walk by, or else a familiar face I'm sure I saw on TV but couldn't put a name to. And there were the people with sunglasses or horn-rimmed spectacles covering half their face, but I used to be able to tell who they were right away like picking beans out from rice. There weren't so many customers in the morning and that's when I liked to size up the book browsers—their clothes and handbags, their shoe styles or facial expressions. I felt like I was searching for a long-lost bloodline! . . . Bloodline, did I just write that?

I'd like to tell you something that happened a while back. I was wandering around the magazine section trying to keep myself from falling asleep on the job, and I came across this photo. I think it was supposed to be some sort of science magazine; it had pictures of a six-week-old human fetus still in the womb, a four-week-old lemur, and a chick that was just a bit past three weeks. Can you imagine what that might look like—the human, the lemur, and the chick? After I looked at the photos, I saw the caption on the side and I was shocked. Sure they weren't fully developed but still, it was pretty hard to distinguish the human from the other two. Without the caption I think I would have mistaken the chick for the human. Really, talk about a wake-up call.

So you see, after the egg attaches to the uterine wall it develops into an embryo and then while it's growing into a fetus, for a good period of time it looks pretty much the same whether it's a human or some other animal. Then all of a sudden it hit me—am I really human? Maybe not, maybe I'm a lemur masquerading as human, or a chicken or a chimp that somehow morphed into a human during the embryo stage. Let me tell you, it was such a disturbing notion that I had to pat myself down—just to make sure, you know. If I hadn't put back the magazine, derailing my train of thought, who knows, I might have ended up doubting the pedigree of my own parents and siblings, thinking that maybe they were actually some other animal whose fate had gotten mixed up while they were embryos. In spite of this, I'd like to believe that I'm still the offspring of a human being.

And I would like to believe that I am connected to my parents and siblings by the hundred thousand kilometers of blood vessels that run through our bodies. I still have qualms about what I saw in those photos. Are we all connected by one blood vessel? Are we all human? For all I know, one mix-up of fate and I could have ended up a chicken or a lemur. And then I wouldn't have been able to recognize the faces of my own flesh and blood passing before my eyes, or the faces of all of you whom I loved so much. Maybe it's that people are meeting people who are actually chickens, or maybe it's a case of chickens meeting lemurs. Yes, "fated to meet" probably means more or less the same as "it takes one to know one." Even so, sometimes we walk past each other without knowing it.

I worked a nine-to-four shift. The lunch hour was a lousy thirty minutes. Somebody from children's books next door filled in for me and I managed to grab a bite to eat. Typically this involved a quick trip to a fast-food place in the underground mall, where I had a cheeseburger and a glass of Sprite that was more ice cubes than soda. Why Sprite? Well, I don't drink Coca Cola. I mean, there's the caffeine issue, and there has to be something more exciting than Coca Cola. It's just so boring.

Anyhow, even that short time was long enough for me to be glad to escape the gloom- and dustball-infested underground for the street outside. That's right, you remember, don't you? The street with all the sidewalk stalls lined up with lots of good food to eat. Those Chinese-style bean jam pancakes, *odaeng*, *ttŏkpokki*, tempura, sandwiches, rice cakes and sweetened chestnuts and such, you know? What a great selection! Typically, I'd pick out one of those places and find a place to sit among people I've never seen before, and I'd have myself some lunch. There's this one place I often went to and it featured omelet-wrapped *kimpap*. Surely you must have seen those mini-*kimpap* that the aunties sell in front of the train station or the park entrance? You remember how they do it; you beat an egg, pour it into the frying pan, then roll up those short lengths of *kimpap* in the egg pancake. You know there's no egg inside, and heck, not even sausage, just some pickled radish and slivered carrots; it's still pretty good, though. Have yourself four or five of those yellow wraps with *odaeng* broth—you'll be full in no time. When I go there I don't even have to order; as soon as the woman sees me, *plop*, the egg is in the pan. The sizzle of the oil is music to my ears.

Wait a minute, I didn't mean to get going on egg-wrapped *kimpap*. I ought to tell you about this guy.

Once a week—and it was always the same time, on Friday afternoon—he came up to me. Well, "came up to me" isn't really the right expression. He was just another customer who needed some business cards. He didn't want to customize his cards like other people; you know, with something like "Call Me Anytime" or "Best Wishes." What I remember about him is the way he looked and the clothes he wore. But that's not all. Actually, he was a plain-looking man you could bump into just about anywhere along Chongno. And there was nothing special about his clothing—the heels of his shoes were worn down and his navy blue trench coat had gone out of style a long time ago.

This man went by a different name each time he ordered a set of cards. One Friday it was Kim Ch'ŏlsu, the next Friday it would be Pak Minch'ŏl, then Yi Sŏkho, and then Chŏng Ch'angi. I've lost track of them; after all, I must have produced well over twenty different cards for him. Once I greeted him, "Oh, Mr. Chŏng Ch'ansu, I believe?" He shook his head determinedly. "No, it's O Chŏngsu, O—Chŏng—su; that's how I want it." Not just that particular time, but he always stressed the individual syllables like this, as if he was stamping out the cards himself. I never questioned him; every Friday I made him a different card with a new name, just like he wanted. Which ultimately, as far as I was concerned, made him the name-of-the-week man. That's about as close as I got to him. We all have our own way of loving someone, right?

And my way applied to my pet turtle too. That may have been the reason it got sick, I'm still not sure. My turtle was about the size of a fist, and one day when I was changing the water in the tank I discovered its eyes were so swollen they were bugging out. There was something gunky and gooey on them that was really milky white. My turtle never moved around much to begin with, so if it wanted to stay glued to one spot, like the flowerpot of perennials by the window, that was fine with me. That little critter has lived with me in the same room for two years now. In the summer, my place smelled like rotting duckweed root. But it still beat the nuisance of taking care of a dog or a cat. My turtle never ventured outside its rectangular tank. These were the things I liked about my turtle. All I had to do was change the water every now and then and feed it. But before I knew it, this turtle of mine had gone blind.

The man who ran the fish tank shop took a look at my turtle's eyes. It was a virus, was his verdict. I should have been changing the water regularly, he said. And he figured that a virus in the dirty water had blinded it. He sold me a bag of powdered medicine that cost a whopping ten thousand *wŏn*. The owner told me first to clean the turtle's eyes and then to pour the remainder into the tank. He made a point of mentioning that I should give it three months or so to see how it went.

As you might have guessed, it's not that I don't love my turtle—I just didn't want to get too attached to it. I didn't want to lose my turtle or that man either. Before I knew it, there she was, in my imagination, that girl that I loved dearly, so long ago.

. . . Wait, don't put this letter away yet. There's something I have to tell you today. And another thing—this is the last letter I'll be writing to you.

242

What have I got to lose—this was my mindset when I called the department store. I wasn't really expecting anything to begin with, because I honestly didn't think they would do alterations on a garment I bought from them years ago. What I was told by the woman I spoke with, who had called the main store about alterations, was that shortening the coat was the only option. I guess I should be thankful that alteration was even an option at all, but I had to stop and think for a moment. I thought maybe they could line the hole with a similar fabric, but guess what? They said that's not an option. But the problem was, if they shortened the coat, it would only be knee length, when it used to go down to my ankles. In fact, the coat's very charm was its line from the high waist all the way down to the ankles. There wouldn't be much charm in a long coat that wasn't long anymore.

I made a couple of big circuits around the women's section on the second floor and then said to myself, what the hell, better to wear it altered than not wear it at all, so I left it with them. Besides, it was my one and only winter coat, and there were still a good two months of winter left. If you've ever been out in the rain without a proper umbrella, you'd understand where I'm coming from. The woman at the store told me to come back in a week.

So that's why I showed up at the wedding wearing a black shawl over my thin black dress—the shawl the yarn shop woman had asked me to knit.

I wasn't invited to the wedding, but that's another story. The important thing is, it was at that wedding that I happened to see for the first time in a long while the woman I dearly loved.

No one had ever taught me the way in which you could love someone. I was only seventeen back then, and no different from all those girls who were all so clumsy when it came to loving someone else. This friend of mine and I were in the same class at school, and along with the woman who got married that Saturday, we made an inseparable trio. My friend's name was Sinae. Han Sinae. Among all the business cards I made, never had I seen a name so beautiful.

Han Sinae—I wrote it down in the back of all my textbooks. Her face, though, wasn't as beautiful. It was splotchy from a sprinkling of pimples, and she had a snaggle tooth that really stood out. I can still picture everything about her—the curve of her fingers holding a neatly pressed pink handkerchief, that bubbly handwriting she was able to produce with her half-a-millimeter-tip pen, the school shoes with the white socks neatly folded at the ankles, or the play of her lips as she ate noodles wrapped around her fork . . .

Oh, and there was something else too. She always excelled at subjects like history and Korean, but if she had a weakness, it was math. Math was my subject—meaning that I didn't like it a whole lot, but I worked at it harder because I knew it was difficult for her. Every class, the teacher put some questions up on the board and looked down his class list and called half a dozen students and made them solve those questions. My friend Sinae was always miserable on the days when we had math. She wouldn't even eat her lunch, and sometimes she would say she was sick and take refuge in the nurse's room. One day it was her turn again and the teacher called on her. Her head dropped. And at the same time, I nonchalantly stood up and approached the blackboard. The teacher didn't know the difference and fortunately no one told on us. And on those unfortunate days when my number and hers were both called, the friend who got married filled in for me. And so, from that day on, whenever my friend Sinae was called upon, I went up to the blackboard. It wasn't something she asked me to do. That pretty much put an end to her wishing upon the stars for her bus to crash into the river before it could deliver her to math class.

I never left her side. I had lunch with her, I walked home with her after our catch-up classes, and I always waited for her when she went to the bathroom. I even went to a stationery shop outside Ewha University to buy the same wrapping paper she used for her books; I had to take two buses to get there. In no time I had the same handkerchief she did, I wore the same shoes and even the same brand of socks. I loved her so much.

And it was twelve years later, at our friend's wedding, that I encountered this friend that I once had loved so much.

Around the time I turned eighteen I discovered in my schoolbag a letter from her. I didn't want to understand the meaning behind the cursory sentences, but the result was that we no longer hung out with each other. Beside her now was that friend of ours, the one who got married. I was left by myself. I ate alone; I studied alone, and I walked alone the long way to the bus loop. We graduated and I never saw her.

Every once in a while I thought about her. I wondered what had compelled her to write that letter. Was it the identical handkerchief? Was it the socks? The blouse? The textbook covers, perhaps? Or was it that the way I talked or the expressions I used had, without my knowing it, become like hers? What would you say it was—I mean, the reason for our parting, or actually the reason she called an end to our friendship? I don't think I ever consciously decided to copy her, I just wanted to love her in my own way.

I was in the bridal room with the bride and bridesmaid when I heard a voice:

"Sukcha, you're Pak Sukcha, aren't you?"

I turned in utter astonishment. Carefully, as if I were considering the stained pages of an old book, I raised my eyes to hers. She wore a flimsy smile, and you know, she still had that snaggle tooth at the left side of her mouth. But she no longer had that way of looking right through me. And she no longer had the pink handkerchief in her hand, nor was she wearing the neatly folded-down cotton socks. As I recall there was a brief awkward silence between us. For one thing, the person I used to know was no longer there; instead, I saw before me the face of one of those strangers who bumps into you or steps on your foot and continues on her way without a word as if nothing had happened.

After the ceremony, a few of us high school friends ended up at a café nearby. And Han Sinae of course was among them. There commenced an endless round of gossip from these women who had just entered their thirties.

By and by it was her turn.

I want to tell you about this group I started up six months ago. I call it the Letter Exchange. I ran an ad in one of the lifestyle magazines and you wouldn't believe it, inside of a week the letters were pouring in! Letters to me, a complete stranger! It was the craziest thing. It's kind of a hassle, but since I promised, I make sure to answer all of them. Sometimes I wonder, what's the point? Actually it's quite simple. What they want is the feeling of contact with another person— to feel like they aren't alone in this world.

Just like always, I couldn't take my eyes off her, and I was all ears for whatever she had to tell us.

Life can be a real bore—it can get real tiring. That's why I thought I'd like to see what's on people's minds. I have to confess, when I'm reading their letters I feel like I'm watching a movie or reading a book—that's all they are to me. So they're fun to read, but when it comes to answering them it's not as easy as you think. These people are always really tired or absolutely lonely. You have to give them a pat on the back and make them feel better. And the most important thing, you have to give them hope.

She was rather solemn and serious, she had the look of a doomsday high priestess or one of those bogus sect leaders, take your pick.

My dear friend, would you excuse me for a moment while I get myself a drink of water? I'm feeling thirsty all of a sudden. There's more I want to tell you when I get back.

Remember the place where I used to work? It's different now. It's a bargain bookstore called Book Mart. On one of the pillars at the front of the building was a poster that read from top to bottom *Sale, 30 to 60% off.* It looked like this bargain bookstore had also taken over the space right next door where the children's bookstore used to be. And now the children's bookstore was directly across the way. The place where I used to sit all day making business cards had vanished. This new bookstore was as crowded with strangers as the old one; I didn't recognize a single soul.

The day I discovered Book Mart, I was wearing the very same coat I had had altered. You have no idea how awkward it felt; I was used to having it nice and snug around my ankles, and now it felt shorter, no, too short. Though it was much warmer than the shawl, I couldn't get rid of the feeling that I was wearing someone else's clothes. Back when I was making business cards I used to wear it on really windy days. If that man remembers anything about me at all, I'll bet he remembers that coat. I made a couple of circuits through the bookshop, worming my way among all the strangers who were browsing the shelves and the tables or else standing about with expectant looks on their faces. Even inside, far from the entrance, I couldn't find my old workspace. I had brought with me, stuffed in a paper bag, a camel-colored sweater that I'd made for that man—it was all guesswork, though, because I didn't know his size. I gave it a pine needle pattern front and back—which is very complicated, by the way—with a nice tight weave. I had worked on it in my spare time when I wasn't filling orders from the yarn shop woman.

It had been a few days since I'd visited the yarn shop. I had run out of yarn with one sleeve still left to do on the man's sweater, but when I arrived at the shop I found the door locked. In addition to the sweater sleeve, I needed enough yarn for three women's wool hats that I had to finish by Saturday. So I went to the altering shop next door and that's where I learned that the Yellow Woman had run off with the yarn shop owner's share of the money in the neighborhood credit association. So saying, the altering shop woman gave me a concerned look and asked if I had been taken in too. And so to get my yarn I had to go to an old-style market that was four bus stops away. It was the same camel-colored yarn, but I somehow convinced myself it was different, so I ended up carefully comparing this yarn with the parts of the sweater I finished, namely the front, the back, and the other sleeve. That night I finished the remaining sleeve and the sweater was done.

He asked me out for dinner. It was the day he ordered a set of business cards under the name of Kim T'aeju. He wore a very curt expression—I think he was trying hard to look macho. He wouldn't look me in the eye this time either. Instead he directed his gaze somewhere above the top of my head. My eyes traveled up his chest and past the coils of scarf about his neck and when I reached his face, I quickly changed my own face back to default. And then it hit me—the tension between us had broken long ago.

"I get off at four," I told him. My tone was calm and composed. Even now I remember that day with picture-postcard perfection. It was five minutes past two when I gave him his Kim T'aeju business cards. I was wearing a thick gray polo shirt under my coat, and for lunch I had five pieces of egg-wrapped *kimpap* with tempura soup.

Around the time the man was supposed to show up, two young women were caught shoplifting. I watched silently as the male employees we called "the librarians" took them back to the office. Just then all the lights went out, plunging everything into a dark haze as if someone had pulled a thick curtain over the surroundings. This blackout, short though it was, instantly threw the darkened bookstore into bedlam. People started screaming and I heard from the vicinity of the door a thud, followed by the sound of something hitting the floor. In the confusion, I crawled under my desk, like I'd been taught to do if I ever felt an earthquake that registered 3.6 on the Richter scale. It certainly wasn't any brighter there, but it somehow made me feel as if I were immersed in the stillness of some distant place, like say, Île d'Orléans, which I've never been to in my life. Maybe I was experiencing a moment of solitude—what do you think? It was my great good fortune that the lights came back on in no time.

It was the winter solstice, when there's the longest night of the year. Can you see how that day remains in my memory? The man had said he would meet me at four, the time I got off work, at the

248

Chongno side of the building. In the bathroom I put on a new coating of lipstick and applied some Vaseline to the backs of my hands.

To make a long story short, he never showed up. It didn't help that the person who worked the shift after mine arrived ten minutes late—of all the luck! I snatched my bag and scrambled toward the exit on the Chongno side. I tried to convince myself that he couldn't have come and gone during those ten minutes. If he had arrived by the usual route, I would have seen him from where I sat in the bookstore. You see, he always came in from the Kwanggyo side and after I completed his order and gave him his cards he would walk past my desk and go out through the Chongno side exit. The bottom line was, it got to be past 7 o'clock and he still wasn't there. And that night I came down with a bad cold and had to miss work the next two days—at least I think it was two days. I kept myself hunched up so my depression wouldn't sink its teeth into my heart.

Two weeks later I lost my job. In all that time the man never appeared.

You're probably wondering about that sweater. Well, I never meant to make a big production out of it. And in fact it was no big deal. I didn't think I'd see him again. And yet, I still returned now and then to that bookstore where I once worked. I would focus on the faces of people passing by or else just hang around there. I don't believe in coincidence. Even though a lot of time has passed since then, I have to admit, I still find myself wondering if that man had a change of heart and eventually showed up where we were supposed to meet. I wonder if he's wandering the city even now, making a new name for himself each new day.

It was very early–maybe six? Or even five. In the alley, there wasn't a soul to be seen heading off to work, only the clean scent, like that of wet grass, with which the delicate winter rain had freshened the air. The garbage truck had come and gone. I made myself anxious with fantasies of someone suddenly appearing around the corner, penetrating the sight-obscuring gloom that

blocked my way. I tightened my grip on my turtle's tank, so it
wouldn't drop to the ground and shatter. I plodded down the alley.

The door to the aquarium shop was locked. For no reason, I
alternately shook the metal grate blocking the entrance and looked
up at the unlit neon sign. Even as I did this, my turtle remained
motionless on its rock, with what I think were its arms and legs
stuffed up inside its shell—it must have been the cold. I'd applied
the solution to its eyes and mixed some in the water, but the slime
covering its eyes hadn't begun to go away. Worse, my turtle looked
like it was eating a lot less. Maybe I should have picked something
clever for a pet, like a dog or a cat. I remember the aquarium shop
owner saying I should give it three months or so. But you never
know, maybe by then it would be blind forever, or, the worst-case
scenario, it could end up dying. For all I know its life had been slowly
slipping away as it sat in its tank in the corner of my room, apart
from the rest of the world. You can't see what's going on inside my
turtle, but there is a virus that is consuming it. I have no confidence
in anything—not even in myself, not even in my ability to dispose
of my turtle when it dies, and even if the slime does go away, the
damage has been done, and how could I look into its ruptured eyes?

I lingered near the shop as if waiting for someone, holding
the rectangular tank. Finally I set it down carefully on the cement
sidewalk beneath the metal grate. As I did so, the water inside the tank
sloshed around and a few drops went over the side. The turtle looked
soulless, not like a living creature of flesh and blood. It didn't even
budge—as if it had already died. It looked just like a rock, a smooth,
blue rock, a shell with a head crammed inside. I don't know how long
I was huddled up there in a kind of trance before I decided to leave.

I wonder, will it ever open its eyes?

At this point, I pored over my letter from the beginning to
see if I had left anything out. If we should ever run into each other
again, I wonder if you would be able to recognize my face?

The yarn shop had not reopened. It was impossible for me to
complete the three wool hats I had promised, and I couldn't buy

any more yarn either. To get it, I'd have to go a long way, about ten bus stops. I started to take apart the man's sweater—first I undid the front, then I moved to the back, followed by both arms. The pine needle pattern that had taken a week and a half of effort slowly disappeared before my eyes. In the resulting mass of yarn I found one of the ends and began to make a ball out of that strand so the yarn wouldn't get tangled up. In connecting the strands from the front, the back, and the arms of the sweater, I made sure the knots wouldn't be visible. I boiled a pot of water and steamed the yarn. All the curls straightened out and the yarn was like new again. With this much yarn, I can probably make a whole coat, except for the sleeves. With nice roomy pockets and buttonholes as well. And by then, the yarn shop will probably be open again and I can buy the yarn I need.

And now for the very first time I'm knitting something for myself—a large coat no less. I'm so hopeless when it comes to picking out a pattern, or determining the gauge—you'd think I've never seen a bamboo needle before. I have no idea when I'll be able to finish my camel-colored winter coat. But soon enough I'll be inside my new coat, shopping for nice ripe kimchi cabbage or taking a long walk on a snowy day. There's still a good two months of winter yet to come.

My fingers are tightening around the pen—I'm about to bring this letter to a close. There's only one thing left to do.

I just can't find the right way to say it. The way you put it was something like this, though I can't remember exactly: "There is a plant that blooms when its leaves have fallen, and makes leaves when its flowers have fallen. The leaf and the flower long for each other, but they're fated never to meet. For the flower you long to meet, please contact the Letter Exchange"—maybe I should phrase it the same way? It all seems so long ago. Can you imagine? I'm going to have to come up with a new name for myself, just like you did. And I have to remember to make a small addition to what you wrote: "Contact the *New* Letter Exchange."

Five Poems by Jang Jung Il

Translated by Tae Yang Kwak

Hiding in an Underpass

Like an air raid, there's a sudden downpour of the sky's blood
As if it were a Civil Defense drill, pedestrians without umbrellas
Scramble about seeking shelter to wait out the rain
Without time to consider and find a proper place
I descend into a nearby underpass to escape the rain for a few
    minutes
Starting from the steps, rolling mood music covers the underpass
Safe from the rain, this underpass seems impenetrable
Even if a million megaton neutron bomb hits
If again there's forty days and nights of flood, this underpass will
    stand unscathed
I idly walk the underpass from end to end
This would be a pretty nice stroll if I had like a black dog on a leash.
As I steal furtive glances at the shop windows, young saleswomen
    say
"Please come in!" and "Are you looking for something?"
Offering every type of clothing and product, as well as restaurants
    and bathrooms, this is a nearly perfect underpass
So I entertain a daydream. I meet a woman here

We fall in love, have children, and we could live our whole lives in
    this place. . . .
Whether the rain has stopped or not outside, it's utterly impossible
    to know from here
Does the utter impossibility of knowing the climate outside make
    this place a tomb?
Ornaments and figurines, handmaidens and silk fabrics, jars of seed
Is this a tomb of the ancients buried with such funeral articles?
Walking along the underpass again from end to end, a face reflected
    in the window
I stare at it. A pale face. Oh, is this my tomb?
Now that I think of it, this time none of the saleswomen calls to me
    or asks me in.
Yes, I am a ghost. Even if the rain has stopped, I don't want to return
    to the surface
Walking with nothing to do, if I happened to run into a close friend
    who just came down
I would happily shake his hand, and I'd want to hear news from the
    surface world
No, I'd want to hide completely. I'd hide here for three days
Then I'd climb the stairs and return home. That'd be interesting
Without a phone call or message, if I vanished for three days,
    without a word
How sad would my mother be? Twice I was arrested and tortured
She'd have to file a missing person's report in the likes of the very
    police stations I most revile.
But I deliberately return, and I am resurrected
I kick away the tomb of civilization, brilliantly illuminated by 100-
    watt light bulbs
I spring forth. Listen! If I claim to be the Second Advent of Christ
The people will believe it. They won't believe it. They can't help but
    believe it
They can't help but not believe it. Oh, whether they believe it or not
There was a time when I escaped the rain and hid in an underpass

254

A Meditation on Hamburgers

—a poem written for use as a home recipe

In the past I meditated on money or dreams
On very concrete or transparent things
But now I meditate on mushy things as well

The meditation I'll show you today is making hamburgers
Anyone can do it, doesn't require many ingredients to make this
    meditation
Yet it's a meditation that's delicious and quite nutritious
How could we divorce ourselves from the "tribe of hamburger eaters"?
Now, let us me begin our meditation on hamburgers
I'll first tell you what we need. The ingredients:

hamburger rolls 2
butter 1½ tbsp
beef 150g
pork 100g
onions 1½
eggs 2
breadcrumbs 2 cups
salt 2 tsp
black pepper ¼ tsp
lettuce 4 leaves
cucumber 1
mayonnaise dab
steak sauce ¼ cup

The above ingredients aren't difficult, and in your own neighborhood
You can find them at any reliable grocery store. —At the grocery store
Each item will be safely and hygienically plastic-wrapped. Shop at
    the grocery store—

First we finely mince the beef and pork.

At this point, cast off your idle thoughts. This is the first step in
     achieving our meditation

In order to make this a more perfect meditation

An order has been very carefully designated

If in this first step, you cannot cast off your idle thoughts, your
     finger might be cut off by a

Sharp knife, and you'd be forced to abandon this meditation

After the beef and pork have been finely minced,

Finely chop one onion, place in an oiled pan, and

Sauté until the edges brown, then let cool.

The sizzling oil and pleasing aroma

Will make you mildly excited and quicken your pulse

This means you are feeling aroused by this meditation

But if you aren't aroused, it'll be impossible to meditate

If you aren't aroused, there'll be no world.

After you've done this,

Take the minced beef and pork, breadcrumbs, eggs, sautéed onion,

Salt, and black pepper, and knead thoroughly with your fingers until
     it congeals.

How thrilling a meditation this is. Like touching that part of a lover
     in bed

This moment of sensual bliss,

Exactly this moment,

Of kneading food with our fingers

When the mixture becomes sufficiently sticky

Divide it into four round patties and cook well-done to the core.

At this point our meditation will also mature. Place the formed meat

On a heated frying pan for one minute, then flip and fry for another
     minute

After slightly browning both sides, reduce the flames—in order to do this

You must have a gas range—cover with a lid and over the low flames

Cook thoroughly to the center. At this point

Your mind must be completely meditating on making hamburgers.

Not just on the surface of your mind but to the core of your mind,
    completely!

After this,

Cut the remaining half onion into rings and

The cucumbers diagonally

Wash the lettuce leaves

Even in these final touches

This meditation is not just realized in our minds

But demonstrates another marvelous product of labor.

When this work is done,

Insert a knife into the rolls, split, and spread on the butter

Lay down the lettuce and spread the mayonnaise. Now, this act of
    spreading

Will block any potential resurfacing of idle thoughts.

So don't just slap on the butter and mayonnaise together

But slightly, spread to infusion.

When this is done,

Place the meat and pour on the steak sauce to taste, and add the
    onions and cucumber.

This is how the meditation ends.

Isn't this a valuable meditation?

After an intricate and highly detailed meditation

You've made a delicious and highly nutritious American-style
    snack.

The Cook and the Anorexic

1

The woman who lives in 301. She is a cook. Every morning her
kitchen brims with fruits and vegetables as well as meat and fish
delivered from the supermarket. She roasts or boils them. She is
lonely, and a full stomach is the only thing that allows her to forget
her loneliness for a while, a little while. And so she cooks without
rest or eats without pause, and usually she does both at once. What
shall I make and eat today? Her bookshelves are full of all kinds of
cookbooks, and she constantly indulges in new dishes to sate her
loneliness. Her kitchen constantly billows with smoke, and she gives
fancy names to the dishes she's invented. Incessantly, she offers her
plates to the woman in 302.

2

The woman who lives in 302. She is an anorexic. She takes
the food just delivered by 301, and wraps it in a plastic bag and
discards it, or abandons it in her refrigerator until it hardens. She
takes pains to eat almost nothing at all. She is lonely, and a deathly
hunger seems to offer the only respite from her loneliness. How can
I fast to the point of having just one gulp of water? Her bookcases
are full of research on fasting and records of her anorexia, and
lying on the floor exhausted, she takes pleasure in writing of
her loneliness. Often, she fasts and writes at the same time, and
endlessly she submits her unacceptable drafts to literary magazines
and newspapers.

3

One day, after having tasted all the dishes of the world, 301's loneliness went so far as cannibalism. So she took the emaciated 302, made a soufflé out of her, and ate her. Of course, 302, exhausted from loneliness, went to 301 willingly. So does the loneliness of these two people come to an end? 301 is still lonely. Therefore 302, who has become 301's flesh and blood, is also still lonely.

1

I write. Love in Germany.

Yes, this is the title. How much did I want to write this?

Love in Germany. And I write it like this,

German roadside trees are evergreen trees

Not knowing to shed their leaves even in winter, German roadside
    trees are evergreen trees

German lovers walk under the evergreen tree in winter

When German lovers smile, their lips turn green.

I'll continue to write.

When Michel goes to meet blond Margaret

Michel is awash in green as he walks under the evergreen tree.

Blond Margaret says to Michel who shines green

"You look like an evergreen person."

What does Michel say to such an adorable woman?

When German lovers meet, they whistle.

In the manner their forefathers called forth Jews.

In the same manner, but not necessarily for the same purpose.

Isn't that history?

As German lovers whistle, they call forth a flock of doves.

German whistling sounds green under the evergreen tree

German lovers dance a dance jumping to the heavens.

Instead of making their Hebrew slaves dance, under moonlight
    green from the snake of life's embrace

German lovers dance.

Oh, Love in Germany.

Using Korea as a desk on which I lay, I write.

Love in Germany. Ah, how much did I want to write this?

Let's write like this. How time passes,

That stars rise and float in the German sky

That stars as vibrant as the evergreen tree rise above the German
   lovers' brows.
And let's also write like this. Then,
The German lovers under the shade of the evergreen tree
Whisper under the green stars.
"The stars that have risen tonight are green."
"Yes, the stars that have risen tonight are as green as the ocean
   herring."
They undress their shadows to the moon
And swiftly, they become earthly stars rising in flame.

2

Korean roadside trees are ginkgo trees
Korean lovers walk under them when autumn comes
Walking under the ginkgo tree's yellowed leaves are Korean lovers
Korean lovers receive yellow draft cards in autumn
Korean lovers are gunned down in autumn.
"I've been drafted to the army this winter."
Men depart, and they live in low barracks
In the longest winter nights he writes a letter to his woman left *in
   her own hands.*
To Suk, my black-haired darling. . . .
Writing like this, it seems too tacky. Crumples the page
Then writes again. To Suk, my slim hipped beauty. . . .
Then writes again. This seems too vulgar. Crumples another page
As more days go by, the harder it seems to go back to yesterday. . . .
Just then, a command is given to assemble
Ah, I hate red words. I hate blue words too!
The crew-cut private puts the barrel of a gun to his temple, and then
"Bang—" he fires. Just then
Above one man's life
Crawling by like a crab, the words "The End" stream by.
The falling ginkgo leaves are yellow cards.

3

Love in Germany. I saw this some time in some movie magazine

The title of a German movie. I was fond of the title

Soon, I wanted to try to paint Love in Germany.

Tidy streets

Rich tables

Brimming beer steins

And the world's greatest soccer

Cute Beetle cars

That grand German philosophy!

In the context of these things

I wanted to write a heart-wrenching love story of a happy couple.

But why did confusion break out?

I keep confusing the story of Love in Korea, with

The story of Love in Germany.

Let me go, Korea!

Love in Germany, Love in Germany, I want to write of Love in
    Germany.

I pulled my love from the River Rhine, or

Ahah diddid bababa let me undo your necktie with my hands, or

I wonder who'll come to my house tonight in a Volkswagen,
    perhaps

Without a past, there's no future, such

Melancholical rhetoric evenly mixed

To restore sensation ancient yet modern

I wanted to write a great love poem that would be on everyone's lips.

But why do I spoil the taste with

The story of Love in Korea? I

Hate Korea. To be frank.

4

She is a member of the White Rose Society[1]
She throws rocks at the giant Nazi posters
She sings angry songs
And reads subversive poems.
She is to the bone, a totally committed student activist.
But her lover, he fears the nightstick.
She tries to raise his consciousness with simple words
But he just shakes his head.
"I don't want the whistle or the nightstick or to be cross-strapped to
    the iron chair!"
"I hate red words. I hate blue words too!"
The moment he shakes his head, she is wanted
The moment he shakes his head, she is reported
The moment he shakes his head, her head sits smiling on their
    platter.

5

Have I been vague in this poem?
Have I forsaken Korea and run away to Germany?
Have I employed irony?
Have I seen through the happy 21st-century Germany's silhouette
    into the dark, fascist, anti-democratic, police-state past of
    Hitler's Nazi Germany?
Have I awoke from my dreaming?
Have I been living in Germany and written a letter to Korea?
Or, has my body remained in Korea as my spirit went to Germany?
Have I avoided censorship?
Who am I, what am I?

1. An underground student group that opposed the Nazi regime.

I will answer.

. . .

. . .

I tear up this poem,

"Ri-ip——"

Catching a Taxi in Kiran[2]

I went to Kiran.
It's a rustic place, Kiran.
It was getting close to night in Kiran. That's what
I wrote. And how
many, introductions had I started?
Reloading the typewriter paper, I
reorganize my thoughts. I write.

   I went to Kiran.
   It's a beautiful, rustic place, Kiran.
   In Kiran night draws nearer.
   The stars rise.

I write this, and before writing more
I stop. With fast, accurate hands
I pull out the loaded page,
crumpling and discarding it. Why's this guy's poem
so damn trying? I
want to pursue the tension between technology and nature
in modern man. A new page
loaded, I write again.

   I went to Kiran.
   I wait for a taxi in Kiran.
   No taxi comes in Kiran.
   I was able to catch a taxi in every other city.
   But in Kiran it's difficult to catch a taxi.

I stop writing again. It's too stiff

2. Kiran: A rural district in the outskirts of Andong.

isn't it? All the stanzas, they end.
With periods. It has the awkward smell of a
translation about it. Regardless
I hear such things pointed out to me a lot, don't I?
I pull out that page crumpling it, and load
another sheet. I write.

> I went to Kiran.
> I saw no taxi in Kiran.
> I was easily able to catch a taxi in every other city
> But it's difficult to catch a taxi in Kiran
> And all of the sudden stars spill over every streetcorner.
> Suddenly Kiran feels inconvenient.

I stop writing again. A little
smoother, a little more concrete depiction of the landscape
in the introduction from which it must be able to develop.
After depicting the beautiful, rustic landscape of Kiran
the place where the traveler waits for the taxi that doesn't come
I must draw an image of that brash traveler.
I pull out the page crumpling it, and a new sheet
loaded, and I write.

> The mountains are tall in Kiran
> And its rivers clear. The trees of Kiran are verdant
> And the flocks of doves over their branches form white clouds
> As beautiful and splendid as architecture.
> To see it not from a distance, but from within
> How beautiful is Kiran?
> The traveler takes his suitcase which is as large as German bread
> Sets it on the roadside, and waits for a taxi.

> Right about here I stop writing for a moment.
> Although I'm not fond of it, as a beginning it suitably

whets my appetite, and it's lighthearted enough
to get the reader to continue reading on.
Now as night falls on Kiran, I intend to make the traveler
reach ontological self-cognizance. I write.

    For some reason no taxi comes for a long while
    And for as long as he'd waited, it was getting close to night.
    Nameless leaves rustle,
    The traveler realizes that he is alone.
    Nameless flocks of birds steal pieces of the sunlight
    Carrying them off to the west, and
    As if jars of sand were spilt, nameless stars are scattered.
    Forty years of city life have erased his youthful rural knowledge
    Of the names of flora, fauna, and constellations. It's all
    Nameless. Suddenly the traveler
    Was overwhelmed with shame.

I stop writing again. The traveler's solitude
is too unrealistic. Where did he come from, and
where is he trying to go? Forty years of city life,
just came out of nowhere, didn't it? A certain publisher
a poet who is a senior of mine, is one of those people who've
criticized me for making sudden leaps. Actually, I detest
poems that aren't concrete. I discard
what I've just written, and I load another page. And
I resolve to write concretely. I write.

    Having left his hometown and having lived in the city for forty
        years,
    He is in his fifties and though he hasn't seen it for a long time
    He has returned to his hometown. Kiran. . . .

I let out a sigh. Seizing the page
I toss it away. This guy's poem is killing me.

I wanted to expound on the contradictoriness of
antimony related to the use of technology. Namely the convenience
of the use of technology, and the consequent interconnectedness of
modern man. And also, his enslavement to technology
and when modern man is confronted with a
natural situation where he cannot use technology
I wanted to depict his anxious response. How can I do this?
When he is confronted with this kind of situation for the first time
he might feel the inconvenience of technology, and might rather be
angry at nature that has not been technologized.
I load a new page, and I write.

I went to Kiran.
I cried for the beauty of Kiran.
Darkness fell on Kiran.
I saw no taxi in Kiran.
I think of the people waiting for me outside of Kiran.
Inconvenient is Kiran.
Scattering my appointments and sitting on them is Kiran.
Uneasy is Kiran.

I'm flying a kite, and stop for a moment. I'm writing in this tone,
I'm firmly resolved. No matter what anyone says
I think of it like this. Just like a stamp collector who collects stamps
the way he collects stamps in his own stampbook
is poetry-writing, and the way I collect poems
in my own heart! The desire to write new poems
is no different from the eccentricity of a stamp collector
who wants to possess the Bolivian mountain butterfly stamp
a stamp he doesn't have in his stampbook. Stamp
collectors want to acquire a stamp no matter how hard it is to
      acquire and
possess, even though the world doesn't change because of it
Poets, no matter how good the poems they write, the world doesn't

change

for it. Between the stamp collector and the poet, who is more
noble? When we don't distinguish high and low, the stamp collector's
satisfaction, in order to enjoy such fulfillment I must write poems.

These are the kind of
bottomless, endless thoughts I have, I return to the typewriter keys and
tap away.

> When I am outside in Kiran, I think of drinking coffee from a
>   vending machine.
> I want to escape from Kiran.
> There is no means of escape from Kiran.
> It feels like a riddle, Kiran.
> Revolting are the mountains and rivers of Kiran.
> Sticking out like phantoms are the trees of Kiran.
> Ah, such off-putting nature
> Incomprehensible nature.
> It's frightful this uncivilized Kiran.

I'm flying a kite, and rest for a moment. The traveler is already
sufficiently anxious, and he is feeling the obscenity of
the natural state of Kiran which has not been
technologized. Then at this point
I bring up the place where he has to go, a meeting of modern men
I'll produce and conclude. I
write.

> But where shall I go?
> Where is that place I must go?
> In order to easily catch a taxi
> First I must slip out of here where it's hard to catch a taxi
> But then to where?
> Indeed, if I leave Kiran, will I be able to return to Kiran?
> For the first time in Kiran

I'm struck by the uneasiness of the outdoors in Kiran.
For me, for you, every road
Is a road that leads us where?
There's no place for us to be.

Finished writing. A poem of three years.
I try reading it. What a mess!
I sigh. What a difficult poem.
It's such difficult work, and my whole life
it's been my dream to do this! I
tear up the poem just spent three years writing. I brew some coffee
and drink a cup. My thoughts are connected. Aren't poems like
games of Chinese jump rope the girls used to play
when I was a child? Step by step emerging into a new world.
    Repeatedly
raising the jump rope to higher levels and delighting in the distress,
Delighting in the distress! I must finish writing "Catching a Taxi in
Kiran" tonight by any means. I frightfully load
a clean white page. I write again.

    On a patch of overgrown grass
    A lone traveler holding a black suitcase
    Waits for a taxi.
    Little by little the sun was setting
    But no taxi could be seen, however
    The traveler showed no sign of giving up easily.

Let's stop here for now, the morning is bright. I get up to wash my face.
As if I were dreaming all night. Staying up all night has left me
numb. To cold water, I mix in just enough hot
water. The thought arises.
Dreams mix with life, invisibly
like water mixes with water.
I will continue, to write.

Needle

by Cheon Woon Young
Translated by Sora Kim-Russell

He asked me to give him a tattoo of the world's biggest spider. The print he brought looked more like a giant red crab. It was called a Goliath bird-eating spider, the biggest spider in the world.

"Look at that perfect symmetry. Doesn't it look like it was folded in half and cut out?" he said, his eyes fixed on the print. "Draw it exactly the same way, exactly. Including those soft hairs all over its body."

What he wanted wasn't the spider's hairs or its long, symmetrical legs. He wanted the skin of the Chelicerata. Spiders can overpower other animals despite their small size because of their hard outer skin. Most of the people who came to me wanted to get this tough Chelicerata skin from me. This is because human skin is closer to that of fruit than of insects and is wounded easily. Yet, because the skin is so tender, it makes it easier to draw spider skin on human flesh.

While I was spreading a towel on the bed, the man had undressed and was holding the photograph of the spider against himself to decide where to place the tattoo. It didn't look like there was enough room to draw a huge, thirty-centimeter-long spider on his chest or back. An elaborate butterfly was fluttering its wings around his navel. The bamboo climbing from wrist to shoulder was girding his forearm.

271

I lit the alcohol lamp and burned some incense. The pine-scented smoke floated around the room like a ghost. I felt like I was going to have a seizure, needle clenched in hand, if the scent faded. I would have to keep adding sticks of incense until the job was done. I took the #5 needle from the needle case and heated it over the alcohol lamp. The needle turned black in the flame then flared red.

"Nowadays, everyone uses tattoo guns because of AIDS. The color comes out evenly and it's much safer. But I like the hand-pricked tattoos you do with a needle. Tattoo guns remind me of sitting in a dentist's chair. You know that sensation when the needle pierces your gums? You're numb and feeling like you just bit into an unripe persimmon, and meanwhile, the doctor is treating the patient in the seat next to you first after anaesthetizing you. The sound of the drill gives me the creeps."

He spoke slowly, watching as I sterilized the needle. I set the needle down silently and swabbed my hands and the man's thigh with alcohol.

I don't talk while doing tattoos. Even at other times, I'm not much of a talker. To me, the desire to divulge, to convey my thoughts, feels like a rotten tooth. A decayed tooth that keeps getting in the way of your tongue and hurting you, even while, planted deep inside your gums, it reminds you constantly of your own existence. And by the time you're ready to pull it out and expose it to the light of day, it's already reeking and falling apart.

He would probably keep talking, demanding responses, until the job was done. He should have known better after two sessions with me, but like most people who ask for tattoos of things like spiders or scorpions, he couldn't master his fear in silence. I handed him a glass of strong cognac without ice. He wasn't allowed to use drugs or smoke weed in front of me. Only a person who can overcome pain is qualified to wear the skin of the Chelicerata. He was nervous, probably because I was drawing directly with the needle instead of outlining the tattoo with a marker first. I'm more careful when I'm doing the outline than when I'm coloring it in—I make a shallow cut that swells and flares red but doesn't bleed—because this is where the indelible shape of the tattoo is determined.

I picked up the needle and began tattooing the body of the spider about a hand's span away from the man's knee. The body formed a perfect octagon. There was a pattern covering it, but I had to draw the silhouette first. The tail portion on the underside of the body was plump as if clear thread would spin out without stopping. Just as the man had said, the four supplementary angles formed a perfect symmetry. The spider was slowly emerging from the tip of the needle.

The man had his eyes closed and was breathing evenly. Lying with his arms raised above his head as if cheering and his legs uneasily spread, his pose suggested that he knew what it meant to surrender. A needle is not a fatal weapon, but if I were to attack, he would be as helpless as a butterfly trapped in a spider's web.

Tattooing the thigh takes a lot more focus than tattooing the back or chest. You have to work while straddling the person's shin and staring at the hairs that stick out from beneath his underwear. The breath from my nostrils and mouth was enough to warm his crotch. His penis would gradually begin to stiffen from the moment I touched the needle to his body, and he would have a raging hard-on by the time the outline was complete. But so far, no one had ever propositioned me once I began a tattoo.

"It's a good thing you're not even the slightest bit pretty. I get so horny by the time you're done tattooing me. But even though I like your tattoos, I never feel like doing you. I'm sure if all the guys you've tattooed had stuck it to you, you'd probably be popping antibiotics every day."

My sharply protruding cheekbones, the round hump of fat on my back and neck that made me look like a hunchback, my voice like nails on a chalkboard, my stubby toes . . . these were the reasons he said he didn't want to sleep with me. While listening to him, the abstract word "ugly" seemed to unfurl before my eyes and take concrete shape. I even stuttered when I spoke. But no one would ever look at the tattoos that came out of the tips of my needles and associate them with ugliness.

I went to the cabinet that held the dyes to color in the spider tattoo. I chose Venetian red, India ink, and zinc oxide for the burgundy of the spider's body. For the plump, hairy legs, I would use chrome green and cobalt blue indigo dye. Titanium would work to bring to life the hairs that the man wanted to emphasize. Titanium is a metal used to build jets and rockets, but it can also be used as a pigment. Because of its shiny silver-white color, I sometimes used it to tattoo metallic blades or arrows. It could even enhance the effect of hairs standing on end, like on the Goliath spider.

I sterilized eight needles in the flame of the alcohol lamp and ran a silk thread through each of the eyes. I carefully wound the thread around the needles, leaving half a centimeter from the tips uncovered. When you wind the silk thread, you have to be careful not to overlap it. You have to do that to keep the ink from clumping together or coming out all at once. You also have to remember to leave about a centimeter of the eye uncovered so you have room to hold the needle. I coated the silk thread in Venetian red first.

The first stitch in skin. I love this moment the most. When I hold my breath and place the first stitch in the surface of the skin, blood instantly wells up in the slit. We call that the first dew. At the same time that the first dew is forming, the ink held in the thread slowly spills down along the needle. Crimson ink reaches the tip of the needle and quickly seeps into the small wound that has opened up in the skin. It's the same feeling as when the words that have been stuck inside my head finally come spilling out of my mouth. When I make my stitches, I do not stutter.

I blotted the blood with gauze and checked the intensity of the ink. Once I know the first stitch is successful, my hand begins to move faster. You can't lose speed. That's the most important trick to keeping the color even. I adjusted the amount of ink on the thread and planted the skin on the spider. The spider was soon revealing its bright red inner skin. Now it was time to wrap that skin in bone. Unlike humans, spiders wear their bones on the outside. It's called an exoskeleton, but I preferred to think of it as hard skin. I completed the skin with India ink and zinc oxide. As the chrome green blended in, the spider now had a perfect exoskeleton.

Once I blotted the ink and blood from the man's skin, the shape of the tattoo stood out vividly. The Goliath spider looked like it was enjoying a walk in the jungle after finishing off a rich meal. I became a spider hiding in the jungle, a spider gliding on eight slender legs along a clear web reflecting the morning sunlight. I felt a light twitching in the tips of my toes. The careless blue-green butterfly flapped its wings, caught in my web. I waited quietly until the butterfly's beautiful cyan wings were worn out. Then I gently wrapped my prey in the fine thread coming from my legs, as gently as stroking soft fruit, like caressing a man's body. Then, I sank my fangs into the butterfly's body, as if inserting a hypodermic needle.

"The bitches'll go crazy when they see this, huh?" he said, tapping my shoulder.

I'm totally worn out after every tattoo, like after having rough sex. As if all the strength in my body was sucked up into the spider's fangs. I smoked a cigarette. The man lit one as well and examined the burgundy Goliath spider. Now he had a palm's worth of exoskeleton. I didn't know whether he had become one palm stronger.

A man calling himself Detective Moon ordered me to present myself at the police station in a few days as a witness regarding the murder of the head priest of Mirŭk'am Temple. The name Mirŭk'am beat inside my chest like wings.

"Are you there? Kim Hyŏngja is your mother, right? They say Kim Hyŏngja killed the head priest of Mirŭk'am. No proof and no witnesses—why does it have to be so complicated? Ms. Bak Yŏng-suk, you'll have to talk to her. Hello? Are you there?"

Detective Moon kept demanding a response from me. But my tongue had turned to stone.

"Do you know Kim Bonghwan, the head priest of Mirŭk'am? His Buddhist name is, let's see . . . Ah yes. Hyŏnpa. He's called Hyŏnpa."

I had absolutely no memory of the name Kim Bonghwan. But when I heard the name Hyŏnpa, I felt a heavy wave break and stir up white foam in my head. I managed to recall a monk with peach-colored skin. The monk's shaved head looked like it was painstakingly groomed, and the salt and pepper stubble sprouting out of it was beautiful, seeming to sparkle like silvery gray sand. Even the monk's old robes were dazzling. I couldn't believe he was dead.

I yanked out the phone cord. The long black telephone line was like a conduit for malignant insects. My mother's hands, which had sewn traditional Korean *jŏgori*, were like fine embroidery stitched in fabric. The time she had spent drinking tea with the monk, the jade-colored tea that spilled from her fingertips, which were softer and straighter than the bamboo painted on the tea set— could those hands truly have killed a monk? I stared at my own rough, calloused hands, as if I were the one who had strangled the old monk. But I immediately felt indifferent, like a person rejected by her parents. I did my morning chores and ate breakfast as usual. I made a list of the inks I needed to buy and checked how much bottled water was left in the fridge.

The big discount store resembling an enormous grain silo was bustling with shoppers pushing carts. I put a pack of bottled water and several kinds of hard liquor in the basket then headed straight for the meat section. I selected a piece of fresh pork belly, a chunk of marbled beef shank, and a pork backbone with lots of meat on it. I'm not that fond of beef, but I picked up one pack each of tough sirloin and tenderloin steak.

I eat meat unseasoned. I like beef sliced finger-thick and grilled until it's just a little bloody and pork boiled with garlic and onions. I don't eat it with vegetables like lettuce. The best match for grilled meat is not vegetables but white rice. When the slightly darkened blood from the meat soaks into the clear rice, cooked until the eye of the rice, the embryo, is almost visible, the flavor of the meat is at its peak.

On my way out of the meat section, I stared vacantly at the red lumps of flesh set on trays. The round shape of the meat reminded me of the monk's shaved head. His clean-shaven skull looked like a sun on the verge of rising, and there seemed to be a whiff of the animalistic about all that dignity. I sometimes wondered how his hard, round head would look with a Maori tribal tattoo, while the animality of his shaved skull got mixed up with my own warped desires, causing me to picture a woman's fine hands clutching the monk's head during intercourse.

A cool breeze surged out of the freezer. Fine volts of electricity seemed to flow through my legs. A long forgotten sensation pricked my whole body. I recalled the numbness that used to march up my stomach and chest like a flash freeze, and the seizures that laid me out on my back with my fists clenched tight. I remembered holding my mother's hand and climbing the sloping road that led to Mirŭk'am in search of a cure for the epilepsy, my mother's endless bows and the sound of the monk's wooden bell, her prayers to Buddha wrapping around my body like a magic spell.

I shook my head hard and rushed out of the store. The shopping bags were heavy, stuffed with bottled water, packs of meat, and the toilet brush I had impulsively grabbed in the cleaning supplies section. The closer I got to home, the faster I walked. I wanted to rush inside and boil the meat in a large pot so I could fill my mouth with its taste. The warm juices already seemed to be pooling in my mouth and seeping between my teeth.

The elevator had stopped for a long time on the seventh floor before descending to unload a swarm of people onto the first floor. Because of the toilet brush, one plastic bag was on the verge of bursting. I got into the elevator carefully and pressed the close button several times. The double doors closed slowly, as if taking their own sweet time. Just before both doors shut completely, a hand shot inside. The doors opened again and a forearm, shoulder, and head squeezed in turn through the narrow gap between the doors. When the left leg was completely inside the elevator, the doors flew open and slowly closed again. The man was puffing for breath with his back turned to me, his shoulders rising and falling heavily.

The elevator didn't budge. It was still stopped on the first floor. We had been standing there without pressing any of the floor numbers. I shifted the bags to one hand and pressed the button for the eighth floor. Right when the green light lit up behind the number eight, the man's finger pressed my finger. At that moment, the plastic bag that had been barely holding together ripped apart, spilling its contents onto the floor. The elevator began moving, and I lost my balance and fell onto the bloody packs of meat. I gathered the stuff up with one hand and barely managed to right myself. The man picked up the rest of the things that had fallen onto the floor and placed them in my arms.

The elevator doors opened with a metallic sound. Getting off, I went right while the man went left. After dropping my things in front of my door, I turned my head to see where he'd gone. He had walked at nearly the same speed I had and was standing in front of the door at the end of the hallway, looking for his key. Since the apartment at my end of the hall was #806, his was #801. He and I had been riding the elevator to the same floor, walking almost the same distance, and opening the door and returning home alone. If the building were folded in half around the elevator, the man and I would intersect in the same place. Like the supplementary angles of a Goliath spider.

I pictured the man's face, as clear and white as rice. It seemed a beautiful face. I pushed my purchases inside with my foot and closed the door. Blood was leaking out of the packs of meat lying on the floor. I was famished. I felt like sitting down right there and tearing the plastic open, grabbing the meat in my bare hands, and eating it raw. I wanted to feel the satisfaction of frenzied eating with blood smeared around my mouth like a wild animal.

But did my mother really kill Hyŏnpa?

Two in the afternoon. I left my house and began walking along the elevated highway next to the Han River. The road stretched through the center of the city like a long, thick tendon. Seen from above, the city would resemble a person's skinned body, veins and tendons racing to reach every corner of that body.

Thinking about the monk's death, I remembered the kitten at Mirŭk'am Temple. A large number of cats used to prowl around Mirŭk'am. Wandering brazenly around the courtyard or even the sermon hall, the cats had frightened me. But they were beautiful. It seemed like all manner of beauty was wound up and hidden like springs inside their small, soft bodies. They were soft and warm and a little scrawny. The monks sometimes tossed fish heads or pieces of meat brought by the faithful to the cats in front of the dorm. Each time, I stared at the cats as they enjoyed the taste of meat with gleaming eyes through my own jealousy-filled eyes.

One day, when the air was swirling with pine pollen, I found a newborn kitten between some woodpiles used for firewood. I measured the kitten's warm body against my hand. Just then, the mother cat appeared from out of nowhere as if for a surprise attack and arched her back aggressively. I took the kitten and ran. I was almost stopped by the mother cat's keen wailing, but I managed to get away. My hair stood on end. I felt like I was running in a loop rather than along a mountain path. It felt unreal, and only the wind lashed at my ears. I arrived at a village at the base of the mountain and hid inside a public outhouse. The kitten in my hand was small, soft, and beautiful. I didn't hesitate for even a second to toss it into the latrine. I watched for a long time as all traces of the kitten disappeared inside the latrine bucket that was frantically crawling with worms.

I had arrived at the War Memorial. I bought an admission ticket and went inside. Most memorial buildings or museums have artifacts that were either excavated or preserved on display in glass cases in separate rooms according to time period. If you take a closer look, you can tell that they are well-made models crafted from plastic or beeswax. I took the weapons out of their glass cases one by one and began my attack on the monk.

The whistling arrow sang as it left the bowstring and pierced his heart, and the seven prongs of the *chiljido* sword sliced his internal organs to pieces. Blood spurted from the monk's feet as they were torn by the staple-shaped caltrops, which were once scattered on the ground to stop horses from charging. I tried every type of weapon, from submachine guns and .45-caliber revolvers used by the Commies even to tanks, but none could satisfy me. I needed something stronger and crueler, something that didn't leave proof, something my mother could have used.

A painting of the Battle of Kwiju at the end of a corridor caught my eye. I was drawn to the strong, savage-sounding name of Kang Kamch'an. But the painting of the Battle of Kwiju seemed more soft than savage. It looked like a landscape painting of grass moving in the direction of the wind. Soldiers running with spears and horses charging with steam rising from their nostrils were heading steadily in one direction, like a clump of grass whistling in the breeze. The horses' manes fluttering in the wind looked supremely soft, and even the soldiers facing their deaths looked like they were dancing. It was unacceptable. The war I pictured wasn't a black and white landscape painted in India ink but a realistic painting interspersed with the screams and sufferings of primary colors. The blood and casualties that are always present in war were nowhere to be found.

I was dizzy. My stomach heaved, and my ears were ringing. I stumbled in search of an exit. But the fluorescent arrows pointing in the direction of the exhibits determined where museum visitors could walk. You could only get out by passing through each of the inner rooms of the museum. Squirming like a midget held by the nape of the neck in the hand of a giant, I passed each room and grabbed the last opportunity. The war experience room.

I bought a separate entrance ticket and squatted in front of the steel door to the exhibit. Each of the children waiting to enter had a small notebook in their hands. After a long time, the door opened and the ticket agent came out. He meticulously collected each ticket and directed everyone inside. I lagged behind the others who rushed in, and handed him my ticket. He was putting the tickets in one hand and reaching out to collect them with the other. I lifted my head and looked up at the ticket agent. The white nape of his neck was visible over the sharp collar of his stiffly ironed uniform. It was the man from #801. The ticket slipped from my hand and fell to the floor. He bent at the waist to pick it up. I rushed inside, avoiding his gaze. The inside of the room was pitch black without a single source of light.

Shots rang out in the dark. The smell of gunpowder stung my nose. Lights flashed below my feet, and I heard the sound of bullets flying overhead, the shouts and screams of soldiers, voices on the radio calling for backup, sergeants barking out orders. Suddenly, I felt a cool breeze in the darkness where a fierce battle was under way. Fine shivers like the warning signs of a seizure ran through me, like the fidgeting of a beast of prey waiting in the darkness for a chance to pounce. The sound of tense, close breathing raised the hairs on the back of my neck. I could feel someone's warm breath on my earlobes. The breathing grew faster and rougher. The bombing stopped. The breathing stopped at the same time. My collar fluttered as if stirred by a breeze. A red light came on, and the children darted out, shoving past me where I stood uneasily. I looked around the red room and went outside.

I didn't see the man from #801. Was it his breathing that I heard? My nose tingled from the heavy smell of gunpowder. I passed the last room where a life-size tank and helicopter were on display and exited the War Memorial. All the strength had drained from my body. I lay outside on the lawn beside a tank. It seemed like I could hear the faint sound of a wooden bell and my mother's prayers. The smell of gunpowder turned into the delicate scent of incense.

A long sword I had seen inside the War Memorial flashed before my eyes. It was a beautiful, glorious sword with a fine, sharp blade and an elaborately engraved pattern of a tiger. I dreamt that I knelt before its beauty and licked the metallic edge of the blade like a dog. The tingling sensation on my tongue was like both the bloody scent of steel and the scent of incense or gunpowder.

"There was no autopsy, but it's been determined for now that he died of natural causes due to old age. The members of the temple opposed the autopsy. . . . Of course, it seems the monk was practically a walking corpse before he died. I don't know why she insisted that she killed him, but thanks to her, innocent people have suffered."

Talking absently without looking at me, Detective Moon's words cut deeply, piercing all the way to the bottom of my lungs like a cigarette smoked at dawn on an empty stomach. Since it was morning, the station wasn't busy. Nevertheless, Detective Moon kept shuffling his papers and avoiding my eyes.

"So, what you're saying is that my mother didn't kill the monk?"

"That's what I'm saying. Kim Hyŏngja was released from custody. She's probably home by now."

Detective Moon hurried away saying he had work to do. I sat on the stairs at the entrance to the station and stared at the tips of the shoes of people passing by. Home. Did she have a home to return to? Did she go back to Mirŭk'am? Uneasy questions were pouring out of me. I felt like a missing child. Like the day I sat stock-still in front of the *hanbok* store and stared at the corner where my mother had left me.

Once the seizures stopped, my mother and I had no further reason to stay at Mirŭk'am. Raising the dust-covered shutters of the *hanbok* store, I decided to erase my memories of everything that had happened at Mirŭk'am—the cat I killed, teatime with the monk, even the heavy scent of incense and the sound of chanted prayers. I would learn how to make *hanbok* from my mother and make clothes as fine as hers. I would begin by dyeing fabric or winding thread onto bobbins, and stay right by her side until I could backstitch the sharp line of a front collar. That's what I thought.

But Mom thought otherwise. For four days, she worked on a cotton jacket and pants dyed with charcoal and a robe dyed with gardenia seeds. When it was all done, including the starching and ironing, she handed me something wrapped inside a mustard-yellow cloth. Inside the cloth were rolls and rolls of bills. She took the monk's clothes and left the house. "I have to go back." Those were the last words she said to me.

My mother wasn't what killed the monk. Maybe her thinking that she killed the monk was just an intent to kill that couldn't be realized, like the weapons displayed in the War Memorial. But just as wars are glorified, someone could have covered up the incident in order to preserve the monk's beauty. I headed toward Mirŭk'am.

Surrounded by forest, Mirŭk'am was silent, as if returning to forest itself. There were no signs of life. The main hall and the Hall of Maitreya were tightly padlocked. The courtyard was piled high with dry pine needles, making it seem like I had arrived at an abandoned house. The front gate to the dorm was likewise bolted shut. I tightened my emotional screws, which were loose and rattling. I climbed on top of a discarded wooden crate next to the gate and peered inside the dormitory. Mirŭk'am was so deeply quiet it was uncanny. Where had all those cats gone? I stretched my hand inside and unlocked the bolt.

The kitchen was clean and in perfect order. There wasn't a single grain of rice left in the drain. A kitchen knife, long sharp chopsticks, a cast iron pot, firewood in the hearth, Freon gas that could be used to set the dormitory on fire—with determination, anything could be used as a weapon. But I didn't see any proof anywhere that my mother had killed the monk.

I went into the room where my mother and I had stayed. Except for some clothes that looked like she had worn them and a damp-smelling blanket stuffed in the corner, the room was empty, with no furniture. On top of a ramen box in the window sat the devotional book she read every day, her straw sewing basket, and some cheap, half-used cosmetics. I turned the sewing basket upside down and spilled the contents on the floor. A spool of white thread rolled away. There were buttons, chalk, and a tape measure packed inside a clear bag, a needle case made from silk, a 24-pack of Japanese Kirin-brand gold-plated needles, a sky blue plastic comb, and a black hair band.

"If you put a strand of hair inside, the needles won't rust," she had said every time she opened her needle case to insert a strand of hair.

She used to roll up her long, jet-black strands of hair and place them inside the needle case. Sometimes she lovingly wound one of my own stiff, thick hairs, which fell out in clumps, and put it inside as well. I stuffed my mother's needle case and the pack of needles in my pants pocket. She wouldn't be needing them anymore. I would take the needles and make beautiful tattoos with them. I pocketed the needles like a war trophy, but my heart kept beating violently.

President Kim brought a man in his late forties who had spent his life roaming from one gambling den to another. His unusually thick hair was dyed jet-black, and he had large, round eyes like a calf. He had a blue anchor tattooed on his shoulder, a large square in the middle of his chest, and five rectangles on his stomach.

"This one was a group tattoo from when I was working on a ship, and this square is the letter *miŭm*. I asked the guy who was doing the tattoos to write Masan Forever, but he only wrote the *miŭm* and took off. How could he have written all of Masan Forever when he made the *miŭm* so big? Ever since then, my life has been all screwed up. I can't show my face in Masan again, let alone call myself a success."

While he talked, he stroked the tattoo, which was just an empty outline. He said the five rectangles were supposed to be the five high-scoring *kwang* cards in a flower card deck. A few futile lines were all that was left of his hope that by carrying the cards on his chest, he would finally be on a roll.

After I returned from Mirŭk'am, a couple of people had come to me for tattoos, but I couldn't help them. If it weren't for President Kim, I might have spent days locked in my room, just eating meat and drinking bottled water. Kim sometimes brought customers to me like this without notice, asking for tattoos. Most of the people he brought needed me to fix botched tattoos or wanted complicated drawings that required me to spend the whole day with needle in hand. There was even one person who asked me to tattoo a samurai sword on his penis, and I couldn't refuse that unreasonable request either.

President Kim was the one who taught me how to handle a needle. After my mother left, I met Kim while loitering in front of the *hanbok* store. When I saw the bluish marks on Kim's iron-like forearms, a strange feeling I had never felt before came over me. He had a scent about him like something you might smell on a welder working in an iron foundry. It was like the smell of sweat mixed with the bloody scent of iron. The blade tattooed on his forearm was beautiful. I followed him to Seoul. If my mother used needles to embroider fabric, I would embroider soft human flesh. President Kim was the light that aided in my molting.

The *miŭm* in "Masan Forever" engraved at the center of the man's chest looked more like a small picture frame than a letter. Words inscribed in flesh are good clues to the state the person was in at the time of the tattoo. That was always the case with words like "effort" or "savings." The will or determination to live a better life enabled people to overcome the pain of having their flesh carved into. Conversely, the tattoo also included the trials they would have to endure in the future.

Something that coexists between the flesh and the words inscribed upon it. That something is a beautiful wound or a painful adornment.

I drew a tiger inside the man's small picture frame. The tiger with its sharp canines glared as if ready to spring forth at any moment. I ground some charcoal to a fine powder and carved stripes deep into the torso. The tiger trapped inside the square was not just a symbol of Masan but the pattern used for the embroidered insignia worn by military officials in the Chosun Dynasty. Inside the five rectangles, I drew the five *kwang* cards: January pine, March cherry, August pampas grass, November paulownia, and December willow. He would do well at any flower card game with the five winning *kwang* cards hidden inside him. Wouldn't it be nice to have such a strong, hidden hand in life?

He looked at himself in the mirror and grinned brightly. After a while, the forgotten pain would come rushing back, but when he walked out with his finished tattoo his shoulders exuded confidence. I puffed on a cigarette and stared blankly at the needles and bottles of ink littering the floor. The same five cards I had tattooed on the man's chest were stuck fast there. Though it hadn't been that difficult a tattoo, I couldn't move, as if all the strength had drained from my body.

With the cigarette still in my mouth, I picked up the ink bottles and the pieces of gauze I had used to wipe away the blood. Just then, there were two long rings on the doorbell. President Kim must have left something behind. I could barely manage to stand up and open the door.

It was the man from #801. He was standing at attention in front of the door. Had I been waiting for him to come? I slowly opened the door as if guided by some force and stepped aside so he could enter. He walked across the living room to the sofa without any hesitation, as if he had been coming to my apartment for a long time. Then he sat on the sofa with his knees neatly pressed together and stared at me. He didn't take his eyes off of me until I closed the door and went to sit beside him. He turned his head away and abruptly began speaking.

"I wondered what was on the other end of the path I take every day."

He talked without looking at me. I looked up at the side of his face. His flushed cheeks glittered with peach fuzz. He pressed his lips together then spoke again.

"I mean, I wondered what would happen if I went right instead of left when I got off the elevator, or if I crossed the street in the morning and got on the same bus but going in the opposite direction."

Each time he spoke, his eyes looked like he was deep in meditation. His words caught the light and flashed like fish leaping out of a deep sea. I opened my mouth as if to catch the tail of a flopping fish.

"I saw you at the War Memorial."

My voice was stiff and hard. Compared to his flashing voice, mine was like the sound of a pot breaking. I closed my mouth and waited for his next words.

"When I ran into you in the elevator, you stank of gunpowder. Or maybe it was the smell of disinfectant. Every day, I smell gunpowder and hear the sound of cannon shells. You probably already know that."

" . . . "

"Sometimes I go into the monitor room to listen to the sound of bombs. If I sit in there with my eyes closed, I can feel the sound of the wind. It's the sound of shells falling, like a stream of air from a B-29 bomber."

"Why do you listen to the sound of bombs?"

"I like war. War is strong. Strength comes from power. The most beautiful thing in the world is power."

"There's no such thing as war here."

"I know what you do. I know that the men who sometimes come to your door have to ring the bell twice before you open it. You never open the door on Sundays for the salesmen or newspaper deliverymen who only ring once."

"Have you been spying on me? What else do you know?"

He smiled faintly.

"They come out looking stronger than when they went in. I know why they look that way. Last month, one of the men who came out of your apartment showed me his sword. I mean the sword you tattooed on his forearm. He knows. The power of weapons, that is."

"Beautiful people like you never get tattoos."

"Beautiful? Look at me. Look at this pale skin, like a corpse. My skin is naturally too white, so it doesn't tan easily. I once spent a whole day tanning to try to make my skin bronze. But it only turned bright red, then returned to normal the next day. I always look weak and timid. I hate it!"

He narrowed his eyes and glared at me. The faint smile visible just a moment ago was nowhere to be found. His light brown eyes resembled those of a cat. They were filled with doubt, like the eyes of a girl just before she offers up her virginity. He continued talking with a cautious and desperate look on his face, as if revealing an old shameful part of himself.

"When I was in the army, the senior officers always gave me the worst punishment drills for being pretty. I really fought hard. But, one night, I woke to discover the senior officer who slept beside me pulling my pants down. I couldn't move."

" . . . "

"That's when I knew. There were two ways for me to survive. To get soft or get hard. Which one do you think I chose? I have no choice but to get hard. You can do that for me."

"Me?"

"Fill my body up with the strongest weapons. Knives, arrows, missiles, planes, whatever."

He was staring straight at me. His hardened face was insisting that he would never back down. I spoke slowly.

"It's like a hymen. Once it's broken, you can't stitch it back together again. It will be a part of you until you die. Do you still want to do it?"

He reached his hand out and took my hand. His was warm and soft like a freshly boiled piece of fat.

I put a thick steak on top of the grill. The cold meat sizzled and shrank when it touched the hot pan. Flipping the meat after it was cooked on one side, I pictured a piece of pastry stuffed with custard.

A soft, sweet cream puff that makes you heave a very delicate sigh. Just then, the phone rang.

Detective Moon, who had told me about the monk's death, said my name. He paused like someone about to make a grave decision. I took a bite of meat and waited for Moon to speak. As I chewed through the tough piece of meat with my molars, Moon told me my mother was dead. She had killed herself. Her body had been found at the lower reaches of the Mt. Kŭmjŏng gorge. He stammered, saying that I should go to the morgue and collect her body. The voice inside the receiver sounded like that of a messenger from the underworld reading off the names of the dead.

I put down the receiver and took another bite of meat. I put some thinly sliced garlic on the grill. Grease dripped onto the flames, filling the room with the smell of burning protein. I put a piece of garlic that had absorbed the juices from the meat into my mouth. The undercooked garlic made my tongue tingle. Chewing the garlic, I tried to imagine my mother torn against the rocks. But all I could picture was a woman's pale, naked, slashed-up body and not my mother's face.

I looked for my mother's needle case and the pack of needles that I had brought from Mirŭk'am. After returning, I had completely forgotten that they were stuffed inside the pocket of my pants. I thought I would remember what her face looked like if I saw the strands of her hair. I opened the needle case. I turned the case upside down and shook out the contents. Short strands of hair and needles spilled out. The hair looked too short and rough to be my mother's. I licked my thumb and picked up the hairs that had fallen on the floor. It was the monk's hair.

I pictured my mother shaving the monk's head with a razor. She used to kneel and shave his head with one hand while resting the other on his shoulder, pressing down lightly. The image of the monk's hairs falling gently from the end of the razor was a very tranquil one. I could see my mother's delicate hands gathering up every single one of those fallen hairs and placing them lovingly inside the needle case, just the way I could see my mother and the monk drinking tea around the low tea table without saying a word.

Why did she say she killed the monk when she didn't? And why did she end her own life? I opened my mother's treasured pack of Japanese needles. The gold-plated needles shone where they were pinned, from #1 to #20. I took them out and felt their fine curves with the tip of my finger. Suddenly, all of my nerve endings were drawn at once to the tips of the needles. I squinted to take a closer look. The twenty needles were broken off at the tips. The needles were blunt as wire, having lost their points. She had deliberately trimmed the tips of the needles.

"Chop the needle finely and put it in the vegetable juice he drinks every day. The fine, sharp needle shards will swirl around inside his intestines and make lethal cuts. They will travel through his veins to his heart and stop his pulse, summoning death, and leaving no external injuries."

Her voice echoed loudly all around me.

He gets off the elevator every night and turns right. Though he doesn't ring the doorbell twice, I know he is coming. I can sense his soft steps and deep breaths outside the door.

I drew a single needle the size of my little finger on his chest. The needle, tattooed in titanium ink, looked like a small gash. A narrow slit like the genitals of a little girl. It seemed like the universe would be sucked into that gap.

Now he carries the strongest weapon in the world. The thinnest, hardest, and softest needle.

Looking at
Clouds

305

Looking at
Afternoon
Sunlight

To the Kennels

Pyun Hye-Young

Translated by Yoosup Chang and Heinz Insu Fenkl

When he opened the front door a letter fluttered to the ground—he was leaving the house on his way to work in the city. The envelope had been stuck in the doorjamb and it was crumpled, as if someone had tried to force it in. There was a white birdhouse mailbox in front of the house, but the envelope had been stuck in the door as if to draw attention to it. It was nothing remarkable. What caught his eye was the red print on the envelope. Any other time he would have dismissed it as a flyer from the local pizzeria or a mailer from a new herbologist, but as soon as he saw the red text he knew this was a special kind of letter—an eviction notice.

He slowly picked up the crumpled envelope. The notice meant they could barge into his house any time they wanted. His wife, who had come out to see him off, glanced at the envelope in his hand and immediately gasped. She also knew it was from them. Her face went white. She screamed, *Aaah!* What do we do now? Her voice was full of fear, as if she thought they might come charging in right then. Now his mother screamed from her room, not even knowing why his wife had screamed, and his wife grew even more scared because of the noise. His mother was suffering from dementia. She would not stop screaming. He frowned slightly in annoyance.

They had climbed over the fence last night like thieves to stick the notice in the door. They might have been hiding there last

307

AZALEA

*To the
Kennels:
Pyun
Hye-
Young*

night by the newly paved road—so dark you couldn't even see your toes—watching him return from work. He looked toward the length of new pavement that led to the village entrance as if to stare them down. He couldn't be sure they weren't still there, spying on his family and the anxiety they had caused.

That morning in the village was no different from any other. The heads of the single-story houses got into their cars in unison for the commute to the city. Every day, they got into their cars at approximately the same time and squeezed out of the village. Those who didn't leave then usually couldn't get to work by starting time at 9 A.M. The cars carrying the breadwinners disappeared in an orderly line over the new road, and mixed in among them were three or four of the same make, model, and even color as his. Typically, he would also have been mingling in the parade to the freeway. To leave the house at the same time every day, he got up at the same time, and to do that he went to bed every night around the same time. For him, even sleeping, eating, and sex followed a schedule.

The wives leaned against their fences and waved to their husbands leaving for work, then exchanged greetings with their eyes as they headed inside. After the wives were back in their houses, he continued to glare toward the new road until all the cars were gone. Only a thin, early morning fog from the hills lingered on the new road; there was no sign that the men who had stuck the notice in the door were hiding anywhere. He could see the sound wall of the highway beyond the fog, but the rumbling noise of a vehicle was still clearly audible through it. It was probably an overloaded freight truck or a semi. The new road shook slightly, as if startled by the noise.

The envelope was thin, like it was empty. He was upset that his daily routine was ruined by this flimsy envelope. Normally he would have left the new road and been on the highway by now. He stared at his and his wife's names for a long time—in stiff, bold print—at the bottom of the envelope. The longer he did this, the more unfamiliar the names got, and that feeling made him nervous. The bankruptcy was entirely his fault. He had known a letter notifying them of the eviction would come eventually. Still, now that he had actually received the notice, anger rose within him uncontrollably. Exactly what had he done wrong?

He clenched the envelope and tore it up without even checking its contents. His name and address, the red letters of the notice and eviction date, the name of the marshal—all torn to tiny pieces. His startled wife stared at him. His screaming old mother stared at him. His son, clutching his wife's skirt, stared at him. Then, sensing the gravity of the mood, the boy burst into tears without even knowing why. His wife patted the boy's back, looking dumbstruck. No one stopped him. His face must have looked fierce and unapproachable as he ripped the envelope. He must have looked angry, too, and that attitude strangely put his wife at ease. She hadn't noticed his hands shaking as he tore the envelope—she took it to be his resolve to protect the family. He regretted it immediately because now there was no way of knowing when the marshals would come barging in. Should he have gone to them and pleaded to have the eviction date pushed back? Before he could change his mind, he tossed the fragments into the toilet and flushed. The shreds of the notice were sucked down into the whirlpool with a gulp, and the water cleared once again. He hid his still-trembling hands by shoving them into his pants pockets.

When are they coming? his wife asked in a slightly lowered voice. Instead of answering, he opened the living room curtains, revealing the smokestacks that had not yet been torn down. The village was built on the site of an abandoned industrial chemicals factory, which had been dismantled to convert the lot to residences, but here and there parts of buildings and smokestacks were still standing. White smoke seemed to rise from one of them. It must have been fog rolling down from the hills, or scattered clouds—smoke couldn't be coming from the chimney of an inert factory. When the fog lifted, the new road was empty, and in the morning sun he could see the dust floating around inside the house. His wife frowned. He was confused—was it because of the sunlight, because he didn't answer, or because of the eviction notice? He shook his head at his wife, not knowing. She went into the bedroom with a gloomy look on her face. What's certain, he mumbled—looking at the back of her head, white from the sunlight—is that we are going to be kicked out of this house very soon.

He had no choice but to accept the fact that he was bankrupt, and—needless to say—flat broke. He also had debts that he could never in a million years repay. He could no longer borrow money from his friends, let alone from a bank. And he had no family or relatives he could ask, either. Even if there had been someone, it would have been a nuisance to go into a long-winded explanation of his bankruptcy and then listen to their lectures in order to borrow the money. But even if he could have endured a lecture, he wouldn't be able to borrow any money because. . . . Thoughts arose in a jumble; he wanted to prioritize things. The first thing . . . , he muttered, and realized that he hadn't left for work yet. He had to go to work, just like any other day. Self-pitying thoughts like "Do I have to go in on time even on the day I got my eviction notice?" did not occur to him. The money he earned would all be taken by them, but it was important to stick to the routine. He glanced at the clock on the wall. He should have been approaching the tollgate by now. It was all because of the notice that he was this late.

There's probably a little time left before the eviction. I just have to find another house to live in by then, he said as he stuffed his feet into his creased, black shoes. The heels were worn out on the inside and made his back hurt after just a few steps. His wife looked at him without a word. He gave her a broad smile. The process begins with the delivery of the eviction notice but they have to go through more legal steps to confiscate the assets of the bankruptcy filer, he said. He had no way of knowing when the marshals would appear, either. But the moment he said this, he was sure that the eviction would be postponed and that they would find a new place to live in the meantime. It was a ridiculously optimistic thought.

~

He passed by fourteen houses to get to the village entrance. There were a total of twenty-two houses in the village, standing along the new road in a gentle curve—so as not to block the light—toward the hills. House #1 was at the entrance, and the numbers got higher as you approached the hills. Mr. Y, the broker who gave tours of the development, said that buyers were flocking in for the beautiful scenery, thanks to those hills behind the village. They weren't very high, but they were enough to attract people from the nearby city to come and forage for hazelnuts and chestnuts. It was nothing but some low hills, though, as far as he was concerned. From the new road, you could see patchy pine groves and bald spots here and there, where small grave mounds stood out like scars. There were probably more graves hidden up there. He didn't much care for those hills. Forests with no distinct paths and unexpected, hidden graves. Forget about hiking. He was the type that thought, "What's the point of struggling to get to the top if you're only going to come back down?" He knew this sort of sentiment would make him seem stubborn and simpleminded, so he didn't share it with anyone.

The houses appeared to be wooden at first glance, but they were actually steel-framed. The cost of steel was much less per square foot than wood, and once a site was selected, it took barely ten days to build the house. With modular materials, construction was just lining up corners and tightening them with screws, fitting the houses together like gigantic Lego blocks. Maybe that was why they all looked the same, like they were mass-produced. Little things, like the placement of windows or the exterior walls, were slightly different if you looked closely, but from a distance, they all looked identical: a parasol in a white pebble yard, a low-rising flowerbed encircled by a latticed fence, identically sized birdhouse mailboxes standing by a swinging gate. On weekend evenings when the weather was nice, the neighbors would roast the same cuts of meat under their parasols. As they put their lettuce wraps into their

AZALEA

To the

Kennels:

Pyun

Hye-

Young

mouths, one family would catch the eye of another and give a wave, and only after waving back from under their own parasol—at the same angle and the same number of times—would the neighbors also eat their own.

He had decided to move because he really wanted a single-family home. Their three-story housing project in the city was so crowded it was always bustling with activity. Though he did not like them much, he felt special for having hills behind the house. It meant that he was actually living in the country, and that they had escaped the city. He knew how hard it was to leave the city. Before moving, he had never lived outside the city, but he had never actually lived downtown, either. Where he was born, where he grew up, where he started a family—it was all in the suburbs on the outskirts. Never living downtown but never going outside the city—that was a typical city person.

Once he left the new road, the sound of dogs barking was especially loud. There were kennels, where they bred dogs, near the village. Mr. Y said that since the breeder was unlicensed, the kennels would be shut down by the local authorities and would soon be gone. They had tried to force the kennels to relocate, but had only succeeded in slowing their growth thus far. His wife was hesitant about the move when she heard, but it didn't concern him. Even if the breeder's dogs were ferocious enough to maul each other to death, they would be no problem unless they were somehow to attack a family. In their cramped cages, the dogs would consume the same feed, sleep and wake up at around the same time, be sold off to this place and that according to whim, and in the end be gruesomely roasted to death. No matter how ferocious, they would never leave the kennels unless they were sold off to die or died in their cages. The loud barking might be a problem, but he thought he could endure it. In the city where he had lived all his life, noise—and not quiet—was the norm.

But the dogs' barking was hard to bear. It sounded like every dog at the kennels was barking at once. When one started it sounded like hundreds of dogs barking at the same time. The noise never stopped all day. A rumor started to circulate among the residents that they were breeding fighting dogs at the kennels. There were lots of other rumors about the kennels: dogs being starved to make them more vicious, dogs pitted against boars in the same cage. There was even a story that the kennels were also a slaughterhouse. The dirt there was suspiciously red, and there was a strong smell of blood— proof of the butchering. There was even talk of the kennels' owner living in the village. Maybe that was why wives sometimes asked the women next door what their husbands did for a living. Rumors were thick, but not one person could say they had been to the kennels. He often turned his head towards the noise. The barking sounded muffled, as if the kennels were far away, but it also sounded close, as if they were right next door. But with the noise of trucks passing on the highway and the mechanical sounds from under the floor mingled in, it was hard to guess at the precise direction.

It was already past his commute time. Normally, he should have been in his office reading the paper and sipping coffee. No coworkers called, concerned by his lateness. They probably wouldn't notice his empty cubicle because of the high partitions. There was an important meeting scheduled for that morning. He tried to remember what the topic was, but couldn't. It was probably written on a Post-it, stuck to a corner of his monitor. He realized that he was entirely unprepared for the meeting if he couldn't even remember the topic. If he did somehow get to the office in time for the meeting, he would not be able to make any useful suggestions. The department head would probably scold him, asking sarcastically if he wore his head just for show.

He became more anxious the moment he had that thought. He turned the steering wheel, thinking he might change lanes and speed up. Suddenly, he heard loud honking. He quickly returned to his lane. He was one of those cautious drivers who obeyed the speed limit on the highway. He was afraid of the highway. For some reason, semis and mammoth freight trucks—whose tonnage was

AZALEA

*To the
Kennels:
Pyun
Hye-
Young*

anyone's guess—were on the road around the time of his commute. They made a deafening noise. If a truck carrying industrial chemicals or machinery was behind him, he felt a crushing pressure in his chest. He slowed down to the speed limit and someone honked again from behind.

Only after he looked in his side mirror did he realize that a truck the size of a cruise ship was tailgating him. It soon changed lanes and passed him. He let out a sigh of relief, looking at the rear end of the truck. Soon after, a semi followed him. He pulled completely off to the side of the road and waited until he could no longer see it. He started the car again, but a moment later, another truck approached. He had to pull off again. Only after going on and off the shoulder like this several times did he arrive at the tollgate to enter the city.

As he paid the toll to the female attendant, he rolled down his window and breathed in the friendly and familiar city air, welcoming it into his lungs. The house he owned in the city was at the north end of the river. Despite the problems with microdust, noise pollution, and overcrowding, it was still prime real estate for business purposes. In other words, he had lived in a place like a true city with blowing dust, unending noise, and jostling crowds. His place was in a residential neighborhood crammed with row houses. He had taken out a mortgage and bought a three-story townhouse. He rented to several families—even the basement—but his mortgage payment was still so large he could have covered the floor in 10,000 *won* bills. He wasn't sure if he could pay the place off, even by retirement age, if he wanted to send his son to college. The interest kept growing, and the principal just wouldn't go down. He was floundering in a debt as big as the house, and yet he did not regret buying the place.

It was Mr. Y who suggested the country home when he learned of his situation. Because of the mortgage on the row house, he originally could not even think of moving, and had no desire to move to the country, either. The price of the country house was so great that he would have had to transfer the existing mortgage to the buyer of the row house and take out another mortgage more than half the original value of the new home. The reason he had decided to move despite all this was because Mr. Y had asked him if a house in the country wasn't the ultimate dream of any true city dweller. He thought he should agree if he was truly a city person, and so he had answered—pounding his chest proudly—"My dream has been a white single-story house with a pitched roof and a chimney!" After that, he started to believe that living out in the country actually had been a long-awaited dream of his. He did not hear Mr. Y muttering in a hushed tone, "Why does everybody think a country house is supposed look like that?" In his mind, he pictured a cloud lightly dancing across a blue sky. Every season, he would plant different flowers in the flowerbed in the garden. He would pick lettuce greens and red peppers from the field out back. After he had decided to move, he declared to his coworkers that a home in the country was the ultimate dream of any city dweller. Without pausing to be embarrassed by the pre-packaged phrases, he bragged that his house was a white single-story home with a pitched roof and a mountain for a backdrop.

≈

Even after seeing him hurrying into the office, hardly anyone noticed he was late. The man in the next cubicle asked casually, "Did you overdo it last night?" That was it. Everyone was crazy busy with their own work and the department head would only find out about his tardiness when the weekly time sheets came out. In fact, the morning meeting had been pushed to the afternoon by the department head, so he used the time to think up some ideas. He came up with a few—all mediocre—but they would have been ignored even if they had been good. For important issues, the meetings were usually just a formality, anyway. The important things were already decided beforehand.

AZALEA

*To the
Kennels:
Pyun
Hye-
Young*

The midday hours flew by. In the end, the meeting was postponed until the following week and so he watched for changes in the stock market during work. When prices went up, he lamented not having bought any stock, and when they went down, he bemoaned the weak economy. But there was no way he could have owned any stock. It was just a habit. With the man in the next cubicle, he talked at length about the new city that was advertising for residents. When his coworker said he was seriously considering the solicitation, he mentioned that his own country house was near a planned new city. The coworker wasn't very interested, so he probed, asking if he was tired of living in identical apartments. His tone was unexpected, even to himself. He had never lived in an apartment.

At quitting time those who had finished their work left one by one, but he stayed because of his tardiness and the backlog he had. He liked staying in the office in the city, even if he had no work. He slowly strolled through the empty office at night. Piles of documents like corpses littering an arena after a battle, conference room chairs strewn about in disarray, the large whiteboards with their contents not yet erased, even the coffeemaker with its blinking red light—it looked like his office mates had only left for a moment, not like they had finished their work and gone home.

Before leaving, he went to the window and looked down at the city. Lights from every building were shining in the night. He liked the cityscape, and he especially enjoyed greeting the night from a building in the heart of downtown. The light from the buildings was beautiful and warm. When he worked late, he particularly liked the fluorescent lights in the building that faced his—he could see the people in that building busily moving about. Though it was on the other side of a six-lane road, it was close enough to see clearly into the illuminated offices. He wished he could look inside with binoculars and find out what business kept the people there. Even late at night their phones rang off the hook; people were constantly transmitting faxes, feeding paper into a shredder, wearing serious expressions in a meeting; female workers were chitchatting in small groups. He stood at the window watching them and only left in embarrassment when his eyes met someone else's in the building across the way.

The village, which took two hours by highway to reach, was blackness itself. There was not one streetlamp from the highway exit to the new road leading home. The only light on the road was the headlight beams spewing from the car. He realized again how thick darkness was in the hills. Whenever he entered the village late at night, the hills lay there like giant dogs and abruptly thrust out their shadows. His only clue was the dogs barking from all directions— only when he heard that sound did he feel the security of having entered the right village. He exited the highway, reached the village by following the barking, found his house by fumbling along the dark new road. The dogs were the only streetlamps and security lights in the village.

When he opened the front door and stepped in, his wife came out from hiding behind it, her face pallid. He did not know why she was hiding. He was confused.

I thought it was them, she said in a shaky voice.

He was startled. He realized he had forgotten about them all day. While he was in the city, he had forgotten that he was on the brink of bankruptcy, that marshals would come barging in, that he would have this house taken from him. He hadn't tried hard to forget, nor had he intentionally distracted himself—such things were naturally forgotten in the city. He received large numbers of business calls, and there was enough work to keep him from thinking about his own finances. Talking about stocks and real estate, he confused bankruptcy and bounty. He might have been calmer about meeting them if it was in the city. He regretted leaving the city.

After calming his frightened wife and putting her to bed, he sat quietly in the dark room. He heard what sounded like a machine operating deep underground, so loud he even wondered

Azalea

To the
Kennels:
Pyun
Hye-
Young

if they had buried the thing while dismantling the factory. Before
he knew it, the barking of dogs from the nearby kennels mingled
with the mechanical noise from beneath the floor. He mimicked the
wailing of the dogs and barked—*woof, woof*—in a low voice. From
time to time freight trucks sped by like wind along the highway, and
then he could clearly feel the cracks in the new road. Gradually, it
seemed to him that the house was one huge machine.

~

Several trucks were coming up the new road. His wife became
agitated as soon as she heard the unfamiliar vehicles, and seeing
his mother like that, the boy also became frightened. The moment
he saw the trucks, he too thought that the marshals had come. But
it could also have been new residents moving in. It was a good
weekend for moving. He became depressed at the thought of no
longer having those peaceful weekends. His wife grew paler as the
trucks neared the house. He decided to hand over the house without
a fight, let the marshals lead him to the chopping block. Rather
than cause a scene and let everyone know about the bankruptcy,
it was better just to look like they were moving. Six trucks passed
by his house, bouncing loudly, their cargo compartments stacked
full of metal cages, dense and high, precarious like they were about
to fall. His wife only relaxed her tense features after hearing them
disappear toward the hills.

He wondered if it might be better to leave rather than live
in fear, not knowing when the marshals would come. Not that
they had a place to go. As he sighed and shook his head, his eyes
met those of the man next door. They nodded awkwardly to each
other and said hello. Only then did it occur to him that all the
homeowners uphill from him were standing in similar poses,
watching the trucks. He turned his head and looked downhill. The
houses were lined up at regular intervals along the streamlined
curve of the new road. All the owners of the single-family homes

were outside—either alone or with their families—looking in the direction in which the trucks had disappeared. He was neither shocked nor surprised by that. For him, watching was the only way to show his engagement. The fact that it seemed to be the same for the others gave him a great sense of relief. Though he lived in the country, he was pretty much living the same life as city folk. He waved at the neighbors who were also used to city life. When he waved, the fourteen households each responded in sequence as if they were doing the wave in a stadium. His lips curled back in a smile—he liked such orderliness. In unison, his neighbors also burst into light, mass-produced laughter.

Once the trucks were gone, his wife brought a rubber ball out to the yard with his son—she seemed relieved. His old mother with Alzheimer's followed them out, naked from the waist down. His wife hurriedly covered her. Moaning, the old woman went back inside, pulled along by the wife's arms. He picked up the hose to water the garden, but the pressure was low and the water only trickled out. What a relief, he muttered as he shook the water from the hose, though he didn't know what he was referring to. Eventually the marshals would come and totally destroy their normal lives. As he stood there absorbed in thought, the ball rolled up to his foot. He put the hose down and threw the ball to the child. Every time the ball touched his feet, his son burst into laughter, and he laughed along.

Their laughter was drowned out by the sound of barking dogs, which was so constant it was practically a background noise in the village. But this time the sound was more distinct. Several dogs came running down from the hill, barking urgently, as if they were being chased by something. You could tell how ferocious they were from their barking. The child clung to the fence at the sudden dog noises. He told him to go inside the house because the dogs were vicious. It was obvious once they reached the new road—they had distinct bald patches, clumps of hair missing from mange. None of the village homes had a dog. These must have been from the

AZALEA

To the
Kennels:

Pyun

Hye-

Young

kennels. He suddenly muttered: The kennels must be just over the hill. But in the past, the barking had come from all sides; he could not really guess where the kennels were.

His son threw the ball out of the yard. It skittered down the new road, and in a flash, he had climbed over the fence to retrieve it. Startled, he ran after the boy, but the dogs reached his son before he did. They completely surrounded the boy, drove their ferocious teeth into him. He tried to stay calm, but contrary to his thoughts, his body shook and his legs would not move. He looked around for a weapon to hit the dogs with. Nothing caught his eye. He grabbed whatever he could; he threw the pebbles that were spread over the yard, but no matter how many times he hit them, they were not hurt. In desperation, he yelled at them. His wife came running out, alarmed by the screaming, and his mother came running out, naked, behind her. The dogs refused to let go of the boy. His wife went back inside and came back with a long-handled broom and his son's baseball bat. It was a light aluminum bat—he swung it wildly at the dogs, yelling out to the neighbors at the same time. There was no one to help. They must have heard the dogs and gone inside, locking their doors tight. He should have taken the boy and gone inside, too. He regretted not doing that. In the distance, hundreds of dogs barked at once, as if chastising him for his negligence. The growls of the dogs tearing at the boy mingled with the cries of the dogs howling in the distance. Why were the dogs at the kennels crying so much today? he thought as he swung the bat, feeling as if he were about to cry. He swung blindly—he couldn't even tell if it was a dog or his son he was hitting with the bat. The dogs bit and tore at the boy until they were exhausted, then slowly trotted down the new road.

The boy lay as if he were dead, the flesh torn on his chest and arms. The dog bites swelled up red. When she saw the state he was in, his wife burst into tears. He told his wife—deliriously crying and screaming—to bring a blanket, wrapped the boy in it, and carefully placed him in the car. His old mother hurriedly climbed in, not even properly dressed.

He could not figure out where the hospital was. He just followed the new road down to the village entrance. The man who owned house #6 was outside watering his garden. He asked the way to the nearest hospital. The man put down the hose and excitedly yelled that it was in the direction of the kennels, raising his hand to point toward the hills. He turned the car around and drove back up toward the hills. Just to be safe, he also asked the man from #17— who was out in his yard pulling weeds—where the hospital was. The man also quickly replied that he had heard there was a hospital in the direction of the kennels. From the urgent tone of their voices, he knew that the neighbors had watched his child getting hurt. He gave a halfhearted thanks and sped away. The boy's moaning was settling down. He was afraid that meant he was getting weaker. He wanted to make the boy scream, even if he had to hit him. His wife—cradling the child—kept on crying. He could not concentrate on finding his way because of the crying. He had never gone toward the kennels before. To go there, he had to get his bearings by listening for the barking dogs. He told his wife to be quiet. She sniffled and swallowed her tears.

Before he knew it, they were halfway up the hill. The new road was connected up to there. He stopped the car. The dogs stopped barking. He started again. The dogs started barking again. He could not tell whether it was the dogs' barking or phantom noises made by his ears. Honey, do you hear the dogs barking? he asked his wife. He couldn't stand it, the savage growling around his ears. What are you saying, just go! his wife yelled, choking back tears. Quickly, he started driving again, wanting to cry himself. They crested the hill, awash in the sound of the dogs' barking. A development just like their own village appeared on the other side. He was afraid he might be driving in circles. It was exactly like their village: pure white metal-framed single-story homes all lined up and precisely spaced like dominoes. It looked like if you pushed over the last house, the whole complex would come tumbling down. The new road continued on to the end of the village.

Azalea

To the
Kennels:

Pyun
Hye-
Young

He stopped the car and asked a man who was out in his yard where the nearest hospital was. The man was watering his flowerbed; he put down the hose he was holding. If you go toward the kennels, there is a large hospital, he said. He asked the man where the kennels were, and the man looked around in all directions, confused. There wasn't just one or two kennels, the man said. He'd heard they were over the hill. He pointed in the direction they had come. It's over that hill, he said. I heard dogs barking in that direction. He sighed in despair. He thought maybe he was better off relying on the dogs' barking. The boy was breathing quietly as if he were asleep and his wife's crying had changed to sobs. He wanted to cry like his wife. Anger welled up, but the tears would not come.

He went forward without thinking, just following the sound. The dogs were barking more ferociously than ever. They were barking from all directions. When he went north he wondered if the kennels might be to the south, and when he turned right he wondered if he shouldn't have turned left. He turned the wheel whichever way his arms moved. Sometimes the barking seemed to get closer, and sometimes it faded away. If it weren't for the boy, he would have gone to the kennels first. The dogs that tore his son's flesh were surely being raised at the kennels. He wanted to beat up the dogs in their cages. But what if they weren't from the kennels? They might have been stray dogs you could find wandering in any village, strays that might be even more vicious than dogs from a kennel. He became confused—was he looking for the kennels, a hospital for treating his son, or the dogs that bit him?

On his way down the new road, he unwittingly entered the highway and had to keep moving. Could the kennels have been toward that hill? He regretted only driving over the hill and not looking for other roads on it. If he had gotten off the new road and gone deep into the hills, he might have been able to find the kennels. Before he even had a chance to regret the wrong turn, he heard the barking again. The noise sounded dispersed enough to make the entire city seem like a kennel. It sounded loud, like it was close, but with the wind beating against the window he still could not guess the direction.

The truck that was following him changed lanes and sped in front of him. Another truck rumbled past. Having never exceeded the speed limit on the highway, he decided to tail behind them. In order to take the boy to the hospital quickly, it was better to follow the trucks. Luckily, he could still hear the barking. He casually glanced up at the tailgate of the truck he was following, and was shocked. The cargo bay was stacked precariously high with cages, and in each one was a dog. All the while, the dogs looked down at his car and barked as he drove along. His old mother's eyes grew wide; her body trembled in fear. His wife burst into tears again as she tightly bundled the boy in the blanket. The boy's breathing was still shallow. Following the truck with the barking dogs, exceeding the speed limit, he looked back again and again. He had no idea if he was going in the right direction, toward the kennels. Behind, there were only cars chasing him—speeding, seeming to threaten him like the dogs that bit his son. Darkness was quickly catching up with the cars.

Chasing after the truck, he was soon at the tollgates at the entrance to the city. He could see it beyond the gates—drowned in pitch darkness, without a single light. A female attendant with an expressionless face handed him a ticket. The name of the city he worked in was printed on it, but the lightless city he saw was unfamiliar, and he wasn't sure if he was entering the city or his village. He could not see the truck, but the barking still guided him like streetlights. He picked up speed, following the sound that would lead him to the kennels. The road would end eventually. If he kept following it to the end, he would reach someplace. He thought it would be good if they were headed toward the kennels.

Five Poems by Ra Hee-Duk

Translated by Diana Hinds Evans

Death by exposure

This morning I noticed

An abundance of dried fruit in my room.

The pomegranates and clementines on my desk have become hard
    as stone.

Their fragrance gone, they lie at rest.

Perhaps losing your scent you will gain eternal life,

I whisper as I stroke toughened skins.

Acorns that dropped on my head last autumn

Line up evenly on paper.

When I rattle them a distant bell tolls.

The dried wild rose is still red.

Looking at fresh flowers or fruit

The thought that I should give them a funeral

Before they rot in their own juices

Brought me to subject them to death by exposure.

In the breezy sunshine

I hung the fragrant bodies upside down

If flesh and blood did not disappear

I could have no peace

I placed on the fire flesh pickled in sugar of pain,

Stirred it with a wooden spoon

If I did not run away I couldn't endure

Have I dried up too?

Someone said I do a good job of drying flowers but I said

I'm just putting to rest my nomadic blood

This morning the moment I entered my room,

The scent of dried flowers rushed at me

Those lip-like petals,

Lips that have never grazed a wet thigh,

Faced me all at once and screamed.

Flowers desiccated light as butterflies.

Half moon

Perhaps her cold body was heavy—
At dawn she saddled the ridgeline to rest

Even a god may be caught in the act!

Sometimes she tamps the ground under her feet,
Traces the isolated spur of the mountain; I've watched her
Suddenly our eyes meet
Blushing, she darts behind clouds
Then ventures out again elsewhere

The imprint of her buttocks
Remains on the ridgeline
Trees there have bright scars
Like Isaiah's lips cleansed with a hot coal.

The orchid blooms underground.

Because it never emerges

They say few have seen it.

Only the termite, following its scent in the fall

Through cracks in the dirt, visits it.

The orchid withers when it sees the sun,

The termite eschews the light by digging:

Despite dark determinations, here are bodies of pure white.

Like undeveloped film, the entire plant is a root

It does not rise to the surface

Even the flower

Is only a hidden root

FIVE MINUTES

In the shade of blossoms
My life seems to pass.
I wait and pace
Has it passed already?
Five minutes I wait for the child
White acacia petals fall around me.
In their shade
Suddenly I become a white-haired crone
When the bus rounds the corner
And stops in front of me
No 6-year-old will leap into my arms
A tall youth will walk towards me.
As much as I've aged he will have grown
I'll look at him like we've swapped lives
Even while waiting life flashes past in a blink
I waited in this spot
When for a long time he didn't return
I faced his too distant ebb tide,
The falling petals,
Or the passing bus.
Surely my wait will end as I stand here grumbling.
As I wait, the blanket of petals deepens.
Ah, here comes the bus.
I jump lightly and step out of the shadow.

Only through the weight of their light

Did the stars plug holes in the sky. That night there was a leak; how
    quickly the sky fell!

With each shooting star sky gushed out

Soaked our beds and flowed to the sea.

That early summer night when in the deep well

A scorpion's red heart beat like a drum,

We weren't afraid. There was a house by the shore, without roof or
    floor,

But thin brick walls blocked the wind;

On the cold sand we giggled and pulled and tugged our blankets

And fell asleep.

Sand and sky—our sure floor and ceiling—

Encircled our sleep; afraid the sky might disappear,

I woke from slumber again and again and read that big book,

And read it more. On that night by the waves,

I read all the night sky. But no one knows I

Stole a page and

Tucked it between the leaves of a book.

Lingering Impressions of a Mountain Village[1]
—A Few Paragraphs from a Journal
of Travels to Sŏngch'ŏn[2]

Another
Perspective

by Yi Sang

Translated by John Frankl

More than twenty days have passed since I last savored my fragrant MJB.[3] Here the newspaper seldom comes, and the postman only occasionally appears bearing "hard rolled"-colored news.[4] Both contain stories of silkworm cocoons and corn.

1. This is a translation of the original essay as included in Kim Chuhyŏn, ed., *Yi Sang chŏnjip 3: sup'il* (*The Collected Works of Yi Sang, Volume 3: Essays*) (Seoul: Somyŏng ch'ulp'an, 2005). It was first published in the daily newspaper *Maeil sinbo* from September 27 to October 11, 1935. I must also express my gratitude to Kwŏn Yŏngmin, whose modern rendition of the essay appears in Kwŏn Yŏngmin, ed., *Sanch'on yŏjŏng* (*Lingering Impressions of a Mountain Village*) (Seoul: T'aehaksa, 2006), and proved extremely helpful in sorting out some of the more arcane and idiosyncratic aspects of the original.
2. During September and October of 1935 Yi spent about three weeks in Sŏngch'ŏn, South P'yŏngan Province, where his friend Wŏn Yongsŏk was working at the time. Yi and Wŏn were classmates at three separate schools: Tonggwang School; Posŏng High School; and Kyŏngsŏng Technical High School. Much later, Wŏn would go on to record his memories of his enigmatic friend in two separate essays. "My Last Memories of Yi Sang (*Nae-ga majimak bon Yi Sang*)" appeared in the November 1980 edition of the journal *Munhak sasang*, while the piece "Yi Sang's School Days (*Yi Sang ŭi hakch'ang sijŏl*)" appeared in the June 1981 edition of the same journal.
3. This was incorrectly spelled "MJR" in the original version. There are several similar examples below, and all appear to be due either to illegible handwriting on Yi's part, lack of knowledge on a typesetter's part, or a combination of the two. In any case, it was corrected to "MJB" in the first three editions of Yi's collected works. Only versions two and three, however, felt the need to add the note "A type of coffee." This is interesting for what it tells us about a counterintuitive increasing lack of exposure to Western goods and culture following Korea's liberation from Japan in 1945.
4. The original for "hard rolled" reads "*hadorong* (하도롱)"; it was placed in quotation marks by Yi Sang, and provided with the following footnote by Kim Chuhyŏn:

AZALEA

*Lingering
Impressions
of a
Mountain
Village:
Yi Sang*

The villagers appear distressed about some relatives living far away. I too am apprehensive concerning matters left behind in the city.

They say there are roe deer and wild boar over there on P'albong Mountain. And some even say they've seen a "bear" that comes down to catch crayfish in the gully where they used hold rituals to pray for rain. I continually suffer from the delusion that these animals, which I have only seen in zoos, have not been captured from these mountains and put in zoos, but rather have been taken from zoos and put in these mountains. When night falls, just as men retire to their chambers, P'albong disappears into the lacquer-black, moonless night.

The air is so crystal clear, however, I feel I might easily read my cherished Gospel of "Luke"[5] by starlight alone. And I could swear there are twice as many stars out here as in the city. It is so quiet that I seem to hear for the first time traces of the movement of those stars.

At a peddler's inn, I light an oil lamp. Its subtle odor, reminiscent of the city's evening paper, arouses dreams from my youth. Oh, Chŏng![6] I remember our gluing up packets[7] (paper

---

A durable paper, glossy on one side, often used for wrapping. It was made using a chemical pulp and given a brown color. The name originates from the English "hard rolled paper." It was produced and used for packaging and envelopes up until the beginning of World War II.

Except where otherwise noted, this translation will maintain the quotation marks as used by Yi. And while he most often employed them for transliterations of foreign words, it should also be noted, as will be discussed in the accompanying article, that he at times elected to use quotation marks for certain Korean words, and to omit them for certain foreign words.

5. As mentioned above, Yi places this foreign title in quotation marks; the original reads "*Nuga bogŭm* (누가 福音)."

6. The original reads, simply, "Chŏng *hyŏng*! (鄭兄!). This provides the reader with very little detail, other than that the author is reminiscing about a male friend whose surname is Chŏng. He is, however, most likely referring to Chŏng Int'aek, an intimate friend and fellow writer who worked as a reporter for the *Maeil sinbo*, the newspaper in which this essay first appeared.

7. The original reads "... *pam-i isŭkhadorok* "*hokka*"—*yŏnch'o kapji*— *puch'idŭnsaenggakinamnida* (밤이 이슥하도록 『호 까』— 煙草匣紙 — 부치든생각이납니다)." "*Hokka* (호 까)" is most likely a Korean rendition of the Japanese ほうか (包裹), meaning a packet or pouch. There is a slight possibility,

packets of tobacco) deep into the night beneath such a light. A lone grasshopper perches atop the lamp, and with its light green hue, as if crossing the letter "T" in English, "underlines" the peculiar portions of my languid dreams. Feigning sorrow, I hang my head and stilly listen to its ballad, so like the sound of a streetcar conductress punching tickets in the city. Then that, in turn, becomes like the sound of scissors in a barbershop. At last I close my eyes and calmly, carefully listen.

I then produce my journal and, in wild grape-colored ink, set about drafting the poetic sentiments of this intermontane hamlet.

> Torn up newspaper day before yesterday
> A tarnished white butterfly
> A balsam resembles my lover's beautiful ear
> In that ear stand visible the articles of bygone days

Before long I grow thirsty. Drinking water at my bedside—I consume the liquid, cold as if drawn from the sea's depths. Taking in its quartzose, mineral odor, I feel the path of the mercury plummeting past my lungs. I sense that, if I so desired, I could trace that frigid curve upon a blank sheet of paper.

When the stars shine down upon the bluestone roof, it cracks with the sound of a crock exploding in the depths of winter. The sound of insects is deafening. Because autumn, at this time, has come only enough to fill a single postcard. At times like these, how could I even begin to hope to fathom the mysteries of time? The sound of my pulse turns the entire inside of the room into a clock, and the long hand and short hand's revolving around the drive

---

however, that Yi is referring to smoking a Hokka pipe deep into the night with his friend. The original text is somewhat ambiguous. The fact, however, that Yi was quite poor, and worked several odd jobs while a student, leads me to select the interpretation of *hokka* as envelopes or packets that Yi and Chŏng were filling with tobacco and sealing for later sale.

Azalea

Lingering
Impressions
of a
Mountain
Village:
Yi Sang

screw makes my eyes itch by turns. The smell of machine oil wafts in and out of my nose. I feel sleep approaching beneath the oil lamp.

I have a brief dream in which a young city girl appears; she looks like the "Paramount" Pictures logo. And then, before I know it, in my dream I see the poor family I have left behind in the city. They stand shoulder to shoulder, as prisoners of war do in photographs. And they bring me worry. Which finally wakes me from my slumber. Shall I just die? I entertain such thoughts. I stare at my threadbare Korean coat, which hangs from a nail in the wall. Ah, yes, you have followed me here across the vast northwestern provinces.

I turn up the wick, and, after relighting the lamp, use my pen to plant ultramarine "seedlings" in my notebook. Upon the page, one by one, a wretched population comes to life. A dense population—.[8]

Tomorrow, all day long, I shall spend gazing at flowers. I shall soak a cotton swab in "alcohol" and wipe away all manner of anxiety. I feed on such thoughts. It is because my dreams are so incredibly confused. Flowers in full bloom dreams, "gravure" full-color reproduction dreams—I want to have pleasant dreams, as if looking at a picture book. For which, by way of simple explanation, it would be nice to compose an uplifting poem and lay it out in 7 "point" type.

In the city I have a magnificent hometown. In this village, the mountains are covered solely with broad-leafed trees that occlude the view of my hometown, while the iron skeleton telegraph poles running P'albong's ridges seem to transmit only headlines, and even then only in code.

In the morning I am awakened by the rustling sounds of the courtyard afflicted by the sun's warmth. In the middle of the enclosure, heavy with the "burden" of another day, a crimson dragonfly stirs like a disease. I fell asleep with the lamp on; its flame

8. These two sentences, though quite brief, bring to mind the first-person narrator's musings on Malthus in Yi's acclaimed short story "Wings."

still burns—a trace of the lost night, it lingers like the "button"[9] on my threadbare vest. It is a "doorbell"[10] that allows me to call on last night. Leaving last night's body heat behind in my room, I step out into the court to find a flowerbed in one corner. Blazing cockscombs, and balsams.

I feel my breath grow hot at the passion of these flowers, drawn up from the depths of the earth. Some white balsams are mixed in with those used to color the tips of young maidens' fingernails. I wonder if the white ones will also turn red?—Quite naturally, the white balsams do dye a fine madder red.

On the millet stalk fence, "orange" bitter melons ripen. They commingle with kidney bean vines, making one panel of a folding screen with a "sepia" background. In the vines beyond this, atop an artless yet intrepid pumpkin blossom, sits a lone and "Spartan" honeybee. Reflected in amber hues, it is as magnificent as a "Cecil B. De Mille" film, and extravagant in its golden shade. Listening closely, I hear the sound of the electric fan in the reception room of the "Renaissance."[11]

There is yet another flowering plant; it looks like the "asparagus"[12] leaves placed atop a vegetable "salad." I ask the boy

9. This is yet another example of a Korean word, *tanch'o* (단초), being put into quotation marks. Here it would appear that Yi uses the quotation marks to denote that it is not actually a button he is discussing but a flame.

10. The original here read "*yobiring* (요비링)," a Koreanization of the Japanese *yobirin* (よびりん), or doorbell/call bell. Yi Sang often employed this word when he wanted to evoke the sense of calling something back.

11. The sound he hears is most likely the buzzing of the bee's wings. His immediate conflation of it with the sound of a fan in the "Renaissance"—most likely the name of a café in Seoul—continues his ongoing juxtaposition of country and city, and his own unequivocal identification with the latter.

12. This was misspelled "*masŭp'aragasŭ* (마스파라가스)" in the original. With the level of sophistication displayed by Yi in other portions of this and other writings, it is difficult to attribute the error to him. Rather, as with "MJR" coffee, it is likely that a typesetter not versed in English, and perhaps not able to decipher Yi's handwriting, committed these errors.

Azalea

Lingering
Impressions
of a
Mountain
Village:
Yi Sang

at the inn what it is. *"Kisang."*—He means *kisaeng.*[13] What do its flowers look like?—It has scarlet, silky blossoms.

I reminisce about the actual *kisaeng* in the city—their sort of beauty would not have been approved of by our forefathers—wrapped in "Josette" skirts, svelte as "Westminster" cigarettes. The scent of "Wrigley's Chewing Gum," more pleasingly warm than actual peppermint,[14] the sound of their lips smacking like pages turning in a thick ledger—but the *kisaeng* that bloom out here must undoubtedly resemble those glimpsed in the paintings of Hyewŏn,[15] or perhaps they may be like the *kisaeng* seen in boyhood, red parasols riding in rattling rickshaws, now mere episodes from days gone by.

A pumpkin has fully ripened. It will be sliced thin, dried, and steamed with radish to make rice cakes—led by such delicate aromas, wafting on vapors, do the rustic spirits of our departed patriarchs return on appointed days for ancient rites. But its sense of security, broad and weighty, and its imperturbable color, which first bring to mind farsighted plans for the nation, seem also to await the burly arms of the young heroes of this "generation" that run carrying "rugby" balls.

13. Yi plays here with three different versions of the word *kisaeng*. The first is a type of flowering plant that, apparently, he has not seen before. The boy then pronounces it in dialect—*"kisang"*—adding to the disconnect between Yi and the things and people of Sŏngch'ŏn. Once the urban Yi has "corrected" the rural boy concerning the proper pronunciation of this plant—never mind the fact that Yi was unable to identify the plant on his own mere seconds before—he goes into a reverie concerning actual *kisaeng* (female entertainers). The current ones in the city are dressed in Western clothes and smacking American gum. He appears to appreciate their nontraditional beauty. By contrast, the *kisaeng* he may be able to chance upon in Sŏngch'ŏn will likely resemble those of the past—meaning both Chosŏn dynasty paintings and Yi's own, less modern, childhood. Thus, all three uses of the word *kisaeng* serve to reinforce Yi's emotional and intellectual distance from rural Korea.
14. Yi continues his juxtaposition of nature/real and city/artificial—always preferring the city/artificial.
15. Hyewŏn is the pen name of the Chosŏn dynasty genre painter Sin Yunbok (1758-?). He is especially renowned for his paintings of women, particularly *kisaeng*, some of which are quite explicit.

They say when the citrons ripen, their skins separate to reveal the inner flesh. I pluck one, fasten it to the end of a string, and hang it in my room. Beneath its dripping, voluptuous flavors, I feel as if my own body, even as it wanes gaunt as a pencil, may begin to wax ever so slightly. But this "humorous" figure, neither vegetable nor fruit, possesses no fragrance. Only the carnal redolence of my city, from which another layer disintegrates with each washing, hovers about the room.

Beside the entrance to the narrow grassy path leading up P'albong, a monument erected in honor of a certain Mr. Ch'oe,[16] and another one for the everlasting remembrance of some other fellow, stand like airmail "post"'s.[17] The way I hear it, they are both still living. Ridiculous, isn't it?

I wanted to see a church.[18] I wanted to repent before the god who loves even the farmers of this village, thousands of miles from the holy land of "Jerusalem." My steps follow the sound of hymns. A "goat" stands tied beneath a "poplar" tree. He wears a beard in the style of old. I go before him and gaze into his sagacious pupils.

---

16. The original reads "Ch'oe xx (崔xx)." As Yi is discussing an actual stele dedicated to a person alive at the time, he avoids direct mention of the man's name. This was standard practice at the time, and still is today, at least in South Korea.

17. The original reads "*hanggong up'yŏn 'p'osŭt'ŭ'*" (航空郵便 『포스트』). It is somewhat ambiguous, but most likely means that these steles resembled a certain type of mailbox. Even today in South Korea, many government mailboxes—though they are bright red—are shaped somewhat like stele and have the English word "POST" written across the front.

18. The original is somewhat ambiguous because it lacks the spacing between words that makes at least certain aspects of the contemporary Korean written language so unequivocal. The original reads, "教會가보고십헛습니다," making "I wanted to go to (a) church." another possible reading. Contemporary readers may demand that the lack of the dative-locative "-e (에)" after "church," demands the reading I have chosen. But that would be quite anachronistic; Yi Sang and his contemporaries were not abiding by modern Korean grammar they were inventing it. Both Yi's grammar and orthography quite often flout the conventions that were only later codified and enforced. I have opted for the translation above due to context (there is another reference to seeing a church below) and out of deference to certain eminent scholars of early modern Korean literature who also interpret it as "I wanted to see a church."

Azalea

Lingering
Impressions
of a
Mountain
Village:
Yi Sang

Like exquisite "celluloid" beads wrapped in "*oblato*,"[19] they are clear, transparent, clean, and beautiful. His peach-colored eyes move about, regarding with disdain my inferior physiognomy and meager appearance.

The cornfields are one great military review. When the wind blows, I hear the rustling of armor and helmets. "Carmine" tassels fall from their headgear, curved and undulating at their backs. I hear the report of a gun from P'albong Mountain—definitely the solemn sound of a salute. It was actually the sound of an air rifle right beside me terrorizing a small bird. Then dogs of all kinds and colors—white, beige, black, grey, and then white again—emerge from the cornfields marching in formation. The stimulation of the "sensual" season adds yet another layer of splendor to this "Cossack" parade.

The remnants of newly rinsed cabbage remain on the stepping-stones across this clear mountain stream. The fresh flavor of kimchi prepared with young vegetables brings to mind "Smile" eye drops.[20] As I squat like a crooked letter N[21] atop one of the smooth igneous rocks, two young women, bearing water jars on their heads and hesitating at stream's edge, come into my field of vision. I feel bad and thus stand up, but I then deliberately face them and walk to their side. I brush past. From their "hard-rolled"[22]

19. This is written 『오브라—드』 in the original. It refers to the Japanese *oburāto* (オブラート), which is in turn a rendering of the Portuguese *oblato*, a diaphanous paper made from starch and used to wrap medicines that would otherwise be difficult to swallow.

20. Here, again, Yi juxtaposes the countryside, which he is viewing, with the city for which he pines. Like his earlier paradoxical deployment of "hometown," Yi uses "kimchi" (and all its connotations) here in a most unexpected manner. The flavor of kimchi made from cabbage freshly washed in a pure Korean mountain stream is likened to "Smile" eye drops, an artificial liquid medicine manufactured by the Lion Corporation in Japan.

21. Here, with the letter N, Yi elects to omit quotation marks. This contrasts with his earlier use of quotation marks around the letter T. The crucial difference, not apparent in English translation, however, is that "the letter T" was written out in a mixture of Korean and Chinese script ("『틔』字"), while the N in "letter N" above was simply written using the Roman alphabet ("N").

22. As in footnote 4, Yi uses "hard-rolled" to express a brown color, this time not for envelope paper but for the skin of these country maidens.

skin comes the scent of green vegetables. Their "cocoa" lips are stained with wild grapes and hardy kiwifruit. A processed blue sky is "canned"[23] in their pupils, which do not regard me.

These maidens' skin was exactly the same wheat color as the socks worn by the "Misono"[24] cosmetics "sweet girl" at M Department Store.[25] Ultrastreamlined hats donned at rakish angles, and lithe "handbags" like cats' stomachs adorned with "fasteners"— this is how I remember the modish ladies of the city. I also recall the roundworm-like fingers of the pallid factory girls who pound the "asphalt" at dawn. Will not all the same sorts of ponderous fingerprints fall upon the delicate skin of those various classes of city girls without questions regarding their wealth or poverty?

Despite their poverty, however, it is these comely country lasses, whose skin is tough as canvas yet without blemish, who pluck the fruits out of ground cherries and inflate their husks in place of "chewing gum" and "chocolate," whom I more urgently wish to know. I want to bless them. The church is nowhere to be found. Shrinking before the insidious gaze of the urban dweller, they retreat into the woods, leaving only the echoes of a bell to hover the area like a lingering scent. Or perhaps this is nothing more than a hallucination heard by my restless soul.

In the very center of a field of millet stands a tall mulberry tree. The maidens picking its leaves are near the top, riding high like workers on a telegraph pole. A most delectable fruit ripened in virgin white. Two of them are up in the tree, while one below fills a basket. It is a scene from that folk song in which they only have to pick a couple of leaves before the whole basket overflows.[26]

23. The original reads "『간쓰메』가 되여잇습니다." "간쓰메" is the Korean rendition of "カンづめ," which means "packing in cans, canning, or canned goods."
24. Misono is the name of a Japanese cosmetics brand that was popular in the 1930s.
25. M Department Store most likely refers to Mitsukoshi, the building in downtown Seoul atop which Yi's short story "Wings" draws to a close.
26. This is a reference to the lyrics of the Korean folk song "Toraji t'aryŏng," or "Ballad of the Platycodon"—also set deep in the mountains—which mention a

AZALEA

Lingering
Impressions
of a
Mountain
Village:
Yi Sang

The ears of millet have all dried up and died. Light as "cork," they hang their heads in apprehension. Oh, rain, please come. They long to soak up your waters like a sponge.[27] But, as if rain has been forbidden, the sky is cloudless, blue, clear, and completely dry. So will the SOS of shallow roots reach the subterranean water flowing beneath this rock floor?

Two boys remove their rubber shoes, take them in hand, and wade out into the stream to catch fish. A vein into which runs the ground's resentment—what sorts of fish might live in such foreboding and baneful water—the stream penetrates the earth's fever, and flows out across the inclined steppe. It is a rumor of autumn.

Yes, autumn shall come—does it not whisper its request for permission? The millet ears crumple with a sound like a bride's bowing in a wedding ceremony. The wind, old and cunning, urges the millet leaves to full maturity. But the millet's heart is green and impatient and young.

Who has put the millet field in such disarray?—Millet's no good anyway.—Was it done thinking this? Someone really fouled it up. Silkworms—there are silkworms in every household. Fatter even than millet ears, silkworms devour mulberry leaves in no time at all. This healthy palate is as regal and extravagant as that of kings and princes. Maidens consider gathering mulberry leaves the ultimate glory of their being. But there are no leaves left. The maidens' passion is all aflutter, as if the ceremonial offerings at a wedding had been exhausted.

×

Under cover of darkness, the maidens come out in light attire. In the direction pointed by their blushing faces—there are trophies on the mulberry tree. They need only go there. They

large basket's overflowing after having gathered only a couple of these edible roots.
27. The original sentence, like so many in Korean, does not contain a subject. From context, I have elected to translate it as "They (the millet) long to soak up . . ." but "I" or even "We" would also be possible and make a certain, albeit slightly altered, sense.

trample the field of millet. Their feet, tastily roasted by ultraviolet rays, crush the millet ears where they stand. It is a "scrum." And thus this absolute devotion fattens the sacred, noble livestock housed within the autumn[28] silkworm-raising room. It is a pulpy "romance" that brings to mind Madame "Colette"'s[29] *La Chatte*.[30]

In a room visible from the street, in a house next to the temporary school building, two are chattering away. A young virgin with plaited hair jogs a machine with her bare feet. At which the machine, as if tickled by the long, slender thread brushing against its waist, rolls with great laughter. With one laughing, the other coercing, the famous xx silk[31] is spun into a 15-foot bolt that will be used when visiting ancestral graves, when making festive clothes for children, and will even be used as a dustpan for sweeping away a daughter-in-law's grief, and for obliterating one dream after another—such is my absurd rapture.

This evening's twilight has already been placed in the room beside the cigarette store. In those few "gallons" of somber air, vivid conifers grow luxuriant. On foreign vegetation that lives only in the twilight, that is like an immigrant, ripen untold virgin white and pleasingly oval fruits. Cocoons—naturalized "Marias" gather these fruits of the most current knowledge in a most graceful style.

28. The word translated here as "autumn" is actually *ch'ŏn'go mabi* (天高馬肥). While this is most often employed as a stock phrase to refer to autumn, some of the connotations of the Chinese characters are lost in English translation. Most significant for this essay, and the context provided by the words " . . . fattens the sacred, noble livestock. . . ." is the fact that the last two characters, *mabi* (馬肥), mean fat(tened) horses.

29. This is a reference to the French novelist Sidonie-Gabrielle Colette (1873-1954). Among her representative works are *Chéri* (1920) and *La Chatte* (1933).

30. That Yi mentions this work, *La Chatte*, written in French only two years prior to his essay, is a telling index of certain Koreans' level of knowledge of and interaction with the people and ideas beyond their borders. Although a footnote in the Kim Chuhyŏn volume provides a Korean title (암고양이), the title of this work in the original essay is written in Chinese characters (牝猫). This makes it likely that Yi read the work in Japanese translation.

31. The original reads "*myŏngsan* xx *myŏngju* (名産xx明紬)." The "xx" is used to represent the omission of two syllables. They most likely represent the name of a famous brand of silk or the name of a city or region renowned for producing silk. The same convention was used earlier when avoiding direct mention of a certain Mr. Ch'oe's given name (崔xx).

Azalea

Lingering
Impressions
of a
Mountain
Village:

Yi Sang

Lamenting their son's tragic end, they combine to form a "Pietà" in which a "Christmas tree" is torn apart.

"Cosmos" bloom in the school yard where pupils are learning their letters. They are also working hard at simple arithmetic, converting their honesty and simplicity into resourcefulness and cunning. What a deplorable way to calculate interest. A couple of white butterflies, like pages torn from a genealogy, transitorily flutter above a flower bed that smells of chalk. In turn, the sound of a soft "tennis" ball, like that of a popping cork, seems to transform into traces of a noise and linger as a series of points along a contour line. Tonight in this yard they are going to show moving picture advertisements for a financial association. Cinema? This century's pet child—a "number" reigning over all other forms of art. The victory of the eighth art.[32] What could possibly rival its charm, at

---

32. This appears to be a reference to the work of Italian writer Ricciotto Canudo.

> Italian writer Ricciotto Canudo (1879-1923), who is considered the first theorist of film, considered cinema to be "the Seventh Art."
> As Canudo argued in his manifesto "The Birth of the Sixth Art" (1911), cinema was "plastic art in motion." He understood that film incorporated the distinctive elements of both the spatial arts (architecture, sculpture, and painting) with the temporal arts (music and dance). He later added poetry to the list in his 1923 better-known manifesto "Reflections on the Seventh Art."
> In the 1920s and for some time thereafter, it was common to hear movies referred to as "the seventh art."

What remains puzzling, however, is Yi Sang's reference in this essay to cinema as "the eighth art." Later in this article—on video games—we find the following:

> Today, almost 100 years after Canudo wrote his manifesto, video games have now become part of the "new art" discussion, i.e., *the eighth art*, and employ the elements of film, but add another new and crucial aspect—interactivity. Canudo understood early on how cinema, the medium of the 20th century, was a site of artistic convergence in its synthesis of the other arts. For Denis, video games mark a new site of convergence, one comparable to cinema. Video games are truly characteristic of our new century, in that they involve the audience through interactivity.

Video Games: The Eighth Art - Blog #34
Barry Keith Grant,
Professor of Film Studies

once aloof from the mundane world and dissolute? But the denizens of this place still possess intact their dreams of movies as mere fairy tales. Pictures that can move—they seem at once like conjuring learned from the redheaded barbarians and also like the enviable skill of our own countrymen.

The plain nihility tasted after watching a movie—Chuang Tzu's butterfly dream must have been something like this. Has my entire round, flat head become a camera, and, albeit through a tired "double lens," filmed and projected several times over this early-autumn scene of ripening corn?—shallow pathos flowing in through a "flashback"—it is a heartbreaking "still" I send to my few lonely "fans" left in the city.

Night has fallen. The moon, nearing its tenth day, appears a bit into eventide. Townspeople like those from a folktale gather upon straw mats laid out in the yard. Are they the least bit different from a bunch of North Pole "penguins" tilting their heads before a gramophone? A piece of parchment upon which to record life, at once so short and long—the "screen," amidst this darkness, is the preparatory expression of a "biography." It appears a woman of urbane manner has arrived at the inn across the way, where I happen to be staying. I hear a mixture of dialects coming from its courtyard.

It begins. The Pusan Suspension Bridge appears. Next is Pyongyang's Moran Peak. The Yalu River Railroad Bridge rolls historically forward. Applause and ovation—the finest directors of the West are on the verge of losing face. During the 10-minute break, there is a speech given by the association director through an interpreter.

---

http://blogs.ign.com/silicon-knights/2007/06/21/58004/
Emphasis added.

Yi Sang was obviously familiar with Canudo's work and terminology, a fact no less noteworthy than his earlier references to and knowledge of Madame Collette et al. Less certain, however, is why Yi elected to change cinema, Canudo's "seventh art," into his own "eighth art." Perhaps, like the passage on video games qua eighth art above, Yi was proposing a new "artistic convergence" that would "involve the audience through interactivity."

AZALEA

Lingering
Impressions
of a
Mountain
Village:
Yi Sang

The moon is hidden in the clouds. No smoking—that's what it feels like. They shine the "spot" of electric lights on the director's face as he delivers his speech. All nature must be astonished. Electric lights—the bumpkins here have never seen them, save for the "headlights" of passing automobiles bound for xx.[33] Amidst these blinding rays, the deathly pale director steps down from the stage. Not a single one of these benighted commoners applauded the director's eloquence—of course, I too had no choice but to be one of those benighted commoners—. This evening of cinematic appreciation did not come to its "happy end" until well after 11 P.M. The association employees and film technicians held an appreciation ceremony in this village's one and only eatery. I returned to the inn, turned up the lamp's dying wick, and began to read. It was the exquisite book *The Way of Humanity*[34] by Doctor Kōda Rohan,[35] lent to me as an admonition against my idleness and melancholy by the aged gentleman in the adjoining room. In the distance, a dog barks on incessantly. Unable to forget the refined "high collar" fragrance, the crowd must have yet to disperse.

The clouds break up and the moon appears. Sounding as if the windows to a great dance hall have been opened, the insects are remarkably clamorous. I have an urbanite's nostalgia, a deep longing for strangers by the roadside.[36] Ladies fresh as the cover of a newly published magazine—gentlemen the same age as a "necktie," and my various pallid companions—the hometown that does not wait for me[37]—I want to adapt the words of my naked body and send

33. Here "xx" is used to avoid mentioning a specific city, while the sentence itself reconfirms Yi's distance from and distaste for the "bumpkins" of this place.
34. In the original, the title—『人의道』—was placed in quotation marks. I was unable to find an English translation of this work.
35. Kōda Rohan (the pen name of Kōda Shigeyuki, 1867-1947) was one of Japan's most talented, and prolific, writers of fiction, essays, and drama.
36. This appears to be an oblique reference to prostitutes, of whom Yi was rather fond. I opted for a fairly literal translation, but it might be more liberally translated as " . . . a deep longing for streetwalking strangers."
37. Here, again, Yi toys with and subverts the trope of the "hometown." Rather than the unchanging, eternally waiting rural Eden, it is the city of Seoul, and it surges on, waiting for no man.

them to the city. Sleep—a dream of incoherent printing type, of the printer who was picking type for the Bible when he spilled all the letters and put them back in random order—I too become an apostle, the path before me torn, and deny my starving family not three but ten times over.

Anxiety is larger than the world that subtracts from me. When I open the floodgates, the tides of anxiety permeate this ruined flesh. But I have yet to uncork my "masochist."[38] In the time that anxiety engulfs me, this flesh, worn by wind and reduced by rain, will certainly all wither and disintegrate.

Spreading night's sad air upon my pad, I write a letter to my pallid companions. And with it I enclose my obituary.

38. The original reads "*mesoisŭt'ŭ* (메소이스트)." Although no explanation is provided in the Kim Chuhyŏn volume, given Yi's breadth and depth of knowledge, this also appears to be a typesetting error. Simply changing the "*i* (이)" to "*k'i* (키)" would provide the "proper" pronunciation. These sorts of errors (*masŭp'aragŭsŭ*, etc.) are particularly interesting given the fact that the portion of the essay just above this one actually concentrates on the incomprehensibility caused by typesetting errors ("... a dream of incoherent printing type, of the printer who was picking type for the Bible when he spilled all the letters and put them back in random order"). Perhaps, since this essay was serialized in the daily newspaper *Maeil sinbo* from September 27 to October 11, 1935, Yi was actually reading the errors produced by typesetting in the earlier pages, and then commenting on them, albeit obliquely, in his later submissions.

Marking Territory: Writing against
Nation-based Identity in
Yi Sang's "Lingering Impressions
of a Mountain Village"

Another
Perspective

John M. Frankl

Despite the more than seventy years of nearly constant popular and academic attention given to his life and works since his passing, Yi Sang (1910-1937) remains something of an enigma. Best known today as a Korean modernist/experimentalist writer, Yi, née Kim Haegyŏng, was trained not as a writer but as an architect, and, to complicate matters, often wrote in Japanese. Thus, ironically, a significant portion of his poetic corpus—though proudly and rightfully claimed as Korean literature—is available to many Koreans only in translation.[1] In addition, perhaps reflecting his architectural training, many of his poems appear more concerned with the numerical significances, geometric forms, and spatial arrangements of words on the page than with their syntactic formations. And even when one surmounts these obstacles to concentrate more fully on the words themselves, one is met by a vast

---

1. Nearly half—twenty-four out of fifty-six to be exact—of the Yi Sang poems contained in the most recent and authoritative anthology were originally written and published in Japanese. See Kim Chuhyŏn, ed., *Yi Sang chŏnjip 1: si* (*The Collected Works of Yi Sang, Volume 1: Poems*) (Seoul: Somyŏng ch'ulp'an, 2005). Among those, many were not translated into Korean until between twenty and forty years after Yi's death. However, certain more contemporary anthologies, however, seemingly invested in creating and/or perpetuating the patent myth that Yi and Korean literature were and are somehow "pure," omit any mention of the fact that the poems were ever in Japanese at all. On a more positive note, the above-mentioned collection of Yi's works, not only notes when and by whom each translated poem was rendered but also provides the Japanese-language originals.

mixture of languages, concepts, and figures ranging from French to English, from physics to metallurgy, and from Rosa Luxemburg to Al Capone. All of these combine to create works that are hybridized, idiosyncratic, and particularly resistant to facile interpretation.[2] Yi Sang's prose fiction presents a similar case, albeit without the added complication of having been written in Japanese.[3] I would argue, however, that it is much more his idiosyncracy than the language in which he chose to write that makes him at times impenetrable. This, of course, would have been all the more true during the 1930s, when he was writing largely for an audience of bilingual ethnically Korean subjects of imperial Japan.

Despite, or perhaps because of, the numerous impediments to any semblance of a definitive reading for many of Yi's works, studies of his poetry and prose fiction abound.

His life and (a portion of) his works remain popular topics for established academics and graduate students alike. This is true outside of Korea as well. The volume *Muae 1*, to the best of my knowledge, was the first and only work of its kind published in the United States. It was completely devoted to the works of Yi Sang, yet gave scant attention to his essays. Here I should admit my own positionality as one who often values Korean literary works as primary sources for viewing certain aspects of daily life. Such works are not, of course, transparent windows upon the past, but nonetheless may provide certain personal and quotidian details absent from more "objective" genres and media.[4] Furthermore, all

---

2. The footnotes required to make his poems at least somewhat fathomable to contemporary readers serve as evidence. Extensive explanations are provided for many of the poems in the collection mentioned above; one ten-line poem (詩第七號, pp. 87-88), for example, is accompanied by twenty-four separate footnotes.
3. The short story "Wings," Yi's most famous piece of fiction—the only work of his that many non-specialists have read—provides a case in point.
4. Hobsbawm and others have warned against the value of such sources as newspaper editorials and academic treatises in studies of everyday life simply because they most often represent the views and wishes of an elite minority for a society that does not exist, as opposed to either the desires of a majority or a picture of an actual society. See E.J. Hobsbawm, *Nations and Nationalism since 1780: Programme, Myth, Reality* (Cambridge: Cambridge University Press, 1992), pp. 48-51.

literary genres are not created equally with respect to their value as windows, or prisms.[5] Though it is far beyond the scope of this essay to assess the absolute merits of poetry versus fiction versus essays as sources that can shed light on aspects of Korea's past, it is a fact that while very few serious treatments of Yi's essays have been attempted,[6] scores of works have been written on his fiction and poetry. Furthermore, Yi's poetry and prose fiction appear largely personal, which is, of course, why they so often require major biographical research and scores of footnotes. They were not meant to communicate with the outside world any more than is a diary. Conversely, his essays, despite the relative neglect they have received from the scholarly establishment, are in form and content deliberate attempts to articulate. It is in his essays that Yi, to the degree that he ever does, provides unequivocal information, both about his internal states and about the everyday life of the societies in which he operated. With this in mind, I will explore the essay "Lingering Impressions of a Mountain Village" to see what it might reveal to us about Yi Sang and his world.

Perhaps the most striking aspect of this essay, at least from a post-1945 perspective, is its complete insistence on Yi's own very

5. In Korean literature specifically, the prose fiction works of someone like Yi Kwangsu provide a good example. Works such as *Mujŏng*, though not necessarily unrealistic, were deliberately written to effect social change in the future rather than to describe society in the present.

6. Kim Yunsik's comprehensive treatment of Yi's life and works does, of course, treat Yi's essays. But, due to its extreme breadth, it falls short at times in terms of deep analysis. See Kim Yunsik, *Yi Sang yŏn'gu* (Seoul: Munhak sasangsa, 1987). In English-language scholarship the one notable exception is Jina E. Kim, "A Traveler's Modernity: The Ordinariness of Everyday Space in Yi Sang's Essays from Tokyo," in *Yi Sang Review*, Volume 4 (Seoul: Yŏknak, 2005), pp. 251-274. But this work focuses on Yi's later writings, particularly his impressions of Tokyo and how they affected his understanding of Seoul. "Lingering Impressions" was written prior to Yi's first and only trip to Tokyo, and, as such, provides more of a contrast between rural and urban spaces and practices within Korea, as opposed to a contrast between metropole and colony. Although it does contain some very interesting analyses of Yi's stay in Sŏngch'ŏn, the setting of "Lingering Impressions," they are based on the essay "*Kwŏnt'ae* (Ennui)," which was written in a single day, a year and a half after the actual sojourn, while Yi was in Tokyo. As such, the "pictures" of Sŏngch'ŏn contained in "Ennui" are already both faded and colored to a degree that those in "Lingering Impressions," written only a little more than a month after the actual visit, and prior to the Tokyo trip, are not.

personal, decidedly non-national identity. A large part of (South) Korea's post-liberation history—literary and otherwise—has been devoted to making a heterogeneous population appear homogenous under the totalizing rubric of nation. The word for individualism (개인주의 *kaein chuŭi*) was until quite recently a pejorative term. In fact, among many Koreans it still retains many negative associations. Of course, this is partially due to a misconstrual of the word to mean egoism, but it is also intimately connected to the word's connotations of interests or actions that might not coincide with fascistic orders toward uniformity. Yi flouts such artificial attempts to obscure the diversity that characterized colonial Korean society in the 1930s. He writes not as a Korean, or as a Japanese for that matter, but as an individual. And he dedicates much of "Lingering Impressions" to mapping out and securing his personal predilections, often in opposition to both pre- and post-1945 nationalist expectations.

The opening line of the essay provides a perfect example of this. Having set up his readers' expectations with the rustic and poetic title—Lingering Impressions of a Mountain Village—Yi opens with the following: "More than twenty days have passed since I last savored my fragrant MJB." He is not there to "admire the national territory."[7] Nor is his aim to indulge in the "romantic passion for the pure, simple and uncorrupted peasantry"[8] that swept Europe and later made its way, via Japan, to Korea. Rather, his first remaining impression of the Japanese-controlled Korean countryside is that it lacks the American coffee he so enjoyed back in Seoul. Thus, forcefully, if somewhat obliquely, he begins to stake out his identity not as an undifferentiated Korean indulging in an unspoiled portion of "our" national territory but as a lone urbanite stranded in an inconvenient backwater.

7. This is a translation of the phrase "*kukt'o ŭi yech'an* (국토의 예찬)," which is often used to refer to both the purpose and character of certain colonial period travel writings with which many of Yi's readers were likely to have been familiar.
8. E.J. Hobsbawm, *op cit.*, p. 103.

He continues immediately not to praise but to defamiliarize this Korean place by informing his readers, presumably comfortably ensconced in Seoul, that "the newspaper seldom comes, and the postman only occasionally appears," and that even when they do, they bring only "stories of silkworm cocoons and corn." The human affairs of Sŏngch'ŏn simply have no bearing on his life. As for the natural environment, it too is subordinated to Yi's own natural habitat. Discussing the creatures that inhabit the wilds surrounding the village in which he is lodging, Yi writes, "I continually suffer from the delusion that these animals, which I have only seen in zoos, have not been captured from these mountains and put in zoos, but rather have been taken from zoos and put in these mountains." A man of the modern city, Yi finds nothing "natural" about nature. In fact, as hinted at in the lines above, the only way Yi can digest his new surroundings is by providing nearly everything with an urban equivalent. Retiring to his room, he finds the oil lamp's odor "reminiscent of the city's evening paper," while a grasshopper's song is "so like the sound of a streetcar conductress punching tickets in the city."

Amidst these musings, Yi soon dozes off beneath the oil lamp. He has "... a brief dream in which a young city girl appears; she looks like the 'Paramount' Pictures logo." His mind, as so often in this essay, is on the city and on women. This is not surprising. But what do we make of the Paramount Pictures logo? From the company's inception in 1913, the logo has been a mountain peak haloed by a ring of stars. And while this has nothing to do with the way most young girls appear, it is quite analogous to Yi's descriptions of Mount P'albong at night, the setting of the opening portion of this essay: P'albong, just across from the village, is always in view, and Yi "could swear there are twice as many stars out here as in the city." Awake or dreaming, Yi is continually compelled to transform this foreign space into something more personally familiar to him. And, not so ironically in light of the essay's opening line, this rural setting brings to mind the logo of an American film company and not any romantic notions of the Korean countryside. What is perhaps his definitive statement of identity comes a few paragraphs later: "In the city I have a magnificent hometown." Yi continues to play ironically with conventional expectations concerning city, mountain village, and, now, hometown. Here he takes the trope of hometown, somewhat inviolable in modern and contemporary Korea, and turns it on his head. Even today, some seventy years later, the term often romantically evokes places precisely like Sŏngch'ŏn. Like certain of his contemporaries—Yi Hyosŏk comes immediately to mind—however, he is staking out an individual identity as an author and an urban dweller. His hometown is not a matter of tradition; it is not where his ancestors lived; it is where Yi Sang the individual is at home. He is more concerned with his personal identity than a myth of common Korean-ness.

Upon awaking from his "Paramount" dream, Yi informs us, "I . . . use my pen to plant ultramarine 'seedlings' in my notebook." In the original, the Korean word "mo (모)" or "(rice) seedlings" is also put in quotation marks. Of course, on one level, Yi may simply be denoting the metaphorical sense in which he uses the word. That is, he is probably stressing the fact that, unlike the silkworm cocoons and corn in the essay's opening paragraph, the "crop" he cultivates is not agricultural at all, but verbal. Taken in context, however, it becomes apparent that Yi is also deliberately and simultaneously creating and working according to a very personal definition of "foreign" words. Just as his personal identity is non-national, so is his personal language. Rice seedlings are much more familiar to rural farmers than to urban sophisticates. But these seedlings are completely alien to Yi's experiences and desires. For him, what makes a word foreign is not its etymology or provenance but its intellectual familiarity and emotional proximity. Thus, not only is the work peppered with words from English, Japanese, French, and Portuguese but we also find throughout instances of

"Korean" words being enclosed in quotation marks, while certain "foreign" words are left unmarked.

Although they require further context and examples before becoming clear, Yi's idiosyncratic use of language and definition of words appear from the very start of the essay. In the second paragraph, as Yi continues to describe how foreign he finds his new surroundings, we find the following: "And some even say they've seen a 'bear' . . ." Curiously, Yi elects to put the Korean word for bear, "*kom* (곰)," in quotation marks. At first glance, as in certain of his other works, this particular punctuation appears to be reserved for words of foreign origin, such as "*hadorong*" and "*Nuga.*" Its use here is initially puzzling, but becomes quite clear once one realizes that one of the major thrusts of this essay is Yi's exploration of his own individual identity, and of his resultant "foreign-ness" when placed in the Korean countryside. These quotation marks are just one of several devices he employs in this essay to defamiliarize, and thereby disassociate himself from, the animals and the people he encounters there.

Yi repeats this tactic later in the essay when he places the Korean word for goat, *yŏmso* (염소), in quotation marks. But this very personal use of language, and the identity it implies, moves in both directions. Yi also opts to omit quotation marks for certain obvious loan words. The word for ink is one salient example. The word in the original is "*ingk'ŭ* (잉크)." Interestingly, however, although it is obviously of foreign origin, Yi does not set if off with quotation marks. As we saw with his "seedlings," not coincidentally sprouted from his pen's ink, Yi is a farmer of words. Trained as an architect and working as a professional writer, Yi obviously found his ink—both the word and thing—much less foreign than he did "bears" and "goats."

The entirety of Yi's process of differentiation is not conducted through things and words. In addition to observations of his surroundings and idiosyncratic uses of language, Yi also describes and interacts with the people of Sŏngch'ŏn. But, again, they are not his people. Their shared nationality possesses either no significance or a negative one in Yi's eyes. His attitude toward the people around him, ranging from desirous to demeaning, also serves to distance him and thus reinforce his individual, decidedly non-national identity.

Sitting on a stepping-stone, in the middle of a stream, Yi spots two local women approaching to cross. Using his strategic position, he deliberately forces something of an encounter with them. Although they refuse to look at him, he brushes close enough to register their bodies' scents, their fruit-stained lips, and the "processed blue sky . . . 'canned' in their pupils." Although he feels the need to contrast them immediately with the various women he has encountered in the city, he also confesses that "[d]espite their poverty, however, it is these comely country lasses, whose skin is tough as canvas yet without blemish . . . whom I more urgently wish to know." Far less ambiguous in his essays than in his poetry and fiction, Yi makes it perfectly clear that he uses the word "know" in the Biblical sense. The very next lines provide us with both Yi's intentions and the women's reaction. He first informs readers "I want to bless them. The church is nowhere to be found." Following this, he admits that the women shrink "before the insidious gaze of the urban dweller" and "retreat into the woods." The women, for their part, also appear not to feel any sense of national community.

He continues to desire and objectify other women in the paragraphs immediately following. Yi turns his attention from women gathering water to those gathering mulberry leaves for sericulture. In contrast to the pure and romantic associations of rural Koreans dressed in white that we see in works like Hwang Sunwŏn's "Cranes," however, Yi provides us with the following: "In the very center of a field of millet stands a tall mulberry tree. The maidens picking its leaves are near the top, riding high like workers on a telegraph pole. A most delectable fruit ripened in virgin white." He has gone from wanting to "know" the local women to desiring to pluck and devour them. This sense is strengthened as he describes some of these same women coming out that night to continue their work. He describes their walk across the field to return to the mulberry tree. "They trample the field of millet. Their feet, *tastily roasted* by ultraviolet rays, crush the millet ears where they stand."[9] The original text is rather unambiguous; the exact words used for "feet, tastily roasted by ultraviolet rays" are "紫外線에 맛잇게 쓰실는 새악시들의 발." He is still bent on consuming them.

Yi's gaze, however, is not always so ravenous. At times he takes a more aloof and patronizing approach to the locals. He leaves the women in the millet field to explore other venues, and comes across a local school. In the schoolyard, students are not merely "learning their letters," "[t]hey are also working hard at simple arithmetic, converting their honesty and simplicity into resourcefulness and cunning." Upon viewing this scene, Yi feels compelled to make the following comment: "What a deplorable way to calculate interest." Here, again, Yi adopts something of the foreigner's gaze. In an attitude more recognizable among amateur anthropologists, Yi laments the deleterious effects of the modern education being given to these "innocent" country folk. He uses the word "*sunbak* (淳朴)," which may mean a variety of things including rustic simplicity, lack of guile, and artlessness.[10] It is also worth noting that this approach to other Koreans as "foreigners" is not unique to Yi Sang. Eighteen years earlier, in his novel *Mujŏng* (1917), Yi Kwang-su penned these famous lines: "Hyŏng-sik and the old man were people of different countries, who did not speak or write the same language. . . ."[11] What is interesting, however, is that in 1917 the Korean old man was a "foreigner" censured for his inability or unwillingness to modernize,

9. Emphasis added.
10. For a thoroughgoing discussion of the term and its later appropriation by (North) Korean intellectuals, see Brian Myers, *Han Sorya and North Korean Literature: The Failure of Socialist Realism in the DPRK* (Ithaca: Cornell University East Asia Program, 1994).
11. See Ann Sung-Hi Lee, *Yi Kwang-su and Modern Korean Literature: Mujŏng* (Ithaca: Cornell University East Asia Program, 2005), p. 215.

and thus become part of the new Korean nation Yi Kwang-su envisioned. In this essay, however, it is precisely the effort of these Korean country youths to acquire a modern education that is being criticized by Yi Sang in 1935. What is not so certain is whether Yi actually laments the purported damage it will do to their "purity," or if he merely dislikes the idea of the narrowing gap between their identities and his.

Although the essay does not provide sufficient information to answer the above question, it certainly does show Yi continuing consciously to distance himself from the locals. After a brief but pedantic discussion of his own appreciation of cinema, he shifts back to Sŏngch'ŏn: "But *the denizens of this place* still possess intact their dreams of movies as mere fairy tales. Pictures that can move—"[12] Both the original—이곳 住民들은—and the translation—the denizens of this place—contain not the slightest hint of any connection to Yi. He later establishes an even greater distance from the inhabitants of Sŏngch'ŏn by describing them as "[t]ownspeople like those from a folktale." In all cases, when referring to the people and things he observes, he scrupulously avoids the simultaneously totalizing and reductionist "we" and "our," which are otherwise so common in writing then and now. Such words would connect him—as a fellow Korean—to these people. And, in so doing, they would also at least partially rob him of the individual identity he has worked so earnestly to secure.

As the essay draws to a close, Yi's tone moves from patronizing to disdainful. Continuing with his depiction of the townspeople, he asks the rhetorical question: "Are they the least bit different from a bunch of North Pole 'penguins' tilting their heads before a gramophone?" Here, again, and, I would argue, as strongly as at any point in the essay, Yi truly defamiliarizes and simultaneously degrades these countryfolk. He is essentially likening their reaction to modern, Western, urban technology—movies and records—to

---

12. Emphasis added.

that of dumb animals. He is unequivocal in segregating himself from these others. The film eventually pauses for a ten-minute break, during which a company director gives a speech. In case Yi's readers back in Seoul are still unaware of his personal definition of his identity, he adds a final comment regarding his displeasure at being lumped together with these other, rural Koreans (here pejoratively referred to as "bumpkins" and "benighted commoners") in the eyes of the Japanese director. We know he is Japanese because he uses an interpreter for his speech, and because the construction projects in the film (the Pusan Suspension Bridge and the Yalu River Railway Bridge) were undertaken by the Japanese. We also know that Yi Sang, unlike those other Koreans with whom he is unfortunately conflated, did not require an interpreter to understand the director's speech in Japanese. This, however, does not mean that Yi is either anti-Korean or pro-Japanese, but that he cleaves to his individual identity as a Korean-born, colonially educated, multilingual, urban-dwelling writer who understandably—at least out of the totalizing and artificial context of nationalist politics—may not wish to be lumped together with people with whom he has nothing in common save the coincidence of having been born on the same peninsula.

Yi ends this essay where it begins, physically in Sŏngch'ŏn but in all other respects back in Seoul—"the hometown that does not wait for me." The noise of insects reminds him of clamorous dance halls, while he admits to an "urbanite's nostalgia, a deep longing for strangers by the roadside." Another reiteration of the essay's opening is Yi's mention of his family, the only real gesture toward a non-individual identity in the entire piece. This is the second time he mentions them—the first time they are lined up like prisoners in a photograph—but he settles their importance to his project by writing, "I too become an apostle, the path before me torn, and deny my starving family not three but ten times over." He has cut all ties.

Yi Sang worked deliberately to carve out an identity apart from many of the other inhabitants of the Korean peninsula, to whom his only connection was an accident of birth. Like so many of the things in his brief, intense life, his push toward self-excommunication may have been a bit extreme, culminating as it did in sentences such as "Are they the least bit different from a bunch of North Pole 'penguins' tilting their heads before a gramophone?" One need not be all that familiar with nationalist politics to imagine the reaction, both then and now, to such a rhetorical question were it attributed to a Japanese or American writer traveling through the Korean countryside. Ironically, however, the simple fact that Yi could get away with such a comment demonstrates his failure to achieve an enduring non-national identity. Or, put another way, Yi may have personally believed he had succeeded, but, as was the case with so many of his endeavors, he was a bit premature. South Korea, at least, failed to respect his wishes, to let him go. Of course, he was granted posthumous immunity from prosecution for his blasphemy against the nation, but the price may have been a large portion of what he most valued, his individual identity. For no matter how highly scholars evaluate his idiosyncrasies, at least for now, they nearly always do so under the rubric of "Korean" literature.

David R. McCann

Another
Perspective

The Korea Wave has brought sustained attention to
Korean cultural productions of various kinds, ranging
from the television drama series *Winter Sonata* and its descendents,
through Korean musical and music groups starting with the 1990s
hip-hop group Seo Tae Ji and Boys to the widely reported 2006
Madison Square Garden concert by the singer Rain. Among many
features of the Wave, one less visible aspect has been its cultural
transparency: in China and Japan, Korean cultural creations are
perceptibly *Korean*, but in a somewhat abstract way. For Korean
songs, Japanese- or Chinese-language lyrics may be substituted. For
Korean television productions, the plots turn on what are viewed
as traditional Confucian values, part of a shared Asian cultural
heritage it seems, according to the audiences that have been studied.
A slightly different way to put this point is that the performance,
as much as the given particulars of its contents, seems to attract an
international audience.

If a performance dimension seems a relevant criterion by
which to assess the globalizational adaptivity of Korean cultural
productions, is there any comparable performance dimension to
literature, and to poetry in particular? The question is not simply
an academic one. Many Korean literary critics, as well as readers
and authors, wonder why Korean literature has not found the same

AZALEA

Korean
Literature
and
Performance?
Sijo!:
David R.
McCann

broad and deep international acceptance as have the pop culture constituents of the Korea Wave.

The literary reading tour provides one form of literary performance. Bruce Fulton, at the University of British Columbia, has for many years traveled every fall with Korean writers for a week or more, presenting readings in North American venues of contemporary literary works with English-language accompaniment. The poet Ko Un has traveled all over the world to read his work, and has built a strong and enthusiastic international following among readers and writers including Robert Hass, Gary Snyder, and other renowned poets. Ko Un is a remarkably charismatic artist; his reading of the poem "Arirang" elicited a powerful response from an audience at the Folger Shakespeare Library a few years ago.

There are at least two other performance dimensions to Korean poetry that seem worthy of notice. The pop singer Maya's version of Kim Sowŏl's iconic "Azaleas," on her CD "Born to Do It," completely transfigures the poem, known since its publication in 1925 as a "folksong poem," or *Minyoshi*.[1] One could imagine a concert in which Maya performed her version of the Sowŏl poem along with, perhaps, Yi Sang's famously Modernist poem "Crow's Eye Map," *Ogamdo*, or Manhae's "Ferry Boat and

1.   When you turn away from seeing me
       and go,
       gently, without a word, I shall send you away.

       From Mount Yak in Yŏngbyŏn,
       azaleas
       I shall gather an armful and scatter them on your way.

       Step after step away
       on those flowers placed
       before you, press deep, step lightly, and go.

       When you turn away from seeing me
       and go,
       though I die, no, not a single tear shall fall.

from Kim Sowŏl, *Azaleas, A Book of Poems*, trans. David R. McCann (New York: Columbia University Press, 2007).

Passenger," *Narut'pae wa haeng'in*, to list just two poems that, in a performance style such as hers, might seem quite different from their usual literary construals.

There are, however, other performance dimensions to Korean poetry. "Azaleas" gives a series of directional instructions: "I" and "look at," in the *Na pogiga* that begins the poem, indicate a single point, the "I," and a straight line, "look at." The poem then bends the line away into a curve, with the word *yŏkkyŏwŏ*, a term that reverses the semantic field of what has preceded it, deflecting the happy anticipation of the opening phrase of the poem, "To look at me," into a diametrically contrary reaction: *When, sick of looking at me, you. . . .* That curved line then straightens into the going away, *kasil ttae enŭn*, and a sort of mental dance performance, from point to straight line, through the curve of "*sick of*" and into the straight line of movement away, has begun. The second stanza extends the movements and gestures into the grand invocation of the landscape and the flowers of Mount Yak, while the third brings the dance steps down to the feet, in the intimate treading gestures of the stanza. The final stanza, repeating the first two lines of the opening stanza, ends the poem with an ambiguous rhetorical gesture, perhaps accompanied in the reader's imagination by some hand gesture indicating closure, not weeping.

There are a number of other poems which might suggest a performance-oriented, choreographic reading, ranging from the ranks of running children in Yi Sang's "Crow's Eye Map" to the plucking and offering of the grapes in Yi Yuksa's "Blue Grapes," to Cho Chihun's straightforward "Nun's Dance." To respond literally to the invitations these poems offer might lead to a most compelling evening of dance. To acknowledge the possibility of such a reading, moreover, is to recognize the performance dimensions of the poem text that subtend literal meaning, plot, or content. This is the ground on which lyric poetry rests and moves, rests and then moves again, not as the translation of national historical narrative, but as the reiterated realization of the physical demands of the poem: in

AZALEA

Korean
Literature
and
Performance?
Sijo!:
David R.
McCann

English usage, the step, by the *foot*, upon the verse line, according to a given rhythm or meter.

The question of performance leads to yet another form of analysis and realization. The *folksong poem, minyoshi*, of which Sowŏl's "Azaleas" is the most widely known, is explicitly tied to the idea of performance. But the exploration and practice of the folksong poem have been time-specific, not genre-related. Other poets tried their hands at folksong poetry in the 1920s, but under the press of Modernism, Symbolism, Naturalism, and Realism, Socialist and otherwise, its popularity faded. It enjoyed something of a revival in the so-called Liberation Space, or *Haebang Konggan,* the period immediately following liberation from Japanese colonial rule at the end of World War II, when all sorts of literary and political impulses found expression in Korea, including song-style poems of revolution. The poet Shin Kyŏngnim brought a revival of the idea with his 1973 collection *Farmer's Dance, Nongmu*, most notably in the title poem. Yet the question lingers as to whether there exists a performance-coded verse genre in Korea.

The Essence of Performance: The Korean Sijo

The *sijo*, the three-line Korean vernacular verse genre, descends to the present from a very long and varied past, through a variety of performance vectors. The sijo is presented in sung performance of two kinds, the *ch'ang* or song style, with its emphasis on the breath, deflection and variation in pitch, and the timbre of the performer's voice; and the *kagok* style, with its focus on more elaborate instrument accompaniment and vocal ornamentation.

While syllable count is not a primary organizing feature of the sijo form, it does play a role in patterns of syllable distribution among the four phrases or syllable groups that constitute the lines. For the first two lines, the usual syllable count is 3 – 4 – 3 (or 4) – 4. The third line, with its regular sequence of 3 – 5 – 4 – 3 syllables, coupled with a "twist" at the beginning of the line, brings the poem to a conclusion. A well-known example, on the wanderer theme, is by the famous scholar-poet-official Chŏng Ch'ŏl (1536-1593):

> In the water below, a shadow strikes;
> above, on the bridge, a monk is crossing.
> O monk, stop there!
> Let me ask about where you are going.
> With his staff, he points toward the white clouds
> and goes on, not turning to look back.[2]

Yun Sŏndo's "Fisherman's Calendar" uses an effective relaxation technique applied to the final line. Yun never uses the 3 – 5 pattern, instead deploying a 4 – 4 pattern that serves to reduce the rhetorical pressure toward a conclusion. Yun's final lines all the way through the four seasons of poems provide a relaxed dissolution rather than heightened conclusion, an apt counterpart to the theme in "Calendar" of rusticated withdrawal from the affairs and intrigues of the capital. Contrarily, the overall size of the sijo could at times be greatly expanded, either within the form called the ŏssijo or quite beyond it in the so-called *narrative, sasŏl* sijo, some examples of which might go on and on and on with their playful catalogues and lists.[3]

Other possibilities for variation include use of the run-on line in contrast to the normal end-stopped line, as in Hwang Chin-i's *Ŏjŏ nae il iya*; the play of one discourse realm against another, as also in another Hwang Chin-i sijo, the very well-known *Ch'ŏng salli*, which matches a Korean vernacular second half-line against a Chinese-character initial half-line. In the twentieth century, Kim Sowŏl appears to have had the sijo form in mind for his poem "Cricket." Kim Ŏk, Sowŏl's teacher and literary mentor, in writing

---

2. David R. McCann, ed., *Early Korean Literature: Selections and Introductions* (New York: Columbia University Press, 2000), p. 53. On Yun Sŏn-do's "Calendar," idem, pp. 151-155.
3. See Richard Rutt, *The Bamboo Grove. An Introduction to Sijo* (Ann Arbor: University of Michigan Press, 1998), pp. 223f.

AZALEA

Korean
Literature
and
Performance?
Sijo!:
David R.
McCann

about Sowŏl's innovative verse experimentations described how he took apart the traditional folk song verse line and separated its components into phrases printed one after the other down the page.[4] In "Cricket," Sowŏl took the sijo and broke its initial line into two parts. He also took the final line syllable pattern of 3 – 5 – 4 – 3 and, like Yun Sŏndo, relaxed it to a 3 – 4 – 4 – 3 pattern.

Cricket

Sound of mountain winds,
sound of cold rains falling.
On a night while you talk of life's ups and downs,
country inn fire dying down, and a cricket is crying.

The origins of the sijo remain obscure, for two specific reasons. The sijo is a vernacular Korean-language form, but the Korean alphabet, known as *Han'gul*, was developed in the fifteenth century, by King Sejong (r. 1418-1450). This means that for sijo predating the alphabet's promulgation, such as famous examples by U T'ak (1263-1343) or Chŏng Mongju (1337-1392), ascription is not certain because no contemporary written accounts can confirm it. As a song form, sijo were not collected and printed until the eighteenth century, which makes the trail of authorship difficult to pursue back.

Because many sijo have stories about the characters who appear in them, yet another performance dimension seems to tug at the form. One of the most well known of all sijo, for example, is ascribed to the Koryŏ dynasty statesman Chŏng Mongju (1337-1392). As the Yi family head, General Yi Sŏnggye, worked to end Koryŏ rule and set up a new dynasty of his own, he and his followers kept encountering the stubbornly loyal, highly regarded Chŏng Mongju. The fifth son of Yi Sŏnggye therefore arranged a

---

4. Kim Sowŏl, *Azaleas, A Book of Poems.* trans. by David R. McCann (New York: Columbia University Press, 2007), pp. 194-195: Kim Ŏk's "Remembrance of Sowŏl," published shortly after his former student's death.

banquet, in the course of which he offered a sijo song to Chŏng Mongju urging him to relax his vigilant loyalty, and just live on and on, like the vines on Mansu Mountain. Chŏng replied with the following:

> Though this body die and die,
>> it may die a hundred times,
> my white bones become but dust,
>> what's called soul exist or not:
> for my lord, no part of this red heart
>> would ever change. How could it?

The story goes on that Chŏng was murdered by the Yi followers on his way home from the banquet. It presents a performance, on the stage of Korean history, and adds a Shakespearean denouement, in the midnight murder. The poem itself performs a sort of spiritual dissection, down through the corporeal to the loyal spirit at the center of the individual's existential frame. The *History of Koryŏ*, completed half a century after the founding of the Chosŏn dynasty, does contain an account of Chŏng's death, but very different from the traditional one. Hearing that Yi Sŏnggye had fallen from his horse and was injured, Chŏng went to the house to see for himself what condition he was in, and to assess whether he might make some definitive move to stop him. The fifth son, concerned for his father's safety, as soon as Chŏng had left the house ". . . sent Cho Yŏnggyu and five or six others after him. They attacked him on the road and killed him."[5]

A great number of Korea's traditional sijo, embedded in similar historical narratives, prove equally fascinating and problematic. Still others seem ahistorical in being by or about people who were not part of the ruling *yangban* class. There are, for example, dozens of sijo said to have been composed by *kisaeng* women, members

---

5. McCann, *Early Korean Literature,* p. 39.

AZALEA

Korean
Literature
and
Performance?
Sijo!:
David R.
McCann

of an entertainment profession somewhat like the Japanese geisha. The most famous of all is Hwang Chin-i, "author" of a half dozen truly remarkable sijo, a number of poems in classical Chinese, and with a reputation for her beauty, artistic accomplishments, as well as a singularly independent mind and will. There is something of a Hwang Chin-i "boom" in Korea these days, with novels, TV programs, and other popular culture representations of her life and work. The trouble is, once again, the historical record is scanty.[6]

Though two or three of her sijo poems compete for the greatest esteem, I find one most striking, both for its poignant subject, but even more, its technical accomplishment. One need hardly preface the text with a note that Hwang Chin-i composed the sijo in regret at having sent a lover away.

> Oh no! What have I done?
>   I didn't know what it was to yearn!
> If I'd said, *You, just stay,*
>   could he have gone? But stubborn, I
> sent him away, and now what longing
>   truly is, I've come to learn.

Of the notable features of this poem, one remains lamentably invisible in the English translation. Try as I have, I cannot seem to discover any way at all to register the diction of the poem, entirely and purely Korean-language, with the one exception of the term *chŏng* (longing), feeling. That the vast majority of sijo poems share with the Korean language itself a fairly broad deployment of Sino-Korean, Chinese-origin terms, is not surprising. Especially those

---

6. Three decades ago, when I was a graduate student, my advisor Edward Wagner called me into his office one day to show me a reference he had discovered in an official's collected writings, or *munjip*, that he had been working on. Though it was only a brief mention of the famous beauty Hwang Chin-i, it was dated to the sixteenth century and therefore a confirmation of her reputation at the time. I neglected, unfortunately, to write down the information, and by the time my own path led me back again to Harvard, some years ago, Professor Wagner had passed away.

sijo poems from the sixteenth and seventeenth centuries reflect a mixed Korean and Sino-Korean vocabulary, while those from the later centuries, perhaps indeed reflecting a popularization of the form and practice, demonstrate a drift away from the Sino-Korean. But here with Hwang Chin-i's sijo poem we have an expression of strong, direct feeling pouring forth in nearly pure Korean.

The other technical accomplishment of the poem is its deft use of enjambment at the end of line two, as the sense of the poem rushes past the usual sentence or clause ending form, through the continuative form *kut'ayŏ, deliberately,* into the "twist" at the beginning of line three, where the longing and the remaining turn irreversibly to *sent him away.*

Sijo seem to have served upper-class composers and their friends, political enemies, or consorts for a long interval, but the histories take note of a shift in the seventeenth and eighteenth centuries toward popularization of themes, broader popular production—though in the anthologies, sijo by commoners are the ones labeled as *anonymous*—and some shifting toward an expanded, e.g., less rigorous form known as the *sasŏl,* or *narrative* sijo. A number of these later sijo treat sexual themes, perhaps matching a drift in painting toward similar themes and scenes, and many display a wicked, deadpan humor. One of my favorite examples, which I first encountered in Richard Rutt's book *The Bamboo Grove,* presents an exchange between a young wife and her mother-in-law. The following exchange is quite inconceivable in both of its behavioral dimensions: mothers-in-law were always supposed to be miserably abusive toward their daughters-in-law, and all women were chaste.

> Oh what am I to do, what am I to do?
> Reverend Mother-in-Law, Oh, what am I to do?
> Serving my secret lover his rice, I broke the handle
> on the brass rice server, so now what am I
> to do, Reverend Mother-in-Law?

Oh dear child, don't worry so. When I was young,
I broke it many times too.

AZALEA

Korean
Literature
and
Performance?
Sijo!:
David R.
McCann

Finding a modern mode for the sijo has been a challenge. Does a change in the line arrangement such as Sowŏl's "Cricket" make the genre modern? Or a shift to deliberately chosen modern subjects or images? Many theories and practices were tried in the first half of the twentieth century. For the past half century in North Korea, while the sijo has been denigrated as an upper class literary pursuit, such disapproval seems to miss the significance of the sijo's vernacular linguistic stand against the literary Chinese expression that was in fact always the marker of the ruling class. In South Korea, the sijo continues to have its practitioners, of all generations, with sijo associations, journals, and book series.

Yi Pyŏnggi (1891-1968) remains one of the most highly regarded modern sijo poets. A professor at Seoul National University, he published hundreds of sijo poems, and in 1932 an essay in the *Tong-a Daily* calling for a revival of the form. One of his most beloved sijo is a series called "Orchid." The reader may try to detect what it is that makes this sijo, first in the sequence of four, *modern.*

In one hand holding a book
    drowsing away, then suddenly awake;
the bright sun arcs overhead,
    a cool wind rises.
The orchid, two or three buds
    have opened up, full and wide.[7]

7. The word *book,* in Korean *ch'aek,* is the term for the published item bought in a store, which prompts an image of a modern reader rather than a scholar seated at a low desk reading a manuscript of some kind. There are a number of traditional, pre-twentieth-century sijo that use the rhetorical turn from "in one hand holding . . ." to "and in the other, . . ." Often describing a confrontation with some sort of life crisis, such sijo still treat the situation with humor. See, for example, U T'ak's (1263-1343) "In one hand holding brambles, with the other grasping a big stick,/ I tried to block the old road with brambles and chase white hairs off with a stick,/ but white hairs knew my intent and came on by the furrowed road instead" (McCann, *Early Korean Literature*, p. 48).

The poet Oh Se-young, current president of the Korean Poets Association, has published a number of poetry collections. The cell phone poem below, which might be read as a twenty-first century version of Yi Pyŏnggi's, brings these reflections on the performance dimensions of Korean sijo practice to a trembling conclusion.

Cell Phone

The cell phone that was resting nicely atop the letters case
suddenly shakes its body, trembling and quivering.
Even things, when there's nothing to say, can feel so—
    exasperated!

Contemporary Sijo[8]

Cho Ohyŏn—A Buddhist monk, director of the temple group centered around Paektam Temple in the northeastern part of Korea, Cho Ohyŏn received the 2007 Chŏng Chiyong Literary Award for his book *Distant Holy Man, Adŭkhan Sŏngja* (Seoul: Sihak/Poetics, 2007).

8. The line arrangements of the translations reflect the varied patterns of the originals.

Distant Holy Man

What's a day, this today;
on what's called today, on this day

I saw all the sun's rising,
even watched all of the sun's setting.
Nothing more than that to be seeing,
a swarm of mayflies hatches, dies.

The time to die may well be past
and I may still be living
but seen as if some day to have lived is not that same, that
    one day.

You could live a thousand years, true,
holy man,
far distant, a swarm of mayflies

If I Look at Myself

There in the meditation space
I take a good look at myself.

A single bug, it crawls by;
bunches up its body, it stretches.

Everything, it all goes nibbling
and then it dumps
as it goes on laying eggs.

BUDDHA

Having let river water without river water flow

Having let river water without river water flood

In river water without river water the log bridge swept away

GUILT AND PUNISHMENT

At the edge of our temple's
field, a date tree, lightning-struck.

What kind of sins, and how many,
would leave this one lightning-struck?

Still today with such thoughts as these
I send the sun along its way.

THE SOUND OF MY WEEPING

Half the day from deep in the woods
I listen to the bird's singing

and for half the morning by the sea,
listen to the sound of the sea's music.

And just when will it happen to be
the sound of my weeping that I hear?

Hong Sŏng-ran—A highly regarded sijo poet, and like Cho Ohyŏn, a winner of the Chŏng Chiyong Literary Award, her sijo collection *Winter Promise, Kyŏul yaksok*, was published in 2000, Number 73 in the series *Sijo in Our Times: Poems of 100 Poets*.

BIRDWEED FLOWER

Once I really knew
how life revolved around me

knew how life turned and turned around me,

little girl in a pink *ch'ima*[9]
crouching on a path by the field.

HAWTHORN FLOWER

Such regret,
Having just, just sent you away
brings such regret.

The hawthorn flower beaming alone, its eyes damp.

And another night, not coming back.
Having sent you away
brings such regret.

9. *ch'ima*: A traditional dress.

WINDS BLOW, LONGING DAY

Wrap the warm tea cup, grasp it now the rains have come.

Trembling shiver in the warm air your not being here.

Like the white plum petal falling the wind blows the day is
    cold.

WANDERING

How long, the life of an ant that entered the house?

How far, the wandering of an ant that lost a leg and stumbles?

Eternal interval between the glance back and the going.

Kim Dae Jung—Kim Dae Jung was the seventh president
of the Republic of Korea. At the time of the Kwangju Uprising and
Massacre in 1980, he was under arrest, but then put on trial, on
capital charges, for allegedly having instigated the uprising. During
the time of his imprisonment and trial, he was allowed only a single
sheet of paper, once a month, for writing letters to his family. These
letters were eventually gathered and published, then translated and
published as *Prison Writings* by the University of California Press
in 1987. While I helped with the translation of the letters, I was
surprised recently to learn from Kim Dae Jung that he had also
written a number of sijo at the time of his imprisonment.[10] The Kim

10. The subject of the sijo came up at a luncheon meeting, when I gave the former
president a copy of a sijo poem my father had written: "*East is East and West is*

Dae Jung Peace Center Library very kindly forwarded copies to me, and three are translated below.

On the floor of the conference room,
    the three sons make their bows,
offering best wishes on the New Year
    and birthday, heartbroken.
My dear wife, do not sorrow so.
    For are not these our sons?

Long autumn night,
lying alone in the cell,
thinking of our country's work,
I toss and turn, sleepless.
The bright moon fills all the heaven and earth
while my heart, my thoughts, are dark.

On a road without a promise
    that I may return as now I leave,
but return I shall,
    return like the dawn,
and once back, I'll strike the bell,
    I shall strike the Freedom Bell.[11]

West,/ and never the twain shall meet."/ North is North and South is South./ The twain must meet and meet again./ Otherwise, enmity will ever assert itself, D. J. knew. As I asked for President Kim's understanding regarding the nickname reference in the final line, to fit the syllable count of 3, he replied by asking if I had seen his own sijo. They had not been part of the manuscript for the *Prison Writings*, but they are included in the 2000 Korean-language edition of the *Writings*.

11. The poet Hong Sŏng-ran wrote joyfully about Kim Dae Jung's use of the sijo form for his thoughts, hopes, and feelings during his time in prison. Now that conditions had changed, she noted, she took the freedom bell as also sounding a happy note for the sijo and its use for expressive acts. http://article.joins.com/article/print.asp?ctg=15&AID=2216471

The Sejong Cultural Society Spring 2008 Sijo Contest Winners—The Sejong Cultural Society, in Chicago, sponsored a sijo contest for students in the U.S. Three translators served as judges: Brother Anthony, Bruce Fulton, and David McCann. The prize-winning entries follow.

First Prize was won by Jacob Diamond, a senior at Cypress Bay High School, Weston, Florida. His biographical note says he is a baseball fan and player, He was a bat-boy with the Florida Marlins, where he met the pitcher Byung Hyun Kim.

Cuisine?

I look through the window of the Korean barbeque place.
Ducks, chickens, creatures big and small, hang from the
    gallows of the cook.
Step inside and join the culture, leave your wishes at the door.

Second Prize went to James Meredith, from George C. Marshall High School in Falls Church, Virginia. James is interested in drawing, reading, and video games.

True Beauty

There's a house on the seashore, undisturbed by rot or decay.
In the house, there's a woman, whose beauty outshines the
    great bay.
Yet, her flesh feels cold as ice; her eyes are closed; her breath
    is cold.

Third Prize was a tie. Michael Chung, a fifth-grade student at the Curtis School, Los Angeles, wrote of the sijo form, "Somehow, it seemed easy to express my feelings in this format." He mentioned also that he is a 16th generation descendant of the great sijo poet Chung Chul (Chŏng Ch'ŏl).

DREAM ON A LAKE

I'm floating on the dark lake, dreaming I'm floating on a
    cloud
The surface of my tanned skin tingling as water dries on it
A man yells, "Hello, good neighbor!" breaking my dream to
    pieces.

Third Prize was awarded also to Janelle Torres, a student at the Brooklyn College Academy High School in New York, who noted her interests in writing and music.

WHO AM I? WHO ARE YOU?

You want to know who I am,
    But the true question is who are you?
I have told you once before
    I'm the smoke to your fire,
I'm that lie you can trust,
    I'm you as you come to me in your dreams.

Korea from the Outside

by Yu Hua
Translated by John Kim

Some years ago, in just the past century, an ordinary man unknown to anyone—a worker (工人), to be exact—set himself on fire in a bustling area of Seoul. In his final moments, he expressed a profoundly poignant regret. He had not achieved a higher level of education for himself; he had hoped so much to have befriended a college student, one who had studied law, so that he could have helped them, the workers, somehow use the law to protect their own rights.

The fire that this plain and simple man had lit in self-immolation would never again be extinguished. The intellectuals and college students of Korea had all been living comfortably on the fairly good wages provided by the government, but because of this ordinary worker's death, they began to examine their consciences: what ultimately were the rights of the people? what was the future of the nation? The raging flames of this worker's self-immolation extended into the hearts of countless Koreans and ignited their sense of self-respect and indignation. Then, this nation of song-and-dance lovers began to reveal their strong and steadfast character. From the Kwangju Uprising to the various student movements that swept across the whole of the 1980s, the people began to take back, little by little, their own fate from the hands of the politicians. It was precisely in these times that I was an adolescent in China,

piecing all of this together bit by bit from the newspapers and the black-and-white television sets. One after another, Korean youths who were more or less my age—dying either by self-immolation or by throwing themselves off of buildings—destroyed their own bodies of flesh and blood in order to protest against a despotic regime. Time and again, I experienced what is called "shock," and thought about my own age. I thought about the road of life I had been walking, and the endless experience ahead of me. I thought about the illusion of growing up every day; this kind of illusion described for me a beautiful future. I knew that those Korean peers of mine who had rushed to their deaths were also like me, but their own lives, which they had ended without the slightest hesitation, were, furthermore, taken for the sake of valuable life lessons and countless hopes and dreams. By dying in such sensational ways, they expressed their deep hopelessness toward the present reality; at the same time, their deaths also became a long and powerful cry. Their voices reverberated in the ears of their compatriots, calling them to be forever awakened and not fall asleep.

After I had reached the age of thirty, Korea began coming to China via another kind of image: as one of the four "Little Dragons" of Asia, and as the wealth generated by rapid economic development. Although the interim had been filled with the shadows of the collapses of shopping centers as well as the Han River Bridge, these shadows left a mark only on the minds of Korean people. For the Chinese, this just seemed like a few freckles on a pretty face—it certainly did not affect Korea's fine image. After frequent experiences of political turmoil in China at this time, people began to be weary of politics and began to express unprecedented fervor for economic development. Already by this stage, China did not want to see the Korea of the Kwangju Uprising or the Korea of the student movements. The vision of an era is often the vision of a shopper: only when one needs something can one take notice of that thing. The China of this period wanted to see a Korea that had emerged as an economic miracle and thought that it saw in Korea's development an experience that would benefit itself. Many of China's entrepreneurs were fascinated by the management models of Korean corporations; they thought that expansion constituted development, so they hurriedly boarded planes to Korea—as tourists and as students.

Korea's next image was that of frailty in the midst of Asia's financial crisis. From the Chinese media, which had previously heaped high praise on Korea's economic model, emerged a voice of negative criticism: reports related to Korea in newspapers and on television were all about companies going bankrupt and banks in severe debt, as well as recession and unemployment rates continuing to rise. When the Korean *won* was slumping, Chinese people could not help but consider themselves lucky that their own currency was not yet directly linked with the American dollar. At this time in China the term "bubble" became quite popular, and immediately associated with this word often would be another—"Korea." At this moment in Korea, my Korean friend told me that when people saw each other, they would humorously greet one another with, "You're still alive?" and then say, "Congratulations, congratulations."

After having heard many recollections and rumors about Korea, I came to Korea—this peninsula stretching toward the ocean, this country almost completely covered by mountains and forests—for the first time last June. When I walked out of Seoul's airport, my first impression was one unique to an Asian city—chaotic prosperity. There was no end to the pedestrians and cars; there was a ceaseless hubbub clamoring away at my ears. I supposed that this was the scene brought on by a city's uncontrolled development. When I came to know that Seoul had a population of over ten million, Pusan over eight million, and cities like Kwangju over four million, I wondered just how many of Korea's forty million people were living outside of the cities. This made me think of Korea's fate in the midst of Asia's financial crisis: the expansion of the cities seemed to express the expansion of the Korean economy, and the fate of the cities also seemed to decide the fate of Korea.

When I came to Korea, I wanted to find the Korea of the Kwangju Uprising and the Korea of the student movements. This was the very first impression Korea had left on me, and it was also a memory of my adolescence. In Seoul, as well as in Pusan and Kwangju, I saw the veil of prosperity covering the bloodstains of the past and the tears of today. Everywhere were tall, shiny buildings and bustling markets; people were fashionably dressed and their faces were all smiles. On the streets where the evening's neon lights would flicker, all the hotels and bars were overcrowded, and happy drunkards were walking toward me. I was unable to recognize the Korea of the revolution in the 1980s: it was just that there was no longer a trace of the frail Korea of the financial crisis. I realized prosperity could change people's souls, and this was a terrifying change. It seems like a beautiful dream, seducing people's thoughts and feelings; it makes them believe in shams and be suspicious of the truth. Like the soap operas that fill Korean television and the pop songs that pervade its streets: they just tell you about other people's successful lives, not your own. These commodities blazoned with commercial labels—they are commodities, not art. In truth, they have always been far removed from the masses; they are just like the sunglasses sold in stores, clouding the face of reality.

But Korea also allowed me to see Kim Min-gi's musicals and Chŏn In-gwŏn's concerts. These were unforgettable experiences. In a place in Seoul that was just like New York's Broadway, a place that had many theatres and was brimming with the flavor of business—the street there was filled with posters advertising all kinds of performances; these were all ridiculously stuck on top of other posters. This made me think of the big-character posters pasted all along the street during China's Cultural Revolution. It was there that I saw Kim Min-gi's *Subway Line No. 1*, which moved me deeply. This was a musical accompanied by a rock and roll band, and it expressed the fate of the masses in a very real sense. Then, at Yonsei University's Noch'ŏn Theatre, I watched Chŏn In-gwŏn's concert. This was a rock concert that lasted two days—in other words, this was an exhibition of Korea's rock and roll music. Nearly all the rock vocalists took the stage to perform, and the last to come on was Chŏn In-gwŏn's band, Wild Chrysanthemums. I couldn't understand his lyrics, but I understood his music: his vocal performance made me hear the passion and tenderness of Korea. What I felt ecstatic about was that these works, which excited people's hearts, also possessed the power to penetrate them. When I watched *Subway Line No. 1*, it had already been put on more than a thousand times, but the theatre was still packed, and each spectator was affected by the stage performance: they often burst out with the laughter of recognition, and at other times, seemed moved in the midst of perfect silence. Chŏn In-gwŏn's performance then allowed me to see the spectacle of near pandemonium: when this singer, who looked like a hired mover, emerged on stage, the young audience members rushed the empty area in front of my seat, and I could only stand on my chair to finish watching the show. The entire audience was on its feet, singing and swaying along with Chŏn In-gwŏn's clumsy body. This was the pleasant part of my time in Seoul. These performances do not pride themselves on being pop culture, which the phony soap operas in fact claim to be. The soap operas separate themselves from the masses and drown in their narcissistic, so-called modernism. The concert is the true art of the masses: because it comes directly from the masses and gives itself back to them. This kind of art finally allowed me to see the true face of Korea.

I had seen photographs of the martyrs of the Kwangju Uprising before. On those faces splashed with bloodstains, and on those faces from which life had already vanished, I saw their barely opened eyes, pupils dilated with a seeing blindness; their eyes were burning with a crepuscular radiance. Behind their tranquility was an unfathomable melancholy; behind the haze an inexpressible strength. In the photographs that I saw, there was not one closed eye among the martyrs of the Kwangju Uprising: they looked at me with cool indifference and made me shiver. Then, I understood their eyes to be Korea's eyes.

During my short stay in Korea, my sentiments seemed to be cut in half by a sharp knife. Part of it was the cities' bustling days and neon-colored nights; like an ocean, they drowned out my feelings. It was like falling in love. On the other hand, I also felt that under the calm surface of the sea, there were violent torrents. In Seoul's Sŏnggonghoe University, I saw a memorial hall dedicated to the Kwangju Uprising and student movements; this was the work of my friend, Paek Won-dam, and her colleagues. When the editor-in-chief of the Blue Forest Publishing Company, Kim Hak-won, who was decked out in a suit and leather shoes, stood in front of me with his lovely wife, it was hard for me to imagine that they were once revolutionaries who opposed the despotic regime. They had experienced the torment of imprisonment and the pain of torture. In the tombs of the Kwangju Uprising martyrs, in front of one of the dead students, I saw still unfinished homework that was placed inside a glass case, along with letters that his friends had recently written him. In Kwangju, Kim Hak-won also introduced me to Kim Hyŏn-jang, a national hero in the hearts of many Koreans. That very year, the American cultural embassy in Pusan had burned down. Kim Hyŏn-jang had lit this fire, causing many Koreans to suddenly realize—America was not their friend. After this, Kim Hyŏn-jang spent countless nights and days in prison; he was almost executed several times. He could only say that it was by a miracle of fate that he lived to see this day. That night, we sat on the floor of Kim Hyŏn-jang's house, and I listened to him talk endlessly with Kim Hak-won. I could not understand what they were saying, but I knew they were reminiscing. I could tell from the faces of these two men that they were in the highest of spirits.

I like the Korean poet Kim Chŏng-hwan. Although there is a language barrier between us, I often feel like he has been my friend since childhood; we seem like we had grown up together. He has written a substantial amount of excellent poetry, as well as two thick books about music. What is extraordinary is that his works were all completed while he was not getting enough sleep.

On his face would hang a kind smile, while his eyes were always red and swollen. He would talk with a great sense of humor: he would only have to appear and the people around him would burst out laughing again and again. He still to this day maintains the habits he developed from the start of the revolutionary period: when he would grow too tired, he would walk into the subway, find an empty seat, and lie back. While the subway car was moving forward at high speeds or stopped in traffic, he would sleep for an hour or two.

Many nights in Korea, I wandered everywhere following Kim Chŏng-hwan. At dawn, we would come to some street in Seoul and wave goodbye, but after the curtain of night would fall again, our wandering would begin once more. Kim Chŏng-hwan often brought me to a little bar—I don't remember the name of this bar, but I will never forget its layout and ambiance, which resembled the simplicity and coziness of a home. My friend, Ch'oe Yong-man, told me that revolutionaries of the intelligentsia would gather at this place in the 1980s. Inside, one wall was completely covered in classical music CDs—these were Kim Chŏng-hwan's markers of debt. After he was incapable of repaying his tab in cash, he paid with his collection of CDs. But he often took down these CDs to give to his friends. When we were bidding farewell, Kim Chŏng-hwan found two records to give to me.

The proprietress of this bar left me with a deep impression. She always sat quietly to the side, holding a cigarette between her fingers, and let her customers take a drink or whatever they wanted from the refrigerator. Her eyes were extraordinarily composed, and she seemed indifferent to everything, but this also made me believe that her depths were unfathomable. When she sat with us, and when she smiled and opened her mouth to speak, I noticed that her eyes were still so calm. I can imagine that in the 1980s, after these people—half of whom were revolutionaries and the other half crazy poets and artists—had clashed with police on the street, then come here to drink themselves silly until the break of dawn, and leave all tipsy with an assload of debt, she would look at them with the same calm. I think that these are precisely Korea's eyes.

Last October, I came to Korea for the second time. This time, in the dim light of night, the plane descended into Pusan's airport. As the plane was landing, I saw Pusan's night scene; this city was built on a mountainside so its lights seemed like waves rising and falling. Pusan's lights featured a full spectrum of colors: yellow, white, blue, and red were all intermingled with each other, and it was like a beautiful scene of the human world composed of myriad flowers in bloom. This seemed to be like a wonderful vision you have after getting high on weed; it was just like the glorious scene brought about by prosperity. Its beauty emerges only after more and more truths are concealed. Whether in Korea or China, people sometimes need fictional scenes of beauty; as long as they do not wake, their beautiful dream will never be shattered. When Korea's soap operas were widely welcomed by China's television sets, and when An Chae-uk's concert in the Beijing Worker's Stadium was a big success, Korean weed had already become indistinguishable from Chinese weed. At the same time, after Chŏn In-gwŏn, who used his songs to awaken people, gets out of jail a third time for smoking weed, I think he will probably walk right back through the prison gates for a fourth. Because being intoxicated with song is legal and being intoxicated with marijuana is illegal, I know this is Korea's reality, but I believe it does not reflect Korea's eyes.

Yang Hwa-Sŏn

Journey. 2007, bronze, 60 x 45 x 98 cm.   196

Deviation. 2008, bronze, 44 x 42 x 39 cm.   264

Mountain. 2007, bronze, marble, and sandstone, 56 x 102 cm.   346

Salvation. 2008, bronze, 34 x 29 x 33 cm.   369

Park Youngsun*

Looking at Clouds 1–9.   291–299

Looking at Mountains 1–6.   300–305

Looking at Afternoon Sunlight 1.   306

* *All original images are digital photographs (154 x 102 cm.) taken in color in 2008.*

Lee Woolim

Dream. 2005, oil on
canvas, 91 x 65 cm.   252

K.E. Duffin

Frog. 2008, pencil
drawing, 12.5 x 9.5 in.   232
Attacking Dog. 2008,
cliché-verre 10 x 8 in.   324

Wayne de Fremery

Basketball. 2008, digital photo.   378

*AZALEA generally adheres to the McCune-Reischauer system in transcribing Korean into English. However, many Korean contributors have not followed this convention, and we respect their way of writing their names in English.

Yoosup Chang received his B.A. in Asian studies at Vassar College. He is currently a producer for independent films and a videographer. He has previously translated numerous folktales as well as texts for the Korea Literature Translation Institute.

Cheon Woon Young, born in 1971, is considered a pioneer of a new trend in Korean literature and her works have been the subject of much analysis. Her major works include the short story collections *Needle* (Panŭl), *Cheerfulness* (Myŏng'rang), *I'll Take You There* (Nae ga teryŏda chulge), and the novel *Goodbye, Circus* (Chalgara sŏk'ŏsŭ).

Ch'oe Ryŏn is among the new group of North Korean writers who emerged after "The March of Hardship," the devastating period of natural disasters and economic and social turmoil that characterized the 1990s in the DPRK. Her work is distinctive among her contemporaries not just for its complex aesthetic features and its acute observation of social relations, but for its focus on what she terms the "double hardship" faced by North Korean women.

Wolhee Choe, Professor Emerita of English Literature at Polytechnic University, is the author of *Toward an Aesthetic Criticism of Technology* (1989), *Golden Ark* (1992), *Lyric Brush* (2004), and co-translator of three books of poems, *Brief Songs of the Kisaeng: Courtesan Poetry of the Last Korean Dynasty* (1997), *Day Shine: Poems by Chong Hyon-jong* (1998), and *Windflower: Poems by Moon Chonghee* (2004).

Chong Hyon-jong, born in Seoul, Korea, in 1939, is one of the most respected Korean poets. He has published twelve volumes of poetry, including *The Complete Works* in 1999 and the latest,

Unbearable (2003). His works have been translated into English, German, French, Spanish, and Russian and individual poems anthologized in many languages. He is also a translator of Pablo Neruda, García Lorca, Yeats, and others. Chong is a recipient of numerous prestigious awards including the Pablo Neruda Medal (2004) and the Kyong-am Award (2006).

Chŏn Pyŏng-gu has written poems that attempt to capture ordinary lives in North Korea. "A Birthday Table" is one example.

Wayne de Fremery has a B.A. in economics from Whitman College, an M.A. in Korean studies from Seoul National University, and is currently pursuing his doctorate in Korean literature at Harvard University.

Guy Delisle was born in Quebec City in 1966 and has spent the last decade living and working in France. He has written and drawn graphic novels including *Shenzhen: A Travelogue From China*, and is currently working on one about his experience in Burma. *Pyongyang* is his first graphic novel in English.

K.E. Duffin is an artist and writer living in Somerville, Massachusetts. She studied at the School of the Museum of Fine Arts, Boston, where she learned printmaking. Her work has been exhibited internationally and is in the collections of the Boston Athenaeum, the Boston Public Library, and the DeCordova Museum. She received a Massachusetts Cultural Council Artist Grant in 2005 and a Berkshire Taconic A.R.T. grant in 2007. Her first book of poems, *King Vulture*, was published by the University of Arkansas Press.

Eun Hee Kyung, born in 1959, made her literary debut in 1995 with her novella *Duet*; the following year, her first novel *Gift from a Bird* (Sae ŭi sŏnmul) was awarded the first Munhak tongne Fiction Award. Eun has won numerous awards, including the 1997 Dongseo Literature Award, 1998 Isang Literary Prize, and 2000 Korean Literature Novel Award.

Diana Hinds Evans has two master's degrees in Korean literature, one from Seoul National University and one from Harvard

University. She is a freelance translator and spends most of her time raising her two boys, Emmet and Gabe.

Heinz Insu Fenkl, born in 1960 in Pup'yŏng, is a novelist, translator, and editor. His autobiographical novel, *Memories of My Ghost Brother*, was named a Barnes and Noble "Discover Great New Writers" selection in 1996 and a PEN/Hemingway Award finalist in 1997. He has also published short fiction in a variety of journals and magazines, as well as numerous articles on folklore and myth. His most recent work is *Cathay: translations and transformations*, which includes his own fiction as well as T'ang poetry and the opening of Kim Man-jung's seventeenth-century Buddhist classic, *Nine Cloud Dream*. He currently teaches at the State University of New York at New Paltz.

John M. Frankl graduated from UC Berkeley, earned master's degrees at Yonsei University and Harvard University, and received his Ph.D. from Harvard University. He is currently an assistant professor of Korean and comparative literature at Underwood International College, Yonsei University. He has published translations of several short stories and poems, and recently authored a monograph titled *Images of "The Foreign" in Korean Literature and Culture*.

Bruce and Ju-Chan Fulton are the translators of several volumes of modern Korean fiction, including the award-winning women's anthologies *Words of Farewell: Stories by Korean Women Writers* (Seal Press, 1989) and *Wayfarer: New Writing by Korean Women* (Women in Translation, 1997), and with Marshall R. Pihl, *Land of Exile: Contemporary Korean Fiction,* rev. and exp. ed. (M.E. Sharpe, 2007). Their most recent translations are *The Dwarf* by Cho Se-hŭi (University of Hawai'i Press, 2006) and *There a Petal Silently Falls: Three Stories by Ch'oe Yun* (Columbia University Press, 2008). Bruce Fulton is co-translator (with Kim Chong-un) of *A Ready-Made Life: Early Masters of Modern Korean Fiction* (University of Hawai'i Press, 1998) and co-editor (with Youngmin Kwon) of *Modern Korean Fiction: An Anthology*

(Columbia University Press, 2005). The Fultons have received several awards and fellowships for their translations, including a National Endowment for the Arts Translation Fellowship, the first ever given for a translation from the Korean, and a residency at the Banff International Literary Translation Centre, the first ever awarded for translators from any Asian language. Bruce Fulton is the inaugural holder of the Young-Bin Min Chair in Korean Literature and Literary Translation, Department of Asian Studies, University of British Columbia.

Hong Sŏk-chung was born in Seoul in 1941 and graduated from Kim Il Sung University in Pyongyang in 1968. He debuted in 1983 with the two-volume novel *Nopsae param* (The northeast wind) and has also published short fiction.

Hwang Kyu-Baek, born in Pusan in 1932, studied at École du Louvre. He has had numerous exhibitions including exhibitions at Brentano's Gallery (New York City), Gallery Hugst (Munich), Christie's, Tokyo, and Hyundai Gallery (Seoul). His works have been bought by numerous museums worldwide, including the Museum of Modern Art (New York City), the British Museum (London), Galleria degli Uffizi (Florence), and the Museum of Fine Arts, Boston (Boston).

In the midst of the social and political turmoil of 1987, Jang Jung Ill, then a twenty-something middle school dropout, shook up the Korean literary establishment with his first collection of poetry, *A Meditation on Hamburgers* (*Haembŏgŏ e taehan myŏngsang*). His unconventional poems are highly self-conscious, exquisitely structured, and often focus on the deceptively mundane. A few of his works have inspired feature-length Korean movies, including the 1995 film *301/302*, which was inspired by Jang's poem "The Cook and the Anorexic (*yorisa wa tansikka*)."

Jo Kyung Ran received her degree in creative writing from Seoul Institute of the Arts. Since her debut in 1996 with *Pullansŏ Optical* she has become noted for her delicate portrayal of modern life as an embodiment of estrangement. Her signature works are

Time for Baking Bread, which was awarded the first Munhak tongne Prize for New Writers, *Pullansŏ Optical, My Purple Sofa,* and *Looking for the Elephant.*

Theresa Joo was born in Seoul, Korea. She is currently completing degrees in international relations and Asian studies at the University of British Columbia. She is translating a number of short stories by Jo Kyung Ran. She lives in Vancouver, British Columbia.

Hye-jin Juhn grew up in Seoul. She has taught Korean at the Defense Language Institute in Monterey and at the University of Washington in Seattle, where she resides.

Hyejin Kim, settled now in Singapore after living in South Korea, China, and the United States, has written for numerous publications, including *Global Voices, Asia Times,* and *Ohmynews.* She has a Ph.D. in global affairs from Rutgers University. In 2003 she received the Korean Novelist Association's Award for Best Television Scenario. *Jia: A Novel of North Korea,* her first novel, was inspired by her human rights work with North Korean refugees in northern China.

Kim Jiwon works and lives in Seoul. He studied at Inha University and Staatliche Hochschule für Bildende Künste (Städelschule), Frankfurt am Main, Germany. His work has been internationally exhibited at numerous museums through solo and group exhibitions and collected by the Hana Bank, the Leeum Museum, and the National Museum of Contemporary Art, Korea. He teaches at the School of Visual Art of the Korean National University of Arts.

John Kim is currently a third-year Ph.D. student in comparative literature at Harvard University. His research includes twentieth-century East-West modernism—language reform, the avant-garde, theories and practices of translation, and canon formation.

Sora Kim-Russell lives in Seoul. She was awarded the grand prize in poetry for the 2005 Korea Times Translation Contest and the 2007 Korea Literature Translation Institute's New Translator

Award. She received her B.A. in anthropology from UC Santa Cruz and an M.A. in East Asian studies from Stanford University.

Kim Ki-Su has had numerous solo and group exhibitions in Seoul, Taegu, Kwangju, and Beijing. His works have been internationally exhibited at various art fairs, including Rome, Beijing, Dubai, Taipei, and Seoul, and bought by many museums such as the Busan Metropolitan Art Museum, the Gwangju Museum of Art, and the National Museum of Contemporary Art (Korea). He was awarded the Ha Chŏng-ung Prize for Young Artists in 2006.

Tae Yang Kwak teaches East Asian history at Ramapo College. He received his doctorate from the Department of East Asian Languages and Civilizations at Harvard University. He began translating Korean poetry for *Moim*, an annual student publication at the University of Chicago. Some of his translations are included in *The Columbia Anthology of Modern Korean Poetry* (2004).

Lee Woolim, born in Sach'ŏn in 1972, lives and works in Taegu. He studied painting at Youngnam University, where he earned his B.F.A. and M.F.A. He has had numerous exhibitions, including solo exhibitions at Han Ki Suk Gallery, Kumho Gallery, and Gallery Wooduk, and group exhibitions at the Beijing Art Fair, Singapore Art Fair, and Kwangju Biennale. He was chosen as the 2006 winner of the 21st Century Kumho Young Artist Award, given by the Kumho Museum of Art. His works have been bought by the Seoul Metropolitan Museum of Art and the Kumho Museum of Art.

Li Chong-dŏk is a North Korean poet known for the lyrical poetic style that flourished in the 1990s. "Dandelions," published in 1994, is a good example.

David R. McCann is Korea Foundation Professor of Korean Literature at Harvard University. He has translated the work of many Korean poets—including Kim Chiha, Sŏ Chŏngju, Ko Un, and Kim Namjo—and is the author or editor of many books, including *The Columbia Anthology of Modern Korean Poetry* and *The Way I Wait for You*, a collection of his own poems.

O Yŏng-jae was born in 1935 in Changsŏng, Chŏnnam Province of South Korea. When the Korean War broke out in 1950, he was drafted for the People's Volunteer Army (at the age of 16). He has lived in the North ever since. He is the author of several epic odes, including *The Taedong River* (1985), which is well known for initiating epic odes as a representative of the North Korean poetic style. To South Koreans he is best known for "Mother, Please, Don't Get Older," which he wrote when reunited with his mother in 2000 for the Reunion of the Dispersed Families of the South and North Koreas.

Park Youngsun was born in 1962 and works and lives in Seoul. She graduated from Yonsei University (philosophy major) and the Graduate School of Hongik University (photography major). Her works have been shown in several solo and group exhibitions.

Pyun Hye-Young was born in 1972 in Seoul. She graduated from Seoul Institute of Arts and Hanyang University where she earned a master's degree. She began publishing in 2000 and published two collections of stories, *Aoi Garden* (2005) and *To the Kennels* (2007). She was awarded the Hanguk Ilbo Literary Prize in 2007.

Ra Hee-Duk received her Ph.D. in Korean language and literature from Yonsei University in 2006. She has authored five books of poetry, most recently *A Disappeared Palm* (2004); one collection of essays, *A Water Bucket Filled by Half* (1999); and a volume of literary criticism, *Where Does Purple Come From?* (2003). Among her awards are the Kim Suyŏng Prize for Literature (1998) and the Sowŏl Prize for Poetry (2007). She currently teaches literature at Chosun University in Kwangju.

Ryu Yŏn-Bok, born at Kap'yŏng, Kyŏnggi-do, moved to Seoul when he was in elementary school. He studied painting at Hongik University and after graduation, participated in the wall painting movement and woodcut print movement, as a part of the cultural movement for democratization in the 1980s. Currently he lives and works in Ansŏng, Kyŏnggi-do. He has had over 200 solo and group exhibitions in many countries, including several European nations and the United States. His works have been bought by several museums, including the National Museum of Contemporary Art, the Gyeonggido Museum of Art, Il Min Museum, and Jeonbuk Province Art Museum.

Shin Kyung Sook is the recipient of many awards such as the Manhae Prize for Literature, Dong-in Literature Prize, 2001 Yi Sang Literary Prize, and the 21st Century Literature Prize. Acclaimed works include *Where the Harmonium Used to Be* (P'ung'gŭm i ittŏn chari, 1993) and *The Outer Room* (Oettan pang, 1995).

George Sidney taught courses in American literature and culture at three Korean universities for five years as a Fulbright professor: Sogang, Seoul National, and Sungyungkwan.

Peter Sobolev was born in Leningrad, USSR, in 1973 and has been taking photos since 1997 for his personal website Wandering Camera (http://bcam.spb.ru). His other interests include travel (DPRK, Ecuador, Thailand, Malaysia, China, Indonesia), computer networks, web programming, Argentine tango, and aviation. He is the organizer of the computer art festivals ENLiGHT and Chaos Constructions (http://cc.org.ru). He currently works as a project manager at an IT company.

Chae-Pyong Song is an associate professor of English at Marygrove College in Detroit, Michigan. He has published articles on modern fiction, as well as translations of Korean poetry and fiction, and coordinates the Master of Arts in English program.

Gabriel Sylvian is a graduate student in modern Korean literature. His project seeks to internationalize the Korean glbtiq human rights issue through translations of same-sex works from Korea written by both identitarian and non-identitarian authors, and the production of same-sex discourses within Korean academia (http://www.myspaclve.com/gabsy).

Yang Hwa-Sŏn studied sculpture at Hongik University and printmaking at Sungshin Women's University. She has had numerous exhibitions, including solo exhibitions at Kwanhun Gallery (1988) and Gana Gallery (2002, 2008). Her works have been bought by the Ho-Am Art Museum, the Modern Art Museum at Hongik University, and the Gyeonggido Museum of Art.

Yi Sang (1910-1937), born Kim Haegyŏng, is one of the best known yet least understood Korean writers. Yi blurs the lines among languages, forms, and approaches so that neither his life nor his writings fit into any of the facile categories or "-isms" of which critics seem so fond.

Yi Seong-Bok was born in 1952. His work began appearing in Korean literary magazines in the late 1970s. He has published seven volumes of poetry: *When Does a Rolling Stone Awaken* (Twinggunŭn torŭn ŏnje chamtŭnŭnga, 1980); *South Sea, Silk Mountain* (Namhae kŭmsan, 1986); *That Summer's End* (Kŭ yŏrŭm ŭi kkŭt, 1990); *Memories of the Holly Tree* (Horang kasi namu'ŭi ki'ŏk, 1993); *Songs That Cannot Be Hidden* (Sumkil su ŏpnŭn norae, 1993); *Ah, Mouthless Things* (Ah, yibi ŏpnŭn kŏt'tŭl, 2003); and *The Trace of Wave Patterns on the Forehead of the Moon* (Tal ŭi yi'ma enŭn mulgyŏl mu'nŭi chaguk, 2003). In 1982 he received the Kim Suyŏng Literary Award for *When Does a Rolling Stone Awaken*, in 1990 the Sowŏl Prize for Poetry for *That Summer's End*, and in 2004 the Daesan Literary Award for *Ah, Mouthless Things*. For the past twenty-five years he has been a member of the faculty at Keimyung University in Taegu, where he teaches creative writing and French literature.

Yu Hua was born in 1960 in Hangzhou. He left dentistry for writing in 1983 and has since published more than twelve books. He gained international attention after penning *To Live* (Huozhe, 1992), which was adapted for film by Zhang Yimou and subsequently banned from China. Many of his stories and themes are significantly (and violently) inflected by the experience of the Cultural Revolution. He has been translated into more than ten languages.